ecpr PRESS

democratic institutions and authoritarian rule in southeast europe

Danijela Dolenec

ecpr

First published by the ECPR Press in 2013

The ECPR Press is the publishing imprint of the European Consortium for Political Research (ECPR), a scholarly association, which supports and encourages the training, research and cross-national cooperation of political scientists in institutions throughout Europe and beyond.

ECPR Press
University of Essex
Wivenhoe Park
Colchester
CO4 3SQ
UK

Typeset by ECPR Press
Printed and bound by Lightning Source

British Library Cataloguing in Publication Data
A catalogue record for this book is available from the British Library

Paperback ISBN: 978-1-907301-43-8

www.ecpr.eu/ecprpress

ECPR – Monographs

Series Editors:
Dario Castiglione (University of Exeter)
Peter Kennealy (European University Institute)
Alexandra Segerberg (Stockholm University)
Peter Triantafillou (Roskilde University)

Other books available in this series

Agents or Bosses?: Patronage and Intra-Party Politics in Argentina and Turkey (ISBN: 9781907301261) Özge Kemahlioğlu

Causes of War: The Struggle for Recognition (ISBN: 9781907301018) Thomas Lindemann

Constraints on Party Policy Change (ISBN:9781907301490) Thomas Meyer

Citizenship: The History of an Idea (ISBN: 9780954796655) Paul Magnette

Civil Society in Communist Eastern Europe: Opposition and Dissent in Totalitarian Regimes (ISBN: 9781907301278) Matt Killingsworth

Coercing, Constraining and Signalling: Explaining UN and EU Sanctions After the Cold War (ISBN: 9781907301209) Francesco Giumelli

Deliberation Behind Closed Doors: Transparency and Lobbying in the European Union (ISBN: 9780955248849) Daniel Naurin

Democratic Institutions and Authoritarian Rule in Southeast Europe (ISBN: 9781907301438) Danijela Dolenec

European Integration and its Limits: Intergovernmental Conflicts and their Domestic Origins (ISBN: 9780955820373) Daniel Finke

Gender and Vote in Britain: Beyond the Gender Gap? (ISBN: 9780954796693) Rosie Campbell

Globalisation: An Overview (ISBN: 9780955248825) Danilo Zolo

Joining Political Organisations: Institutions, Mobilisation and Participation in Western Democracies (ISBN: 9780955248894) Laura Morales

Organising the European Parliament: Committees' Role and Legislative Influence (ISBN: 9781907301391) Nikoleta Yordanova

*Parties and Elections in New European Democracies (*ISBN: 9780955820328) Neil Munro and Richard Rose

Paying for Democracy: Political Finance and State Funding for Parties (ISBN: 9780954796631) Kevin Casas-Zamora

Policy Making in Multilevel Systems: Federalism, Decentralisation, and Performance in the OECD Countries (ISBN: 9781907301339) Jan Biela, Annika Hennl and André Kaiser

Political Conflict and Political Preferences: Communicative Interaction Between Facts, Norms and Interests (ISBN: 9780955820304) Claudia Landwehr

Political Parties and Interest Groups in Norway (ISBN: 9780955820366) Elin Haugsgjerd Allern

Regulation in Practice: The de facto Independence of Regulatory Agencies (ISBN: 9781907301285) Martino Maggetti

Representing Women?: Female Legislators in West European Parliaments
(ISBN: 9780954796648) Mercedes Mateo Diaz

*Schools of Democracy: How Ordinary Citizens (Sometimes) Become Competent
in Participatory Budgeting Institutions* (ISBN: 9781907301186) Julien Talpin

The Personalisation of Politics: A Study of Parliamentary Democracies
(ISBN: 9781907301032) Lauri Karvonen

The Politics of Income Taxation: A Comparative Analysis
(ISBN: 9780954796686) Steffen Ganghof

*The Return of the State of War: A Theoretical Analysis of Operation Iraqi
Freedom* (ISBN: 9780955248856) Dario Battistella

*Urban Foreign Policy and Domestic Dilemmas: Insights from Swiss and EU
City-regions* (ISBN: 9781907301070) Nico van der Heiden

*Why aren't they there?: The Political Representation of Women, Ethnic Groups
and Issue Positions in Legislatures* (ISBN: 9780955820397) Didier Ruedin

*Widen the Market, Narrow the Competition: Banker Interests and the Making of
a European Capital Market* (ISBN: 9781907301087) Daniel Mügge

Please visit www.ecpr.eu/ecprpress for information about new publications.

contents

mami i tati

| list of figures and tables

Figures

Tables

| acknowledgements

As is often the case with first books, this one also started its life as a doctoral dissertation project. I took the first wobbly steps in developing the dissertation at Harvard University as a Fulbright visiting student during the academic year 2007/2008, where I had the terrifying luck of having world class scholars read my initial attempts at formulating an argument. In January 2009 I enrolled in the PhD programme at the Centre for International and Comparative Studies at ETH Zürich. It was under the caring supervision of Frank Schimmelfennig that my meandering pursuit of answers was shaped into a coherent research design. Frank's help and dedication to my work has driven me into writing a better dissertation than I thought I could. Even after I completed the doctoral programme and left Zürich, Frank continued to provide me with support and advice as I was preparing the book proposal for publishers, rewriting the argument, agonising over the title and waiting for many weeks before the first good news started arriving. Frank, for this unwavering support you have my deepest respect and gratitude.

I warmly thank Grzegorz Ekiert for engaging with my work from the very beginning and following me through to its completion. It was in his classes at Harvard that I entered the field of post-communist democratisation and began developing an enduring fascination with the history and politics of the region that I come from. Over the years Grzegorz's insightful comments have been instrumental in developing the focus of my work while his criticism always made me go back to the project with renewed enthusiasm. I am especially thankful to Grzegorz for encouraging me to pursue an academic career and supporting me in asking big questions – a disposition not popular in contemporary doctoral programmes in political science.

I would also like to thank Peter A Hall, Milada Anna Vachudova and Charles Ragin for reading various incarnations of the text as it was evolving, generously sharing their knowledge and providing invaluable advice. Ever since our first encounter, Professor Hall's sharp insight, genuine curiosity and a profound grasp of the social world have been an enduring inspiration for me as I search out my own author's voice. In Zagreb, Mirjana Kasapović has been a critical reader of my work, providing expertise on the history and politics of former Yugoslav states. Apart from that, I owe my colleagues at CIS in Zürich warm thanks for providing a supporting work environment. Christa Deiwiks, Edina Szöcsik and Flavia Jurje in particular have my gratitude for bringing warmth and fun to my life in Zürich.

Finally, I want to thank my close friends and family. Group22 is a collection of amazing individuals I grew to know in the course of writing this book. They have encouraged my passion for understanding the world and inspired me to be bold. Karin, Maja and Ogi are my muses, keeping me wonderful company through life's twists and turns. I have mined our friendship for advice, encouragement and much needed distraction. As a friend, Karin has selflessly supported me through the entire book writing process. As a fellow writer, she engaged with my work and helped me reflect on the process, making everything so much easier to handle. Mladen has drawn on his newly minted experience of being a published author to provide both encouragement and many useful tips; the most important one being not taking oneself or one's work too seriously. Slaven clocked the most hours of discussing post-communist democratisation with me, not tiring of debate over breakfast, at the food market, after cinema or in the middle of the night. His passionate worldviews and keen intellect keep me sharp and always learning. In the end, the infinite well of goodwill and love of my parents Nada and Vlado has nurtured every one of my accomplishments. This book is dedicated to them.

I could have not written this book without the time that money can buy. I am thankful for financial support from the US State Department Fulbright programme, the Swiss Government Postgraduate Scholarship, the Croatian Ministry of Science, Education and Sports, the Faculty of Political Science of the University of Zagreb, the Global Supplementary Grant Programme of the Open Society Institute, and travel funding from the ETH-CIS and the US Embassy in Croatia.

Danijela Dolenec
Zagreb, April 2013

| introduction

In the land of absurdity the law is like a designer DIY magazine
Use it to tailor everything, simply follow the instructions
Plug the right hole, this is easy
Being clever means to screw the law
Screw us all, no problem
The law is full of holes like tapestry
Weave your own motif, for yourself, your family and friends.
('Heroes', The Beet Fleet, 2001)[1]

Geographic regions of the world come in and out of fashion with comparative politics scholars. For instance, the Arab Spring of 2011 has brought a revival of interest in North Africa, while the Middle East never really falls off the radar due to its geostrategic importance to Europe and the USA. While the academic field of Sovietology[2] was large and strategically important during the Cold War, the Balkans has never been particularly high on the agenda of comparative scholars. The last time this region acquired international prominence was in the early 1990s, when the violence that erupted in the region reignited nineteenth century narratives about primordial Balkan turmoil (Todorova 1999). When more rigorous academic accounts appeared, they were understandably focused on issues such as self-determination, minority rights, problems of ethnicity, the prospects of secession and the role of nationalism (ibid., Mazower 2002). This focus has, however, meant that democratisation processes in this region have been 'seldom researched and rarely appeared in broader comparative studies' (Džihić and Segert 2012: 241).

Therefore, as a scholar of democratisation I am still puzzled by what happened at the beginning of the 1990s in this region of Southeast Europe. Why is the society I live in so cynical and intolerant? Why does my generation describe the situation in the early 1990s when either both of our parents got fired from factories they worked in, or one lingered on to work in a privatised enterprise that was being deliberately

---

1. Lyrics from the song 'Heroes', sung by TBF, a hip-hop band from Split, Croatia. Author's literal (non-rhyming) translation from Croatian. The song lyrics in Croatian are as follows: 'U zemlji apsurda zakon je ka Burda/ Pa se po njemu kroji sve po zakonu 'samo izbroji'/ I začepi pravu rupu, to je lako/ Kod nas bit snalažljiv je zajebat zakon/ Zajebat sve nas, ma nema problema/ Zakon je pun rupa poput goblena/ Pa vezi sliku za sebe, rođake i priku.'

2. Political and social studies of the Soviet Union and Russia in particular.

destroyed for its property value – as 'typical'? Why do my fellow citizens have little faith in our political institutions (Gallup Balkan 2010)? Why do the majority of Serbs, Croats and Macedonians believe that no political party or politician expresses their views (ibid.)? Why have they had to, as Krastev (2010: 6) has aptly summarised, 'learn to live in dysfunctional states and badly governed democracies'?

In other words, this book questions how consequential regime change in Southeast Europe has been for subsequent democratisation. In its very essence, it proposes a simple answer – the 1990s still matter today. I advance a historical institutionalist explanation which assumes that objective structural conditions formulate various boundaries and constraints on subsequent events (Skocpol 1979), and I argue that authoritarian governance practices from the 1990s have coalesced into lasting obstacles to democratisation in Southeast Europe. In the transformation of these countries towards democratic regimes, introducing the rule of law has been crucial. Unless political elites are forced into accepting firm limitations on their power, the state cannot exert even a modicum of legitimacy. Only legitimate power can in turn guide societal development in ways that can adequately address current political and economic injustices. Therefore, for these societies to begin to engage democratically in improving their lives, the rule of law must be secured.

A proverbial saying credited to Josip Broz Tito, which outlives him in countries of former Yugoslavia, illustrates enduring problems with the rule of law in these societies. Echoing the contempt for the law in the TBF lyrics quoted above, it states 'one should not hold on to the law like a drunken man holds on to the fence'. While state socialism brought many features of modernisation to this part of Europe, the old notion of sovereignty, according to which the state (like the king) cannot break the law since its will is the law, survived (Popović 2010). Tito's quip which compares keeping to the rule of law to a drunk man who cannot walk on his own suggests that not only the state but each man and woman should decide for themselves when bending the law is the preferable strategy. Of course, these social practices neither emerged *sui generis*, nor do they represent the explanation for weak democratisation outcomes. The prevailing disregard for the law in these societies is a coping strategy, an accommodation to a life under political regimes that frequently and blatantly abuse the power vested in them through the democratic process of elections. Before the political elites become constrained by the law, these countries will not move out of the dysfunctionality that currently characterises them. Having said that, available evidence suggests that there are no guarantees over whether these regimes will indeed move forward, since we now know that the majority of third-wave countries have not become well-functioning democracies (Carothers 2002).

Why write this book now? First of all, this account of post-communist democratisation has the benefit of twenty years passed since regime change in post-communist Europe. While it may be true that the recent past is the hardest to understand,[3] a study such as this probably could not have been conducted earlier. As Skocpol has convincingly argued, 'the work of the comparativist only becomes possible after a large primary literature has been built up by specialists' (1979: xv). Access to such literature enables the comparativist to investigate various cases according to the rigorous demands of the comparative method; her task being not so much about revealing new data but 'establishing the interest and *prima facie* validity of an overall argument about causal regularities across the various historical cases' (1979: xiv). Covering fourteen countries over a twenty-year period, this book is designed precisely to tackle such a task of uncovering broad historical patterns beneath the diversity of outcomes in post-communist Europe. Secondly, time passed enables me to abandon unwarranted optimism about the effects of formal institutional design on democratisation. Though democratic institutions that were introduced in post-communist European countries in the early 1990s were supposed to uphold the principle of rule of law, civil liberties continued being curtailed well into the second decade after regime change – reinstating the need for new explanations of post-communist democratisation processes.

Map of the argument

This book explores why democratisation in Southeast Europe has not reached levels comparable to those in countries of Central Eastern Europe, and the explanation is sought in the different configurations of the following explanatory factors: socioeconomic parameters and regime legacies, conditions of statehood, political party dynamics and the EU's democratisation pressure. Eight post-communist countries of Central Eastern Europe included in the study are the Czech Republic, Estonia, Hungary, Latvia, Lithuania, Poland, Slovakia and Slovenia. The six countries of Southeast Europe included are Albania, Croatia, Bulgaria, Macedonia, Romania and Serbia. The analysis covers the time period between the initial period of regime change 1989–1991 and the present.

The crux of the problem lies in the inability of Southeast European countries to secure a functioning rule of law. While many existing analyses of post-communist transformation focus on features of the formal institutional system to analyse democratisation, this book captures governance practices in these countries that ran counter to the effects that formal democratic institutions were designed to have. The argument is that modernisation preconditions and regime legacies drew the perimeter within which the dynamics of domestic party competition interacted with the process of European integration towards more and less successful democratisation outcomes. These factors appeared in different configurations at the moment of regime change in the early 1990s and coalesced into more favourable recipes for democratisation in post-communist countries of Central Eastern Europe

---

3   Judt, T. (2008) 'Have We Learned, If Anything?' *New York Review of Books* 55: 7.   www.nybooks.
com/articles/archives/2008/may/01/what-have-we-learned-if-anything/?pagination=false.

than was the case in Southeast Europe. In Southeast Europe, authoritarian parties that ruled over regime change in the early 1990s produced a mode of rule which represents a lasting obstacle to their further democratisation.

Have we not become tired of studying democracy, described by some contemporary scholars as a new world religion (Brown 2011), generating universal consensus while at the same time being emptied of any meaning? Here I agree with Rancière (2011: 78) in asking what crucial political notion has not been 'torn and frayed by use'? Given the hiatus that separates formal proclamations of regimes as democratic from actual political practices taking place therein (and not only in post-communist Europe), the struggle for democracy as rule by the people remains as pertinent as ever. Democracy is here understood as having both a processual and a substantive dimension. Civil rights are the normatively desirable objective of democracy pursued in this book, while the rule of law is their key procedural safeguard. The rule of law is defined as the principle of supremacy and universality of law (Morlino 2002). Rule of law deficiencies are in the book closely related to corruption which, broadly conceived, stands for the misuse of entrusted power for private gain (Rose-Ackerman 2004, Krastev 2004, Heywood 2009).

Authoritarian party rule over regime change in Southeast Europe produced obstacles to the rule of law through processes of power concentration, power transformation and, paradoxically, power dispersion (Zakošek 1997). In a nutshell, post-communist countries in Europe were engaged in defining rules and institutions to govern their societies, and at the same time they were redistributing enormous societal material resources. In this process a vast space opened for abuse of power, insider deals and rampant corruption across the whole of the post-communist world (Vachudova 2009). In former Yugoslav states, conflicts from the 1990s further aggravated the problem of abuse of power by providing a setting in which this initial capital accumulation by privileged individuals and groups was taking place far away from the public eye. At the same time that formal democratic institutions were being established, longstanding practices of authoritarian rule unconstrained by law were adapting to new circumstances.

When the mayor of Novi Pazar in Serbia lost the 2008 election, the new administration accused him of misappropriating 18 million Euro from the city budget through false public tenders, fictitious public works, favouritism and illegal contracts. Here a cynical observer could perhaps say, very well, but anyone can name numerous similar cases of abuse of power, and this is by no means unique to Southeast Europe. That was not the whole story however. When leaving office, apart from burdening the city with an enormous debt, the mayor literally emptied the premises that he used to occupy; taking the desk and chairs, de-installing the air-conditioning system and even removing electrical sockets from the walls. Since it was his political party's money that paid for decorating the office in the first place, he saw no reason for not taking everything with him on his departure. Though tragicomic, this example serves as a vivid illustration of the lengths that this predatory conception of public office can take.

The first component in the explanation that I propose is drawn from modernisation theory. While democratisation literature has in the past drawn heavily on modernisation theory, a contemporary strand of this scholarship stresses that modernisation propositions should be coupled with an analysis of party system dynamics in order to explain democratisation (Capoccia and Ziblatt 2010). Building on the classical democratisation studies of Moore (1966) or Rueschemeyer, Stephens and Stephens (1992), this strand of scholarship maintains attention to historical analysis, but argues that too much emphasis has been put on the link between socioeconomic development and democracy at the expense of other possible explanations. While pressure from below is a crucial societal dynamic, elite competition from above was also important for democratisation, especially in the case of post-communist Europe. In advancing the study of European post-communist democratisation, Capoccia and Ziblatt's advice should be taken in the opposite direction – by revitalising modernisation theory and the structural perspective more broadly. The bulk of early research on third-wave democratisation focused on theorising democratisation from above, studying elite interactions and employing actor-centred approaches. From the perspective of this book, on their own such analyses are unable to establish broader historical patterns or provide convincing explanations of divergent democratisation trajectories. Drawing on those scholars who combine the study of historical legacies with an analysis of political party dynamics (such as Herbert Kitschelt or Grzegorz Ekiert), this book emphasises socioeconomic development and previous communist regime types as key structural constraints on subsequent democratisation, which are understood to constrain the scope of political agency at the moment of regime change.

The second part of the explanation therefore emphasises the importance of the political dynamic during the early 1990s, focusing on political party system dynamics in the initial decade between 1990 and 2000. I review and extend scholarship on the role of political party systems in post-communist democratisation to argue for the unique importance that authoritarian party dominance during the initial period of regime change has had on subsequent democratisation. Furthermore, while typical comparative politics studies analyse only factors within the domestic political arena, I also consider the relationship between external democracy promotion of the EU and domestic factors that drive democratisation. As a result, this study bridges the disciplinary gap between comparative politics and international relations studies (Schimmelfennig and Sedelmeier 2005, Hobson 2009), following in the tradition of comparative scholarship that does not disregard international factors in structural analyses of political change (e.g. Skocpol 1979).

Thirdly, this book engages with the literature on the roles of conflict, the imperatives of state-building and the obstacles to democratisation in multiethnic contexts, embracing the complexity that this brings into the analysis. In unravelling the ways in which the state-building process proved relevant for subsequent democratisation, I endorse the concept of disputed statehood which enables clear differentiation among countries where acquiring statehood did not have lasting consequences on successful democratisation, versus cases where statehood was disputed either by internal minorities or the kin state. The latter refers primarily to case studies of Croatia and Serbia in Chapters 6 and 7. In cases of disputed statehood I pay special attention to unearthing ways in which circumstances of violent conflict exacerbated authoritarian governance practices. In particular, the extraordinary circumstances of war facilitated greater accumulation of executive power as well as providing cover for political repression. Important domestic voices of opposition in the parliamentary arena and in broader civil society were muted, while both the state and the economy were harnessed by political parties in power.

The presented framework, though creating an interface between structural and contingent factors, clearly predicates structure over contingency. Historical preconditions and legacies influenced whether democratic contenders competed for power, or whether authoritarian parties presided over regime change. The democratisation outcome that emerges from this crucial nexus is further conditioned by the international environment at the moment of regime change. New democracies such as Poland or the Czech Republic where all major parties had credible democratic credentials were also the first to start European integration processes, and on their own initiative. Close international scrutiny from the onset of democratic reform in turn improved their chances of curbing egregious abuses of power perpetrated by political elites. Conversely, in cases where violent conflicts occurred in the early 1990s, as in Croatia and Serbia, processes of European integration were postponed. Once the EU started applying political conditionality in Southeast Europe, it proved to be less of a good fit to given circumstances, and it faced an already solidified authoritarian rule that needed dismantling.

The moment of regime change is understood as a critical juncture, a historical moment of unusually high contingency that proves crucial in directing subsequent outcomes (Brady and Collier 2004). In Southeast Europe periods of regime change were dominated by authoritarian parties whose governance practices were inimical to the establishment of the rule of law. Although in cases where democratisation was stalled, subsequent efforts were made to change direction, this has proven difficult because initial outcomes tend to be strongly self-enforcing (Pierson 2004). Given that entire political and economic systems were being redesigned, at the moment of regime change, political actors had ample room for manoeuvre. Once this critical window closed, however, the collage of institutional features coalesced into a new structure that exhibited increasing stickiness with time (Pierson 2004). What was at one point in time the product of contingent circumstances became institutional architecture that guided actors' behaviour through slow-moving historical processes such as democratisation (ibid.). In other words, after a particular trajectory is established, it gets locked in because the costs of switching increase markedly over time. This argument has been particularly well developed with reference to EU conditionality over potential member states in the process of European integration (Schimmelfennig 2005) and I trace its workings empirically throughout the study. Though I do not claim that inhibiting legacies are impossible to undo, contemporary developments in post-communist Europe speak to their resilience.

Finally, let me conclude by stating what this book is not about. Though the transformation towards democracy and capitalism went hand in hand in post-communist Europe, this study does not include an account of the great transformation from socialist planned economies to capitalism. Alas, such is the fate of analytical endeavours. I discuss economic reform in aspects relevant to establishing the rule of law, but I do not unpack the wide social implications of the introduction of the capitalist mode of production. Political abuse of power and the deeply unjust privatisation process are the root causes of the lack of legitimacy across the region of post-communist Europe and in this book they are identified as chief obstacles to further democratisation. While I focus on ways in which instrumental use of power subverted the role of the state in moderating the complex process of social transformation, other dimensions of the introduction of capitalism such as growing social inequality or the commodification of public goods are equally deserving of careful examination but remain out of the scope of this book. If we agree that economic freedom is a precondition of political freedom, then the nature of the economic transformation that took place across post-communist Europe has fundamental implications for democratisation that are worth a study of their own. This is the research programme that I aim to pursue in the future.

Outline of the book

This book aims to provide an analytically rigorous and at the same time historically grounded account of democratisation in European post-communist countries. The criteria for case selection are discussed in Chapter 1, which elaborates the central argument according to which weak rule of law is the root cause of low-level equilibria of democratisation (cf. Greskovits 1998) across Southeast Europe. The second part of Chapter 1 discusses the overall empirical strategy of the study as well as providing justification for the choice of a mixed method research design. It ends by highlighting the key strengths of both Qualitative Comparative Analysis (QCA) and the case study method.

Chapter 2 weaves together various strands of the political science discipline into a configurational argument that addresses the puzzle of stagnating democratisation in Southeast Europe. Socioeconomic development and historical regime legacies are taken as conditioning parameters (Kirchheimer 1965) for the available palette of political choices at the moment of regime change. In the second part, literatures on party politics and on EU conditionality are extended to argue for the unique importance that authoritarian party dominance has had on subsequent democratisation during the initial period of regime change, as well as for the importance of timing of EU conditionality. Finally, state-building literatures are engaged with to introduce the concept of disputed statehood, enabling the analytical differentiation of cases that experienced violent conflicts from those that did not. Chapter 2 concludes with a succinct formulation of the theoretical argument that guides subsequent empirical analysis.

In Chapters 3 and 4 each of the key explanatory factors is approached analytically, in search of operational definitions and empirical evidence that will enable a better grasp of the political development in each of the country cases.

The main purpose of these chapters is an analysis of diverse post-communist democratisation trajectories and the exploration of bivariate relationships among key explanatory factors and the outcome. Modernisation preconditions, regime legacies, dynamics of party systems, features of EU conditionality, and problems of disputed statehood are analysed with the aim of uncovering patterns of similarity and difference among the fourteen country cases.

In Chapter 5 the theoretical framework is tested through a model that incorporates all explanatory factors. Fuzzy set QCA is used to identify relationships of necessity and sufficiency and to determine the most important elements in the causal chain that generated more and less successful democratisation outcomes.

Chapters 6 and 7 move into a fine-grained case study analysis of two countries, Croatia and Serbia, where a combination of factors has thwarted democratisation prospects in somewhat complementary ways. Here the empirical findings of fsQCA are tested through systematic process tracing, which identifies the most important causal mechanisms. At the same time, the two case studies serve the purpose of theory development since they help identify specific roles that explanatory factors played in given cases. This is particularly relevant with respect to the influence that war has had on democratisation, which is an under-researched relationship in existing literature.

The Conclusion summarises discussions and empirical findings from previous chapters, draws parallels among the two case studies and offers some tentative remarks regarding the future of democracy in the region of Southeast Europe.

chapter one | rule of law as the weakest link

In an important but often overlooked way, regime change after communism did not turn out as expected: Yugoslavia, as the most politically liberalised and economically westward-oriented state in the Eastern bloc, produced the bloodiest conflict (Tripalo 1993, King 2000). While the peoples of former Yugoslavia were fighting, a 'horrified but nevertheless fascinated world wondered how it was possible that a seemingly prosperous and stable country could collapse into such a brutal internecine war' (Stokes *et al* 1996). Due to this fact, among others, scholars have raised the question of whether democratisation in Southeast Europe should be approached as a distinctive model of regime change (Pridham 2000). Perhaps more to the point, scholars did not so much consciously question the existence of a separate democratisation trajectory, as they unconsciously avoided including country cases from Southeast Europe in their comparative assessments of post-communist democratisation. Even today countries of former Yugoslavia remain a blank spot in democratisation research (Džihić and Segert 2012). As a result, the majority of attempts at theorising post-communist democratisation are based on Central Eastern European cases (Bunce 1999, King 2000, Carothers 2002, Ramet and Wagner 2010). This book moves into this lacuna and analyses democratisation in Southeast Europe.

Figure 1.1 displays the puzzle that animates this endeavour. It shows the progress in democratisation that post-communist countries have made since 1991, using Freedom House scores for political and civil liberties. The scores have been combined into a composite following the same procedure as in Inglehart and Welzel (2005).[1] As a result, on this scale zero represents the worst and twelve the best democratisation score. Figure 1.1 shows progress in democratisation over time for the regions of Southeast Europe, Central Eastern Europe, the Commonwealth of Independent States (CIS) and Russia, and it covers the twenty-one year period from 1991 to 2012.

The first characteristic that catches the eye is that the two regions, Central Eastern and Southeast Europe, show progress in democracy scores over time, while the CIS and Russia exhibit stability and deterioration respectively. In the case of Russia deterioration of political and civil liberties is especially pronounced since 1997, while the CIS states show continuity in very low democracy scores. While trajectories of Russia and the CIS also merit attention of post-communist

---

1. In a first step the two components of civil and political rights are summed up, and the sum is subtracted by two in order to obtain a 0–12 scale rather than 2–14. In the second step, the values have been reversed to make the scores more intuitive. These procedures make the interpretation of the scale easier, without affecting scores.

Figure 1.1: Democratic advances in post-communist regions for period 1991–2012

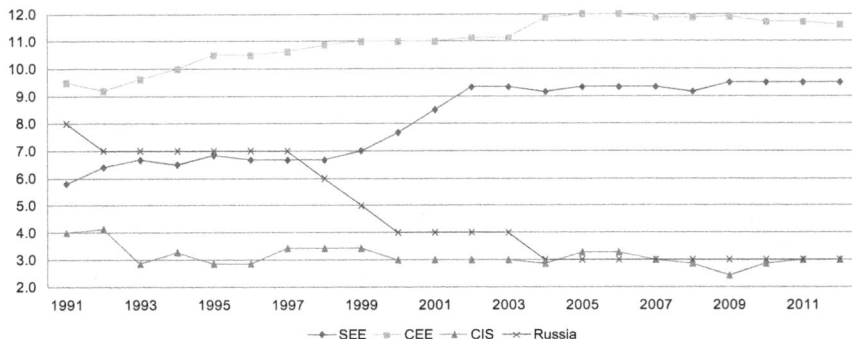

Note: Countries behind regional labels in Southeast Europe are Albania, Bulgaria, Croatia, Macedonia, Romania and Serbia; in Central Eastern Europe the Czech Republic, Estonia, Hungary, Lithuania, Latvia, Poland, Slovakia, Slovenia; and in CIS Armenia, Azerbaijan, Belarus, Georgia, Kazakhstan, Kyrgyzstan, Moldova, Tajikistan.
Source: www.freedomhouse.org, calculations by author

democratisation scholars, they fall outside the scope of this study. Geddes argues that the 'domains of theories of democratisation should be limited to cases that fit their basic assumptions about conditions in the old regime', because otherwise the researcher is pursuing an impossible theory that would explain all outcomes (2009: 293). Following this advice, the domain of analysed country cases is limited to the two regions of Eastern Europe that share sufficient similarities regarding the previous regime. By focusing on Eastern Europe the study introduces two boundary conditions, the first involving constitutional frameworks, the second electoral systems. Russia and the CIS countries are referred to as superpresidencies (Fish 2001), due to the scope of powers vested in the president by their constitutions. Similarly, they are characterised by majoritarian electoral systems. By excluding majoritarian electoral systems and superpresidencies, the analysis focuses on European post-communist countries that had stronger institutional prerequisites for the development of multipartyism and of robust parliamentary opposition – factors which play a key role in the proposed explanatory framework. I therefore apply Geddes' advice about the domain of the theory that I am proposing, both with respect to similarities in the previous regimes, and with respect to the similarity of constitutional setups, in order to increase the validity of the empirical findings. The objective is to extend the empirical grasp as well as revise existing theories of post-communist democratisation by systematically comparing democratisation trajectories of Southeast European and Central Eastern European countries. While for the moment conventional labels of Central Eastern and Southeast Europe are employed, the aim is to analyse the diversity that hides behind these labels and hence the study proceeds with an analysis of fourteen country cases.

Southeast (SEE) and Central Eastern European (CEE) countries have clearly made advances in the development of political and civil liberties of their societies since regime change, and this is particularly true for the improvement of formal democratic institutions such as free and fair elections. At the same time, the two regions exhibit important differences, and their comparison contains the key puzzle of this study. As can be seen from Figure 1.1, the two regions did not have the same starting point, with CEE countries scoring an average of around nine at the very beginning of the process, while SEE countries started from a lower average score of six. Next, in the first decade of post-communist transformation, the CEE group made significant advances, already reaching the average score of eleven in 1999. In contrast, the SEE group of countries spent a large part of the first decade not making any democratic advances. This, however, is not surprising, since the average score for SEE countries was in large part driven by the very low scores of former Yugoslav states that were engaged in wars, especially between 1991 and 1995, but also throughout the decade.

Having this in mind, the explanation for the difference in democratic advances during the first decade after regime change seems obvious, perhaps even trivial. However, it is the difference in trajectories between the two regions since the end of the 1990s that presents a new and unexplored puzzle. In the second decade of democratisation, the CEE group of countries made one more jump forward, in 2004. This is the year that the group joined the European Union, and since then the average score for the region remains at the maximum; though with some worrying signs of backsliding in the most recent years since 2010. The other group of SEE countries, however, made a leap forward between 1998 and 2002 – but has since stagnated. This brief period was characterised by the first democratic alternation of power in Romania, Bulgaria and Macedonia 1996–1998, as well as the 'democratic turn' elections in Serbia and Croatia in 2000 (Schimmelfennig 2005a). After democratic parties gained power across Southeast Europe at the beginning of the 2000s, the expectation was that the following period would be marked by significant movements forward in democracy scores. However, what we have witnessed instead is not democratisation, but stagnation.

How can this stagnation be explained? Pridham (2000) wrote at the end of the 1990s that the demands of state-building, national identity and ethnicity were much more pronounced in Southeast Europe, and that they have significantly distracted these countries from the priorities of democracy building and economic reform. But if the processes of state- and nation-building, as well as violent conflicts, explain why the region did not move forward during the first decade after regime change, how do we explain stagnation after these factors no longer exert an influence? If those are the reasons that the SEE group of countries did not catch up with respect to CEE until the late 1990s, why has the gap between the two regions not started closing in the last decade? Instead, if we look at the period since 2002, the gap between the two regions has actually increased. This is in spite of the fact – it is worth emphasising – that the average scores for the Southeast group include Bulgaria and Romania, two countries that joined the European Union in 2007.

Therefore, the central question is why Southeast Europe has not been catching up with Central Eastern Europe in the second decade since regime change. Focusing on the period after state-building and violent conflicts ceased, the answer as to why countries in Southeast Europe seem to dwell in a low-level equilibrium requires moving away from saying that this was a conflict-ridden region and looking for alternative explanations. The fact that violent conflicts which occurred in former Yugoslav states offer only a partial explanation is accentuated by the cases of Bulgaria and Romania, which did not undergo either state-building or war, but which nevertheless seem to share the fate of post-Yugoslav states when it comes to democratisation trajectories. Observing democratic development in post-communist Europe over the last ten years with these questions in mind reveals a phenomenon well worth exploring.

Democracy is here not understood as a predetermined end state but as an open-ended outcome (Whitehead 2002). In line with this conceptualisation, the term transition is abandoned, having over time become equated with a linear understanding of progress towards a preselected destination of liberal democracy and market economy (cf. Fukuyama 1992). The divergent development of Third Wave democracies, most of which remain in the 'grey zone' between democracy and authoritarianism, testify to reality not following the 'predictable democratisation script' (Carothers 2002: 14). Instead, the key concepts employed to explain democratisation processes in post-communist Europe are regime change and transformation processes that occurred in the economic, social and political domains. The concept of regime change is important because it shifts focus to the critical juncture (Collier and Collier 1991), which opened with the fall of communist regimes at the end of the 1980s. It draws attention to a moment in history which had vast potential for rewriting the institutional rules and endorsing a new set of norms. This study starts from the premise that by unravelling features of this critical juncture it becomes possible to explain long-term processes of democratisation.

The concept of transformation on the other hand evokes the open-endedness of the process of democratisation as well as not prejudicing the outcome. This is important in a study that is designed to explore a diversity of outcomes. In addition to that, transformation assumes a more complex and multifaceted process of change than is implied by the concept of transition. State socialism in Eastern Europe had the misfortune of collapsing at a time when Western countries advocated a very uniform recipe of development that was premised on establishing free and fair elections coupled with the Washington Consensus economic reforms. Notwithstanding that, twenty years later there is a multiplicity of outcomes across the former Eastern bloc, and hence an open-ended concept of transformation seems better suited to the studied phenomenon. The adopted concept of transformation draws from neo-modernisation analysis or the multiple modernities perspective (Spohn 2009). While the basic premises of modernisation theory are preserved, its homogenising assumption, according to which developing countries follow the prescribed Western paths to democracy and capitalism, is rejected (Eisenstadt 2000).

Zooming in on Southeast Europe

If the presented puzzle is considered worth exploring, it immediately opens up the question of differences that lie hidden behind the trajectory line drawn for the region of Southeast Europe. Are Bulgaria and Romania not a separate group, where there was neither war nor state-building? Likewise, should Croatia not be taken out of this group since it is the only country in the region to have completed accession negotiations with the EU? More fundamentally even – where are the boundaries of the region of Southeast Europe and do they make sense? The term Southeast Europe has been politically advanced to replace the heavily burdened term the Balkans as a more neutral reference with primarily geographical connotations. It advanced to common usage through European Union policies towards the region, starting with the 1999 Stability Pact for Southeast Europe. Most classifications of countries that fall under this label include Albania, Bosnia and Herzegovina, Bulgaria, Croatia, Macedonia, Montenegro, Romania, Serbia and, as of recently, Kosovo. In addition to that, depending on whether the discursive context is one of EU regional policy, security policy or enlargement, Moldova, Turkey, Greece and Ukraine are sometimes included under this label as well.

This study operates with a minimal definition of Southeast Europe that includes former Yugoslav countries plus Bulgaria, Romania and Albania. Bosnia and Herzegovina is not included because explaining democratisation in that country requires a different set of explanatory tools from those developed here. According to the Failed States Index, Bosnia and Herzegovina remains exposed to a relatively high risk of state failure (2011). In July 2012 the six-party coalition collapsed after it took fourteen months to form a government. Reports from the International Crisis Group warn repeatedly of state failure and deep-rooted crisis in Bosnia and Herzegovina, while during 2011 and 2012 the EU repeatedly expressed concern over political instability in the country. Therefore, due both to the permanent crisis of governability in the country as well as the unique role that the international community has played in Bosnia and Herzegovina, the theoretical framework developed in this study would offer only limited insights with respect to this country's development.

Kosovo and Montenegro are partially included since these states were established only very recently, in 2008 and 2006 respectively. For the sake of simplicity, throughout the book Serbia is referred to as a country case, even though until 2006 it was not an independent state and its state borders remain contested to this day. At the start of regime change in 1991 it was part of the Socialist Federal Republic of Yugoslavia, morphing into the Federal Republic of Yugoslavia from 1992 to 2003. In the period between 2003 and 2006 it was part of the State Union of Serbia and Montenegro, which ended after Montenegro voted for independence in May 2006. As a result, six countries are studied under the label Southeast Europe: Albania, Bulgaria, Croatia, Macedonia, Romania and Serbia. According to the most recent Nations in Transit report, these countries are semi-consolidated democracies, with the exception of Albania which is classified as a hybrid regime (2012). All eight Central Eastern European countries included in this analysis are, on the other hand, classified as consolidated democracies.

Information provided in Figure 1.1 suggests that these six countries share a stagnant democratisation trajectory in the second decade after regime change. Nonetheless, the reader might contend that the averaging of scores hides actually divergent democratisation trajectories. For that reason the following analyses focuses on the six country cases rather than looking at the region as a whole, with the aim of uncovering those dimensions of democratisation that might lie behind the stagnant trajectories of these states. After the Third Wave of democratisation there has been a proliferation of concepts and definitions in political science literature aiming to capture the specific formations of new democracies, both in post-communist Europe and in East Asia or Latin America. In an effort to distinguish them from old European democracies, scholars have come up with various adjectives to try and capture the degree to which a country may be considered democratic and the type of democracy that emerges (Collier and Levitsky 1996). Among others, the literature has identified hybrid democracies (Karl 1995, Diamond 2002), delegative (O'Donnell 1994), defective (Merkel 1999), authoritarian (Zakaria 1997), Potempkin (King 2001), ethnocratic, limited, false and others.

In this study the focus is on the degree to which a country has democratised, rather than on trying to typify existing democracies as, for instance, Wolfgang Merkel has done. In developing a definition of democracy based in partial regimes Merkel has created a typology of defective democracies, where each subtype signals the key flaw of a given regime that keeps it from becoming an embedded democracy (2004). In contrast to that, I understand democracy as an ideal which serves as a yardstick against which real-life cases are examined. If democracy stands for rule by the people, it requires at very least universal suffrage, free and fair elections, several contestants for power and access to information as institutional prerequisites, as well as sufficient civil and political freedom for citizen participation. These minimal standards are aimed at achieving the goals of democracy, which may be summed up as political and civil freedom, control over government and political equality (Diamond and Morlino 2004). The goals of democratic regimes are in turn fulfilled to varying extent in different empirical contexts. According to this definition, democracy is understood both as a process and as a substantive end. The normatively desirable objectives of democratic regimes are extensions of liberty and political equality, while procedural safeguards for ensuring these objectives are the rule of law, participation, competition for power, vertical and horizontal accountability (ibid.). The analysis of available cross-country empirical measurements of democracy reveal that in post-communist Europe the greatest variety lies in those dimensions that capture civil liberties as the substantive objective of democracy, and the accompanying dimension of the rule of law as their institutional guarantee.

One of many existing measurements of democracy is Freedom House Democracy Score, which defines civil liberties as 'allow[ing] for the freedoms of expression and belief, associational and organisational rights, rule of law, and

Figure 1.2: Civil liberties in Southeast Europe, for period 1991–2012

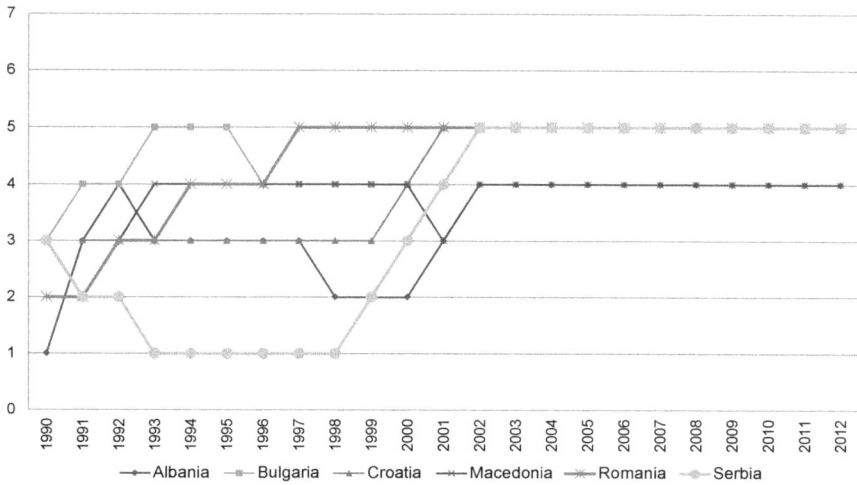

Source: www.freedomhouse.org

personal autonomy without interference from the state' (2012).[2] Since the mid-twentieth century civil liberties have been encoded in international treaties as human rights,[3] and they have been upheld by socialists and liberals alike. Using Freedom House data for the purpose of empirical analysis enables us to move the object of analysis from rating governments and their performance towards rights and freedoms enjoyed by individuals. Apart from conceptual precision, this is also important in order to avoid endogeneity in subsequent analysis since political party system dynamics form part of the theoretical framework, as is elaborated in Chapter 2. Figure 1.2 displays civil liberties scores separately for the six countries of Southeast Europe in the period of twenty-two years between 1990 and 2012.[4]

Figure 1.2 shows the civil liberties scores for Albania, Bulgaria, Croatia, Macedonia, Romania and Serbia. In the first decade after regime change, the scores were unstable and varied across the region, ranging from very low scores for Serbia in the period 1993–1998, to rather good scores for Bulgaria in the early 1990s. After 2002, however, all six countries exhibit stagnation in democratisation trajectories, confirming the argument that the region, which was in disarray during the 1990s, did pick up significantly between 1998 and 2002 – though this rise was

2. Freedom House website: http://www.freedomhouse.org. Last accessed August 23, 2012.

3. Most notably in the Universal Declaration of Human Rights in 1948.

4. Like in Figure 1.1, the scores have been reversed; hence 0 stands for the worst score, and 7 for the best.

followed by a long period of stagnation. Ever since 2002 no country in the region has made advances in the protection of civil liberties. Even though Macedonia and Albania are doing worse than the rest of the group, no country in Southeast Europe has reached the top score in this measurement. In contrast to that, countries of Central Eastern Europe had already reached top scores in civil liberties in 2005 and their scores remain stable.[5] This finding becomes even more important when we acknowledge that the Freedom House criteria of democracy are considered fairly low since they capture only serious deviations from what a democratic regime should guarantee its citizens. Its definitions are only nuanced enough to enable the analyst to distinguish between cases where significant aberrations to democratic procedures are present. After major breaches of individual political and civil rights have been excluded in a regime, it receives the highest score on this ranking and such regimes are classified as securing basic political and civil rights. As Figure 1.2 shows, no country of Southeast Europe satisfies this basic criterion.

Now, as was made evident in Diamond and Morlino's definition of a good democracy (2004), the procedural equivalent of civil and political liberties is the rule of law. The system of rule of law within a democratic framework ensures political and civil rights as well as mechanisms of accountability which 'in turn affirm the political equality of all citizens and constrain potential abuses of state power' (O'Donnell 2004: 32). Institutional safeguards based in the principle of legality and civil liberties are necessary conditions for a democracy, regardless of whether it is conceived as liberal or socialist (Wood 1995). Without functional rule of law 'rights are not safe and the equality and dignity of all citizens are at risk' (O'Donnell 2004: 32). While it is no surprise that countries that emerged from various kinds of authoritarian regimes do not have a legacy of rule of law to lean on (Philip 1999), why defects in the rule of law survive well after formal democratic institutions were established remains unexplained.

According to Carothers, the rule of law can be defined as a 'system in which the laws are public knowledge, are clear in meaning, and apply equally to everyone. They enshrine and uphold the political and civil liberties that have gained status as universal human rights over the last half-century' (1998: 96). In political systems that uphold the rule of law, the legal system is fair, competent and efficient; judges are impartial and independent and not subject to political manipulation. Finally, the government is embedded in a legal framework which is accepted by government officials (ibid.). The centrepiece of the relationship between the rule of law and the ensuring of political and civil rights that I advance is in that the state must respect the law (Morlino 2002, O'Donnell 2004). The rule of law hence stands for the principle of supremacy and universality of law, and is closely related to questions of corruption, organised crime, access to justice, independent judiciary, competent bureaucracy and civilian control of the police and armed forces (Morlino 2002).

---

5. With the exception of Latvia which slid back one point in 2010 and Hungary which slid back one point in 2012.

Though new democracies in post-communist Europe did not have a rule of law tradition to build on, democratic institutions erected through new constitutions and fortified through regular elections were expected to affirm this principle over time; hence these improvements should show up in the development of civil and political liberties. But as Figure 1.2 shows, curtailments to civil liberties continued reproducing themselves over time despite regular elections, raising a pertinent question about how the rule of law can be secured. As the following chapter shows, the difficulty of dismantling authoritarian governance practices from the 1990s helps explain this persistent democratic stagnation in Southeast Europe.

With respect to operational definitions of the two concepts that guide further empirical investigation, Carothers (1998) conceptualises the rule of law as consisting of, firstly, substance of legislation; secondly, competence, efficiency and accountability of legal institutions and, finally, judiciary independence. The substance of legislation refers to whether actual rules and regulations built into the legal framework of a country effectively protect political and civil liberties. Effectiveness, competence and accountability of courts refer primarily to common problems in post-communist judiciaries with respect to large backlogs of cases, excessive length of court procedures and a general lack of transparency in the judiciary process. Finally, judiciary independence is an encompassing term that captures political and other influences on judges and courts, but also more broadly concerns overall compliance of the political elites with the rule of law. Breaches of any of them weaken the rule of law, while successful reforms introduced in any of these three dimensions are considered to bolster the rule of law. These dimensions aim to capture features of a regime where the government is embedded in a legal framework that is accepted by government officials. The key feature of democratisation in Southeast Europe is the extent to which these new states uphold the principle of mutual and self-imposed limitations of power (Kochenov 2004).

When discussing functional systems of rule of law, one threads very closely to the problem of corruption. Corruption may be understood as 'the inverse measure of the rule of law, which is to say, the more corruption there is, the less a system may be said to function according to the rule of law' (Ramet and Wagner 2010: 19). While problems with corruption have been much studied in the context of post-communist Europe, defining the phenomenon remains a longstanding challenge for the social sciences, as was its measurement (Krastev 2004, Heywood 2009). A good basic definition would probably go along the lines of a misuse of entrusted power for private gain (Rose-Ackerman 2004, Krastev 2004, Heywood 2009). Karklins (2002) adds 'at the expense of the public good' to this definition to stress the social costs and the fact that corruption has deep repercussions for questions of social justice. Research has shown that corruption contributes to rising inequality and negatively affects social trust and economic performance, among other things (Holmes 2006, Heywood 2009). Here the focus is not on corruption as a phenomenon *per se*, but rather as an indicator of difficulties in establishing the rule of law. However, since the aim is to explore the extent to which regimes managed to strengthen or thwart the development of rule of law, phenomena such as state capture and abuse of public office clearly enter the analysis.

Figure 1.3 Judicial framework and independence in countries of Southeast Europe compared to CEE average, 2001–2012

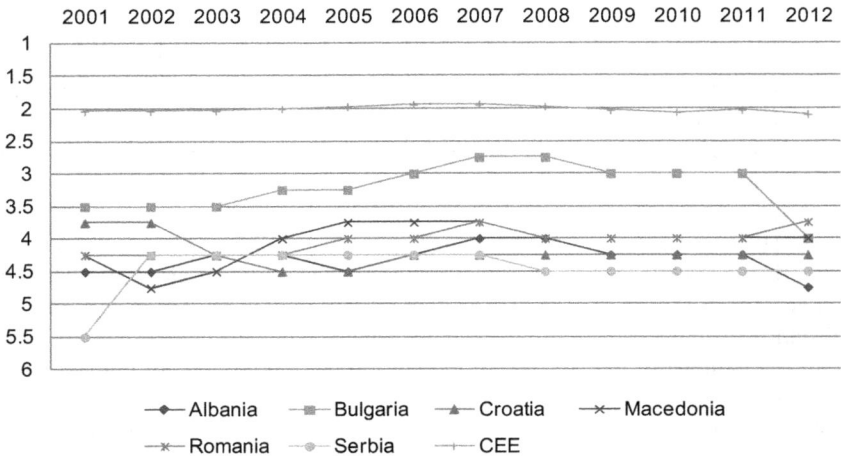

Source: Freedom House Nations in Transit

Previous sections showed empirical data in support of the argument according to which the extent to which civil liberties are secured across post-communist Europe could be an important dimension of democracy that explains divergence among countries of Southeast and Central Eastern Europe. The successful protection of civil liberties is presented as directly depending on the functioning rule of law systems and the related problem of corruption. The following sections again submit these arguments to empirical scrutiny. Figure 1.3 presents Freedom House Nations in Transit data for the dimension of judicial framework and independence, showing scores for the observed six Southeast European countries separately, compared to the average score for Central Eastern European countries, over the 2001–2012 period.

The dimension of judiciary framework and independence reveals a clear distinction between Central Eastern Europe on the one hand, and countries of Southeast Europe on the other. The average score for CEE is high and constant over the entire period covered in the analysis, while the scores for SEE countries are consistently lower, and exhibit both positive and negative trends. While judicial independence in Serbia, Macedonia, Romania and Bulgaria improved in the first half of the 2000s, in more recent years there has been stagnation and even backsliding in the cases of Albania and Bulgaria. Croatia on the other hand witnessed backsliding on this dimension in the early 2000s and has remained stagnant since. Overall, this data shows that there is a noticeable difference among the two regions of CEE and SEE; that the second decade since regime change has been marked by stagnation; and that the rule of law dimension closely mirrors developments in the protection of civil liberties.

Figure 1.4: Rule of law in countries of Southeast Europe compared to CEE average, 2001–2010

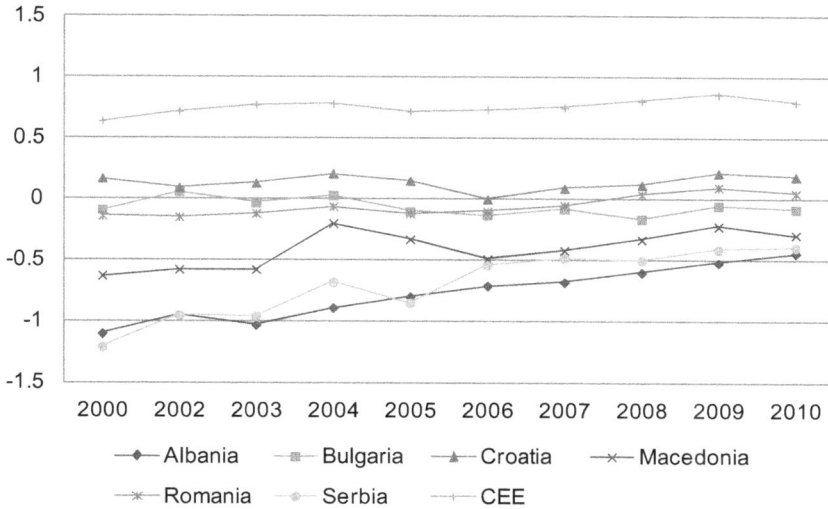

Source: World Bank Governance Indicators. This data is available on the World Bank website, http://info.worldbank.org/governance/wgi/index.asp. Last accessed August 23, 2012.

In order to avert criticism for relying too extensively on Freedom House measurements, Figure 1.4 shows scores on the dimension of rule of law as calculated by the World Bank. The World Bank Governance Indicators (WBGI) project measures several dimensions important for developing democratic governance, with rule of law being one of them. Figure 1.4 shows data for the same countries as in the previous analysis, for the period 2000–2010.

While WBGI measurement captures less movement in scores over time than the Nations in Transit measurement, the essential propositions about the comparative position of countries in the two regions and the stagnation over the second decade hold firm. Similarly, if the Bertelsmann Transformation Index is used to analyse change over time in the dimension of the rule of law for these countries, the same picture emerges. Finally, if the phenomenon of corruption may be understood as the inverse relation to the rule of law, this should also be reflected in empirical measurements. Figure 1.5 shows Freedom House Nations in Transit scores for corruption, for the period 2001–2012.

As in previous analysis, there is a marked difference between the two regions, with the CEE group of countries scoring convincingly better than countries of SEE, where stagnation with some backsliding is the dominant trend. All the presented evidence about individual trajectories of SEE countries shows that the last decade has not seen a catching up process with CEE countries. If this basic argument is accepted as the phenomenon this study sets out to explain, the central

Figure 1.5: Corruption in countries of Southeast Europe compared to CEE average, 2001–2012

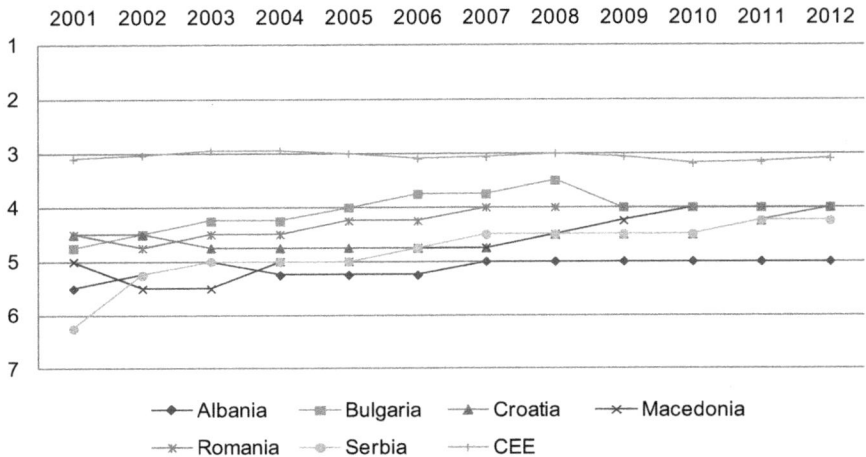

Source: Freedom House Nations in Transit

question then becomes: how can these enduring obstacles to civil rights protection and functioning rule of law systems be explained? That is the task of the following chapters. However, before proceeding to develop a theoretical account of this problem, the following sections first establish the types of practices that lie behind the persistently low scores for civil liberties and rule of law in Southeast Europe.

New democracies in Southeast Europe emerged out of authoritarian regimes where the ruler is sovereign in the classic sense of being able to make decisions unconstrained by law (O'Donnell 2004). Building on this legacy, regime change in Southeast Europe acquired a new morphology through processes of power concentration, power transformation and, paradoxically, power dispersion (Zakošek 1997). Power concentration refers to the domination of the executive over parliamentary and judiciary branches of government. Studying Croatia in the 1990s, Zakošek observed overgrowths of advisory and para-institutional formations around the executive office of the president at the time, Franjo Tuđman (ibid.). In more recent times, the European Commission's progress report for Croatia stated that significant challenges in the area of judicial independence remained, as well as the 'potential for undue political influence over the judiciary' (2009: 9). Furthermore, appointment procedures for the High Judicial Council (HJC) and the State Prosecution did not ensure independence because of potential for political interference. In addition, according to the European Commission (EC), the High Judicial Council did not have 'the capacity to carry out its key functions' (2009: 51). Similarly, the EC Progress Report for Serbia (2009) stressed the weak capacity of parliament and its inability to control the executive branch. In the judiciary branch the report found strong political influence through appointments in the High Judicial Council, even after its reform (ibid.). Vachudova (2005) uses the concept of concentration of power when describing ways in which the Iliescu regime in Romania dealt with any semblance of opposition by abusing power of appointment and patronage, controlling state-run television and other media and, most infamously, transporting armed mine workers to attack pro-democracy protesters in Bucharest in 1990. Similarly, in the case of Slovakia, she describes Mečiar's seizing control over parliamentary committees, excluding the opposition from oversight bodies, passing legislation that violated the principle of separation of power, misusing security intelligence services and seizing full control over the privatisation process (ibid.). Ganev (2007) analysed conversions of power in the case of Bulgaria and found a systematic and deliberate weakening of state capacity on the part of the Bulgarian Socialist Party. All these examples testify to the widespread practice in new post-communist democracies of concentrating power in the executive branch. The centralisation and arbitrary character of state power in these countries manifests itself through weak capacity of state institutions to check abuses by other public agencies and branches of government (Schedler *et al* 1999).

Second, the transformation of power happened as political clout was used for economic gain, transforming political into economic elites. Privatisation processes across the Balkans which transformed political party affiliates into economic moguls and tycoons have attested to this. 'Privileged information, privileged access, privileged loan terms, and appropriations by dubious means helped to build up private fortunes in much of former Yugoslavia' (Ramet and Wagner 2010: 22). In a second step, economic power was used to wield political influence leading to inside capture of the privatisation process (Gould 2003). In Bulgaria organised crime groups have merged with corporations and newly privatised assets, transforming 'accumulated wealth into political and administrative power' (Centre for the Study of Democracy 2010: 6). This political influence in turn allowed companies to corrupt their way to public tenders, avoid taxes and systematically break laws to gain competitive advantages' (ibid.). Some scholars have described privatisation processes in these states as 'daylight robbery' (Eagleton 2011) perpetrated by 'entrepratchiks', which is a term coined to characterise opportunity-seizing insiders (Verdery 1996). In Bulgaria members of the Socialist party (BSP) were involved in asset stripping of state enterprises, appropriation of loans from state banks and lucrative arbitrage opportunities that existed in foreign export business (Vachudova 2005). This poignant summary might as well serve to describe the course of events in Croatia or Serbia.

Even after entering the EU, Bulgaria's main problem remained 'de facto impunity of high level corruption and organised crime' since almost 80 per cent of the pre-trial proceedings initiated for corruption in the 2004–2007 run-up to EU accession did not end up in courts and were suspended or terminated at pre-trial phase' (Centre for the Study of Democracy 2009: 10). In Romania, the CVM report of the European Commission stated that the country did not show 'sufficient political commitment to support the reform processes' in areas of judiciary and fight against corruption (2010: 7). After the accession of Bulgaria and Romania to the EU, in 2008 the European Commission stated that serious problems remained in the area of judiciary reform and the fight against corruption, suspending for the first time in EU history further funding to Bulgaria until EC's main objections had been addressed (EC, IP/08/1195). Serious problems regarding tackling corruption and establishing judicial independence remain open in both countries (Spendzharova and Vachudova 2011).

In Serbia, in July 1992, the Parliament conferred on Milošević emergency powers over the economy, and what ensued was described as outright theft and personal aggrandisement (Ramet and Wagner 2010). The privatisation process was the key instrument of personal accumulation of capital for the socialist nomenclature, resulting in a kind of 'blocked transformation' (Lazić 2004, 2008). Similarly, in Slovakia, privatisation was a 'corrupt system of rewarding loyal Mečiar supporters' (Vachudova 2005: 43). Overall in this process of power transformation and realignment an independent economic sphere as the precondition of control over the political system never emerged. Dvornik[6] has argued that in Croatia the emergence of independent societal spheres was arrested, and instead there was a society without a pluralist structure.

This diagnosis identifies a key problem because however well one designs the formal legal framework, the government cannot be expected to be the sole source of its own control. Monitoring and control should stem from independent sources of power that can counterweight the power of political elites through pressure from below, from citizens and groups demanding fair treatment by government institutions. As a result of power transformation in the 1990s, economic and political power remained completely intertwined, so the only real potential for change exists in the average citizen and in various forms of citizen mobilisation.[7] The extent to which this mechanism of control from below was present in the different post-communist countries probably accounts for some of the divergent success these countries have had with establishing a functioning rule of law and curbing corruption.

Finally, and counterintuitively, in the initial period of regime change in the 1990s there was a process of power dispersion. Since formal institutions and legal instruments were sidelined and disregarded, a re-feudalisation process was set in motion whereby (albeit weak) professional bureaucracies were further weakened through a wide web of informal power coalitions based in party, region or clan affiliations (Zakošek 1997). While I take on board the empirical focus behind this category, I use the concept of state politicisation rather than re-feudalisation, since that term more accurately captures empirical reality in post-communist countries. That state socialist countries were in some respects transitioning to feudalism rather than capitalism was earlier suggested also by Verdery (1996: 208), who focused on processes of 'parcellisation of state sovereignty' into 'competing networks of clients' in Romania. Apart from drawing attention to weakened state

---

6. Author's interview with Srđan Dvornik, Interview No. 15, January 2011

7. ibid.

capacity, the concept of state politicisation emphasises practices of clientelism, patronage, and finally corruption and abuse of public office. By the end of the first decade after regime change corruption in post-communist Europe was 'developing new dimensions, reaching new heights, and posing new challenges' (World Bank 2000: xiii). In the case of Serbia, 'corruption remains prevalent in many areas and continues to be a serious problem', the most vulnerable sectors being public procurement, privatisation and other large budgetary expenditures, but also taxation, customs and licensing (EC Serbia Progress Report 2009: 12). Similarly, in Croatia public administration remains politicised, while 'anti-corruption measures and ethical principles remain to be embedded in public administration' (EC Croatia Progress Report 2009: 8).

In a nutshell, post-communist countries were engaged in defining rules and institutions to govern their societies, and at the same time were redistributing the bulk of existing assets. In this process corruption 'encoded advantages in these new rules and institutions for narrow interests and distorted the path of economic and political development' (World Bank 2000: xiii). The vast space that opened, while rewriting political and economic rules of the game, simultaneously created favourable conditions for abuse of power, insider deals and rampant corruption across the post-communist world (Vachudova 2009). In the case of former Yugoslav states, conflicts that went on during the 1990s further aggravated the problem of corruption by allowing political leaders to exploit extreme circumstances (Ramet and Wagner 2010) in which the initial capital accumulation was taking place far away from the public eye. At the same time, while formal democratic institutions such as elections, the separation of powers or judiciary independence were being inaugurated at the beginning of the 1990s through constitutions, longstanding practices of authoritarian rule unconstrained by law were adapting to new circumstances. The three described processes of power concentration in the executive, the fusing of economic and political power, and finally power dispersion in a web of informal corruptive networks help pinpoint characteristics of these governing practices that were coalescing into a new power morphology within democratic institutions in post-communist Europe. To what extent they were able to negatively affect post-communist democratisation across SEE and CEE countries depended on the varied strength of key explanatory factors explored in this study: socioeconomic and regime legacies, conditions of statehood, political party dynamics and the EU's democratisation pressure.

Empirical strategy

While drawing on historical institutionalism and the assumptions that follow from path-dependency, the study advances a mixed methods approach. Mixed methods research involves the use of two or more kinds of data gathering and techniques of analysis (Green *et al* 2005). The use of multiple sources of data and analytical techniques increases validity and credibility, it enables the development of a more comprehensive grasp of the social world and it allows for capturing a greater diversity of the phenomena (ibid.). In addressing the research question that motivates this study, a combination of cross-case and within-case techniques are employed, analysing fourteen country cases. The eight Central Eastern European countries included in the analysis are the Czech Republic, Estonia, Hungary, Latvia, Lithuania, Poland, Slovakia and Slovenia, while the six Southeast European countries are Albania, Bulgaria, Croatia, Macedonia, Romania and Serbia.

In defining fourteen European post-communist countries as the universe of cases, this study is in a lonely midway position between small-n comparative methods and large-n quantitative studies. In comparative sociology and comparative politics there are many studies at the small-n end of the spectrum as well as at the large-n end of spectrum, while the fewest studies exist in the mid-range that covers ten to twenty-five cases (Ragin 2000). Adopting a midway position enables the study to remain case oriented while the larger number of cases introduces variance both on the explanatory factors and the outcome. Such a design is well suited to the study of diversity that has been established with respect to democratisation trajectories in post-communist Europe. Furthermore, it allows for both theory development and hypothesis testing since with a moderate number of cases it is possible to examine cross-case patterns and still attend to the details of each case (Ragin and Rubinson 2009). Case selection with both negative and positive outcomes enables the exploration of potential causal factors that have led to either outcome. At the same time, unlike in standard quantitative analysis where the impact of individual explanatory factors is examined independently, here cases are understood as 'meaningful but complex configurations of events and structures' (Ragin 2004: 125).

The mixed method research design is appropriate for the study of diverse outcomes since it allows for the application of several methods suitable for comparative research. Once the theoretical framework is set up in Chapter 2, Chapters 3 and 4 mine various sources of data in order to uncover both the proposed explanatory factors and the outcome. Analyses of variance and correlation are used to explore bivariate relationships. These chapters in effect introduce the information and case analysis which is needed for fuzzy set QCA in Chapter 5. The QCA method 'provides analytic tools for comparing cases as configurations of set memberships and for elucidating their patterned similarities and differences' (Ragin 2000: 120). While the application of the method is explained in more detail in Chapter 5, let me emphasise a few of its key strengths here. Probably the most important feature of the QCA method is that its reliance on set theory allows for asymmetric explanations of outcomes, which proves very important in the analysis in Chapter 5. While the positive outcome may be attributed to factors a and b, the negative outcome may have come about as a result of c and d. This kind of analysis is not possible with standard regression techniques, which assume that once association is established it works in explaining both positive and negative outcomes. An additional strength of the QCA method, revealed in Chapter 5, is its focus on identifying necessary and sufficient conditions. It allows the researcher to establish whether a given explanatory factor is a subset or a superset of the observed outcome and as a result deepens the understanding of relationships between social phenomena. Finally but no less important, the application of the

QCA method in Chapter 5 represents a test of alternative theories, and its findings help identify which explanatory factors carry more weight than others.

In Chapters 6 and 7 the case study method is used with the aim of delineating causal mechanisms that link explanatory factors to the outcome. While statistical analyses and fsQCA are used primarily to establish the strength and relevance of relationships between causal factors and the outcome, the case study method is used to test the formulated theory and to establish how causes have engendered outcomes. The case studies of Serbia and Croatia are employed both for theory testing and theory development (George and Bennett 2003). They put the empirical findings of fsQCA to further examination through systematic process tracing. Process tracing allows for distinguishing between spurious correlations versus relationships of cause and effect, and it can identify which causal mechanism is the most likely or most important (Hawkins 2009). At the same time, by focusing on identifying new causal mechanisms and causal paths that explain the 'causal role of a particular independent variable across cases' (George and Bennett 2003: 79) the case studies also serve the purpose of theory development. This is particularly relevant with respect to the influence that war has had on democratisation, a relationship that is poorly researched in existing literature.

Croatia and Serbia have been selected as case studies because even though on the general level they represent similar cases, they actually entail some important differences that help bring nuance and trustworthiness to the specified theoretical framework. For instance, while both cases were characterised by authoritarian party dominance, in Croatia the Croatian Democratic Union party came to power by ousting the Communist party in the first multiparty election, while in Serbia the Socialist Party of Serbia was a fake remodel of the Communist party that won the first multiparty election and stayed in power throughout the 1990s. The analysis shows that these differences in party origin have influenced the differences in the resulting authoritarian governance practices. Secondly, wars and disputed statehood were present in both cases, but they played out differently. Croatia completed the state building project in 1998 and has been able to move the political agenda away from ethno-nationalism, while in Serbia the statehood project remains disputed and nationalism remains an important driving force of politics. Similarly, when it comes to the influence of the EU, Croatia is scheduled to join the European Union in 2013, while Serbia only ratified the Stabilisation and Association Agreement in 2010.

The focus on these two countries as case studies also provides a closer look at the differences with respect to structural constraints that characterised Serbia as opposed to Croatia at the moment of regime change. As the analysis in Chapter 3 will show, Croatia had more favourable historical legacies than Serbia, both in terms of overall socioeconomic development, and of a more favourable previous regime. Building onto that, fsQCA findings from Chapter 5 suggest that Serbia would not have avoided slow democratisation even in the absence of conflicts that erupted, while the same could not be said of Croatia. Case studies in Chapters 6 and 7 analyse this counterfactual proposition and trace how the identified differences between the two cases influenced the democratisation trajectories of Croatia and

Serbia. In a feedback loop, the rich empirical detail that renders meat onto the bones of the proposed theoretical framework and allows for nuanced differences in interpretation should strengthen the overall argument according to which the 1990s still matter in Southeast Europe today.

The primary method of collecting information for case studies of Croatia and Serbia was analysing primary sources and interviewing country experts. Interviews increase both the robustness of findings and the robustness of the theoretical model (Tansey 2007). I conducted eighteen interviews in total, in the time period between October 2010 and February 2011. The list of my interlocutors is provided in the Appendix. Interviews with country experts provided a wealth of factual material that was used to create more plausible analytical narratives. Any biases that the interviewees introduced were, I hope, removed by simultaneously relying on hundreds of primary sources of information on the two countries, including official government documents, international organisations' reports and assessments, studies by specialised organisations such as International Crisis Group, UNESCO and others, as well as domestic and international media coverage of Serbia and Croatia. The use of multiple sources of data and analytical techniques increased the validity and credibility of findings and made possible a more comprehensive grasp of the analysed phenomenon.

In the next step, Chapter 2 critically reviews existing approaches to democratisation in order to distil a working theoretical framework that guides subsequent empirical analysis.

chapter two | explaining democratisation

Democratisation studies are a vast field of scholarship that need viewing through analytical lenses in order to get a grasp of them. One way of sorting through the various existing theoretical approaches to democratisation is through the concepts of structure and agency. Here the debate revolves around whether the proper foci of analysis are actors' strategic interactions, or whether explanations lie hidden in the structural and historical factors. In fact, the best work in comparative politics does not lose sight of either side of the coin, constructing dynamic approaches instead. One such dynamic approach is path dependence analysis, which rests on complex causal processes that involve both structure and agency (Hall 2003). This study advances precisely such a path dependent argument, which rests on the assumption that a crucial choice or event alters the impact of subsequent events, challenging the assumption that factors x and z will have the same impact across cases (ibid.). This means that interaction effects occur over time and can multiply, and it rejects the assumption that an x occurring today has the same effect, y, across all settings in time and space. The world is not inhabited by timeless causal relations, but is rather understood as a branching tree whose tips represent events that unfold over time (Sewell 1996). Also, path dependent analysis is process oriented, whereby both timing and sequence of events matter for the outcome (Thelen 1999, Pierson 2000, Ekiert and Hanson 2003).

In existing democratisation studies, however, the bulk of research takes sides in the structure and agency debate. In his analysis of theories of democratisation at the end of the 1960s, Rustow (1970) saw an emphasis on structural, socioeconomic factors as the main contribution of his generation. The greatest contribution these authors made was to move away from prescriptive and descriptive legalism that characterised earlier work, which focused on the nuts and bolts of constitutions and formal institutions. Together they elaborated what is today known as the modernisation theory of democracy, with Lipset (1959) holding an especially prominent role in establishing the link between socioeconomic modernisation and democratisation. However, at the time of writing, Rustow had become concerned that this focus on structure somehow implied that the actual political process was superfluous, irrelevant for explaining democratic outcomes (ibid.).

Ignoring Rustow's concerns, modernisation studies that developed throughout the 1970s and '80s overemphasised structure and have as a result been criticised as functionalist and overly simplistic regarding the influence of capitalism on democracy (Grugel 2002). Looking back at the twenty years of transformation in post-communist Europe, the view according to which the relationship between democratisation and the introduction of capitalism is uncontroversial seems untenable. Though at the beginning of 1990s capitalism and democracy were embraced in post-communist countries as complementary mechanisms for the attainment of freedom, it has since become clear that rising socioeconomic inequalities and various forms of exploitation coexist uneasily with democratisation. Capitalism is complementary to democracy in that rights of citizenship are not determined by a person's socioeconomic position, but at the same time this civic equality leaves the deeper rooted questions of political and economic equality intact (Wood 1995), seriously limiting the exercise of citizenship.

The so-called mode of transition literature (see O'Donnell, Schmitter and Whitehead 1986, di Palma 1990, Przeworski 1991, Karl and Schmitter 1991) played an important role in the theories of democratisation, since after its rise to prominence it has become 'impossible to formulate a theory of democratic transitions that does not explicitly address the strategic interactions between and within the government and opposition' (Haggard and Kaufman 1997: 265). The mode of transition literature distinguished itself from earlier work on democratisation precisely by shifting focus towards human agency, the analysis of strategic behaviour of actors and elite-based compromise pacts. This was warranted, in part at least, by the fact that these scholars were attempting to account for numerous cases of democratisation in the Third Wave, characterised by high uncertainty of outcomes and the extraordinary weight carried by elite choices. They rejected functionalist determinism inherent to modernisation theories, and embraced emphasis on contingency (Grugel 2002). On the other hand, this literature was criticised for being excessively empirical, a-contextual, elitist, and focused only on the short term (ibid.).

After the collapse of the Eastern bloc, many insights from this literature on Latin American and Southern European transitions were applied in trying to account for post-communist transitions to democracy (e.g. Ishiyama 1997, Bruszt and Stark 1998, Greskovits 1998, Grzymala Busse 2002, McFaul 2002, 2005). While many authors built on the same premise of elite compromise as the most successful recipe for transition to democracy, some reframed the argument in terms of non-cooperative games (McFaul 2005) and competition among elites (e.g. Vachudova and Snyder 1996, Vachudova 2005, Grzymala Busse 2002, 2007). Today, looking back at the twenty years of post-communist democratisation processes, the mode of transition literature looks overly optimistic in placing the weight of their explanations on the interaction of elites and downplaying the influence of historical legacies and structural prerequisites of democratisation. Having said that, I do take on board that historic political and social change comes about through conscious human action (Przeworski 1991, Przeworski and Limongi 1997), and that any attempt at a comprehensive account of change must be dynamic. This realisation is however not new. When Kirchheimer (1965: 965) studied regime change in Russia and Germany in the late 1920s, he theorised that the answers lie in the intersection between socioeconomic conditions and the 'discretionary element left to the decisions of the regime'. In other words, the social and economic frame of a particular society 'lays down a conditioning parameter within which the original choice has to be made and solutions have to be sought' (Kirchheimer 1965: 966). This theoretical insight is of central importance to this study, because it draws attention to the fact that the supply of political parties, as well as elites' and citizens' value orientations are a function of their socioeconomic environment, and that hence the moment of regime change is not as highly contingent as the mode of transition literature assumes.

Kirchheimer's interactive approach was revived by Diamandouros and Larrabee (2000) who argued that structural conditions should be viewed as environments within which choice occurs. The particular trajectory that democratisation will take in a given country depends on how environmental factors combine with political choice (ibid.). In post-communist literature a similar epistemological position regarding the relationship between structural and contingent factors influencing democratisation was taken up, for instance in the edited volume of Ekiert and Hanson (2003), where valuable contributions were made in attempting to explain how historical legacies from pre-communist and communist regimes conditioned political and institutional choice after the fall of communism. Ekiert (2003) in particular argued that without accounting for institutional, social and political legacies of the communist period it was not possible to explain post-communist transformations.

The presented debate can also be applied to the scholarship on post-communist democratisation, which can be analogously organised by grouping explanations into those that emphasise how historical constraints influence long term democratic development, versus those that argue that immediate circumstances surrounding regime change in the turbulent period of the early 1990s were crucial for subsequent developments. Historical legacies explored in the literature on post-communism include geopolitical and spatial, regime types during communism, and, more broadly, modernisation arguments regarding economic development and other development indicators from communist and pre-communist times. These historical legacies have been operationalised as the distance from Western capitals (Kopstein and Reilly 2000), state society relations before the onset of communism (Kitschelt *et al* 1999), the length of democratic statehood before communism and pre-communist literacy (Darden and Grzymala Busse 2006), or simply as the level of economic development. When stressing that legacies can take facilitating or inhibiting forms, Ekiert (2003) was building on Roeder (1999) and others who claim that communist legacies should not be conceptualised exclusively as burdening democratisation, but instead should be understood as also carrying the potential for democratisation. Communist regimes pursued modernisation policies of industrialisation, urbanisation and education, as well as exhibiting relatively low levels of inequality. All these represent important ingredients for the subsequent introduction of democracy (Fish 2001, Ekiert 2003). In addition to that, during the 1980s important economic and political reforms were undertaken in a number of European post-communist countries (not least in Yugoslavia) that facilitated democratic breakthroughs. Taking this on board, Ekiert's distinction between inhibiting and facilitating legacies is adopted in subsequent discussions of structural conditions.

At the same time, numerous scholars of post-communism have focused on the circumstances surrounding regime change, analysing the mode of transition (Stark and Bruszt 1998, McFaul 2002), the availability of opposition and character of political competition (e.g. Grzymala Busse 2002, Vachudova 2005, Fish 1998, O'Dwyer 2004, 2006) as well as the constitutional features of the new regime (McGregor 1996, Fish 2001). In addition to that, important features of the political economy have been identified as influencing democratisation prospects, such as the politics of partial reform (Hellman 1998) as well as the character of the privatisation process (Gould 2003). In the case of European post-communist countries, economic and political dimensions of regime change were frequently compounded by the dimension of state-building. In contexts of state-building it was argued that democratisation would be more protracted and tenuous because the imperative of state-building would take precedence over necessary political and economic reform (Offe 1991). Finally, when analysing circumstances surrounding regime change in the early 1990s, apart from domestic conditions, a number of scholars have looked at the influence of the international environment and the role of the European Union in particular. The influence of the EU in post-communist democratisation has been operationalised in terms of political conditionality (Smith 1997, Vachudova 2005, Schimmelfennig 2005, Schimmelfennig and Sedelmeier 2005) and the different types of leverage that this conditionality entails (Vachudova 2005).

Let me now introduce the main features of the proposed theoretical framework. First of all, modernisation theory is placed centre stage, which has rarely been the case in post-communist studies. As was argued, post-communist studies appeared at a time when modernisation scholars were eclipsed by the mode of transition literature that developed through the study of Southern European and Latin American countries in the 1980s. While post-communist scholars introduced various historical legacies into accounts of democratisation, they rarely referred to modernisation explicitly as a driver of democratisation. In contrast, this study proposes that socioeconomic development together with key features of the communist regime represent the conditioning parameters for political choice at the moment of regime change. In addition, it is argued that the combination of modernisation preconditions with communist regime types as developed by Kitschelt *et al* (1999) effectively absorbs many other historical legacies that have featured as candidates for explanations of democratisation.

The second part of the framework focuses on features of the political process during the early 1990s, where I analyse political party system dynamics and the role that the European Union has played in democracy promotion. Here again a number of potentially important features of emergent political institutions are considered, only to show that party system dynamics have been crucial in engendering vicious and virtuous circles of democratisation after regime change. I engage with excellent scholarship on the role of political party systems in post-communist democratisation, but I extend it to argue for the unique importance that authoritarian party dominance during the initial period of regime change has had on subsequent democratisation. Furthermore, while in looking for explanations of political phenomena, standard comparative politics studies start and finish in the domestic political arena, the theoretical framework presented here includes the role of the EU in post-communist Europe in an attempt to relate the influence of external democracy promotion with domestic factors that drive democratisation. The main argument put forward is that in the case of Southeast Europe the EU's standard toolkit for democracy promotion was less of a good fit than was the case in Central Eastern Europe.

Finally, since this analysis includes former Yugoslav countries, one cannot avoid engaging with the literature that argues for the primacy of state-building, the imperative of a unified nation state and the obstacles to democratisation in multiethnic contexts. These literatures are engaged in another attempt to figure out which features of various existing hypotheses overlap or complement each other in order to enable a comparative analysis across cases. The concept of disputed statehood is put forward, which enables clear differentiation between cases where acquiring statehood did not have lasting consequences on successful democratisation, versus cases where statehood was disputed either by internal minorities or the kin state. The goal is to formulate a theoretical framework that enables cross-case analysis without simplifying the tremendously complex process of post-communist democratisation beyond what is reasonable. The framework, which includes historical preconditions, party system dynamics, EU influence and the problems of disputed statehood, is complex enough to allow for the possibility that countries may have democratised more or less successfully through various combinations of factors. At the same time, the theoretical framework attempts to keep the argument simple enough to endure rigorous formal analysis using fsQCA techniques. In the tradition of comparative politics scholarship, rival explanatory factors are tested against each other in the search for configurations that best explain divergent democratisation trajectories in post-communist Europe.

In the subsequent sections structural factors influencing democratisation are reviewed first, focusing on modernisation theory, the role of historical regime legacies and finally state-building and war which already move the analysis from history towards contingency. This is followed by the exposition of contingent conditions surrounding regime change, focusing on political party dynamics and the role of the EU as external democracy promoter.

Modernisation theory

The initial theory proposed by Lipset (1959) and developed by Moore (1966) and others remains an anchor for discussing modernisation theory. Apart from Duverger's law, the link between economic development and democracy is the strongest empirical generalisation comparative politics has produced to date (Boix 2003). Lipset's key proposition is that the more economically developed the country, the better the chances of democracy. Regarding causal mechanisms, Lipset leaned on Lerner (1958), according to whom the causal chain proceeds as follows: industrialisation brings urbanisation, and in the 'urban matrix' literacy and media grow simultaneously. Literacy in turn is deemed crucial in the development of political participation (i.e. voting). To this analysis Lipset added the role of the middle class as crucial in democratisation, with its demand for moderate politics, and the fact that the growth of civil society seems to be a function of the level of income and opportunities for leisure. Moore (1966) and Lindblom (1977) were among prominent social scientists who reasserted this essentially Marxist connection between a strong bourgeoisie and democracy (Arat 1988). This thesis on the role of the middle class, together with Lerner's causal chain, was later taken up by Huntington (1991). Lipset subsequently also revisited his framework, reemphasising the importance of the middle class which 'can stand up against the state and provide resources to independent groups' (1994: 2).

In modernisation theory, the specification of causal mechanisms linking economic development to democratisation emphasises the role of political culture, a concept that has its origin in citizenship theory and which historically evolved from political liberalism and Lockean ideas of preserving liberties from the state (Somers 1995: 115). It is the middle class that is charged with the historical task of engendering an independent social sphere, i.e. civil society, and the public arena. Parsons and Habermas are most responsible for the theoretical elaboration of the concept and its link to democracy. While for Parsons political culture is defined as internalised values, for Habermas it has an institutional dimension, referring to 'public meeting places, newspapers, and material expressions of public opinion' (Somers 1995: 124). However, in both conceptions relationships among free individuals are the motor for the creation of the public sphere, a civil society which stands for autonomy and plurality of social relations that can stand against the coercions of both state and market (Wood 1995). From this it follows that a certain level of socioeconomic development which releases a person from the everyday toil of work is a necessary precondition for the development of democratic values and principles (ibid., also Howard 2003).

Inglehart and Welzel (2005) explain how the causal mechanism between economic development and the demand for democracy operates on an individual level. What they conceptualise as a process of transformation towards post-material value systems starts with socioeconomic development, by raising incomes, educational levels and diversifying human interaction, reducing 'constraints on autonomous human choice' in the economic, cognitive and social domains (ibid.: 151). This in turn nurtures a sense of existential security and autonomy, leading people to give priority to humanistic self-expression values that emphasise emancipation, liberty, diversity and autonomy. In the final step, increased subjective aspirations lead people to demand institutions that allow them to act according to their own choices, or in other words to seek civil and political rights that define substantive aims of democracy as it is here understood, together with political equality. According to the authors, Lerner (1958), Lipset (1959), Dahl (1971) and Huntington (1991) relied on the same causal mechanism in their explanations of why economic development is conducive to democracy, only earlier empirical testing of this proposition was not possible due to lack of survey data on a wide range of societies. In their longitudinal analysis of Third Wave countries the authors show an almost perfect correlation between self-expression values and the quality of democracy that is practiced in a given society (2005).

The link between democracy and economic development uncovered by Lipset was replicated by numerous studies in the following decades, generating the largest body of research on any topic in comparative politics (Przeworski and Limongi 1997). Przeworski and Limongi's (1997) study in turn provided the most referenced contemporary work revising the original framework. Their analysis supported the exogenous version of the theory, according to which economic development plays a role after democracy is established, while disputing the role of economic development in leading to democracy. However, their distinction between endogenous and exogenous versions of the hypothesis was subsequently challenged. According to Boix and Stokes (2003) socioeconomic development helps existing democracies survive and new democracies emerge. Inglehart and Welzel (2005) also refuted Przeworski and Limongi's finding, using their own data. As a result, the current state of play with respect to empirical verifications of this relationship provides support for both the argument according to which socioeconomic development contributes to the emergence of democracy, and the version according to which it increases the chances of democracy's survival once it has been established.

While the relationship between socioeconomic development and democracy stands firm against repeated empirical scrutiny, the positive link between capitalism and democracy has been empirically disputed. Williamson and Rodrik have argued that more economic openness leads to increased inequality (in Landa and Kapstein 2001), which in effect means that economic inequality that is inherent to capitalism hinders rather than aids democratisation. Boix (2003) has argued that democracy prevails under conditions of economic equality, while a recent study by Acemoglu and Robinson (2006) established that democracy is more likely to consolidate in more equal societies. Similarly, Ziblatt's recent work on First Wave democracies stresses how socioeconomic inequality 'can be a major and underappreciated barrier to the long term process of democratisation' (2009: 1). Other empirical works stress that economic inequality produces divisive social differences, weakens community life, reduces trust and increases violence (Wilkinson and Pickett 2010), all of which are detrimental to democratisation. These findings provide important qualifications to the initial enthusiasm over capitalism's effect on democratisation and emphasise the importance of economic equality for democracy. Therefore, while this study does not deal with the relationship between capitalism and democracy directly, it is important to stress that the modernisation hypothesis as it is used here does not assume that it is the introduction of capitalism that furthers democratisation. Socioeconomic development is a wider phenomenon, and the modernisation hypothesis simply states that a person needs to relieved of the daily toil of securing her material existence in order to participate in the life of the political community. This allows for economic development to stand apart from the concept of capitalism, since economic development may be (and historically has been) achieved through various modes of production. Such a formulation unfortunately leaves aside the fact that economic and political freedoms are closely related, but such is the fate of analytical endeavours. The analysis of the complex implications that the simultaneous introduction of democracy and capitalism has had on post-communist societies over the last twenty years is something I hope to tackle in future research.

As has been shown, claiming that economic development advances democratisation is a hollow proposition without an attempt to specify the causal mechanism, and specifying the causal mechanism has led to the application of macro concepts of civil society and the middle class, or self-expression values as the equivalent micro-foundational concept. What lies at the heart of the causal mechanism that links economic development with democracy is a large enough independent social sphere, which is necessary to limit political power and create bottom-up societal pressure for democratisation. In the context of communist Eastern Europe civil society stood for opposition forces against state oppression (Wood 1995). While the concept of the middle class does not travel to the post-communist setting unharmed, its crucial features stand. In the post-communist setting the middle class stands for social groups which have sufficient education and material means to generate an independent public sphere and pressure the state to establish an impartial rule of law system that upholds human rights. Additionally, the presence of an urban middle class plays a key role in breaking down clientelism and patronage as a model of party-citizen linkage (Kitschelt *et al* 1999), which is of direct relevance for establishing a functioning system of rule of law. In Kitschelt's definition (1999) the middle class combines features of advanced education with higher income expectations, and creates pressure for the establishment of the rule of law. Henceforth, the empirical analysis of modernisation preconditions in the subsequent chapters relies on indicators of levels of economic development, urbanisation and literacy in the fourteen post-communist countries.

In the following sections the structural precondition of economic development is related to features of communist regimes as historical legacies that influence democratisation.

Historical legacies

Already by mid-1995 it was possible to distinguish the more from the less successful democratisers in previously communist Europe (Kopstein and Reilly 2000, Vachudova 2005). Poland, the Czech Republic, Hungary, Slovenia, Slovakia and the Baltic states had made significant progress, unlike the rest of Eastern Europe. Kopstein and Reilly (2000) wondered at the apparently complete overlap between being successful at democratisation and being close to the core of Western Europe. They undertook an empirical investigation of the effect that the distance from the European core had on the prospects of successful democratisation only to find that this relationship was actually more complex. As Darden and Grzymala Busse (2006) noticed, judging on proximity to Vienna and Berlin, Belarus should have been doing better than the Baltic states. It seems reasonable to assume that spatial distance is closely related to historical and cultural ties among states, as well as strength of norm diffusion among neighbours. Surely Slovenia's democratisation was aided by the fact that it is surrounded by Austria and Italy on its western borders, but this type of explanation loses power as one moves away from the elusive Western border.

The proximity factor probably overlaps with other structural cultural and political legacies of these states, which are investigated next. In the investigation of historical legacies, the main question is how far in the past is one willing to travel. Putnam (1993) famously traced the causal chain of divergent governance performance among Italian regions all the way back into the Middle Ages. I follow Kitschelt's advice (2003) of not incorporating causal factors which are either too close to the phenomenon of interest to effectively carry any explanatory weight, or go so far back into history that the unravelling of the supposed causal mechanisms poses an insurmountable obstacle. Hence the argument advanced here does not travel far back into previous centuries, but instead focuses on illuminating those historical legacies that can be tied to the type of causal mechanism proposed by modernisation theory. In that respect Kitschelt *et al*'s (1999) typology of communist regimes seems relevant.

Even though Kitschelt *et al* (1999) do not explain democratisation *per se*, but rather the features of post-communist party systems, their regime typology can be used to help explain subsequent democratisation trajectories. Their typology partly relies on establishing the extent to which the rule of law was present as a pre-communist tradition in each of the examined states, which links their work directly to this analysis. In addition to that, their regime typology aggregates several dimensions of historical political legacies that have been argued in the literature to play a role in the success of subsequent democratisation. Hence the application of this typology enables a simplification of the theoretical framework by reducing the number of analysed factors. Their regime typology is based on two pillars: the extent to which a formal bureaucracy existed within the communist regime, which was usually a vestige of the pre-communist democratic statehood experience, and the balance of power between communists and political society, to employ Ekiert's (1991) concept that refers to independent social and political movements and organisations.

The first regime type in their classification is patrimonial communism, in which rational bureaucratic institutionalisation in the state and party is low and instead political power is concentrated around a small clique or an individual ruler. Any opposition is repressed or co-opted, and there is effectively no separation between party and state. Such communist regimes evolved in rural societies, with weak cities and effectively no proletarian base. Having presided over heavy industrialisation, these regimes had no rivals in alternative visions of modernity. In other words, in these societies communism was the force that brought social progress, and it had widespread social legitimacy (Elster, Offe and Preuss 1998). On the eve of the moment that would bring regime change, patrimonial communist states faced 'no significant opposition movements except dispersed isolated dissident intellectuals, unable to produce a sustained discourse or organise a professional cadre advancing a new vision of political-economic modernity' (Kitschelt *et al* 1999: 24).

The second regime type Kitschelt *et al* (1999) identify is national-accommodative communism, crafted to capture regimes that had a modestly professional bureaucracy but for which the central defining feature was an accommodative relationship between the communist party and the political society (ibid.). This was especially relevant in attempting to accommodate appeals to national autonomy with the official communist ideology, as was the case in the more developed republics of Yugoslavia: Croatia and Slovenia. Similar features were present in countries under Soviet domination that emerged from semi-authoritarian interwar polities with established interest groups and political mobilisation, such as the Baltic states. Instead of relying on a strong working class base, in national-accommodative regimes communist parties had to balance urban-rural conflicts. The cognitive legacy, as the authors call it, of national-accommodative regimes is the experience of conflicting visions of modernity, with communism never acquiring hegemonic ideological power.

Finally, bureaucratic-authoritarian communism is characterised by a powerful rule-guided bureaucratic machine on the one hand, and a harsher oppressive relationship of the communist party towards opposition forces on the other. These regimes relied on a technocratic class of professionals in the bureaucracy and a hierarchically stratified communist party. However, with respect to accommodating potential outside challengers, these regimes were rigid and oppressive, tolerating no political diversity. This type of regime occurred in countries with considerable democratic experience in the interwar period and an early, more advanced industrialisation, such as the Czech Republic and, to some extent, Poland. Hence, while in patrimonial communist regimes opposition was feeble and easily quenched, in bureaucratic-authoritarian regimes the opposition was potentially much more powerful, but the state was comparatively much stronger and able to repress political pluralism. With respect to cognitive legacy, these regimes carried within them the most pluralistic array of competing models of development.

How does Kitschelt's communist regime typology relate to other historical conditions that have been advanced in the literature? Kitschelt *et al* (1999) acknowledge that their regime typology relies on modernisation theory in that their regime types imply a movement from an agrarian to an industrial society. However they also argue that by the 1970s and 1980s the relationship between regime type and level of economic development was no longer close (ibid.: 28). Initially economically more backward regimes managed to catch up and it was the political institutions of communist rule rather than levels of economic development that were key determinants of subsequent political transformation strategies. Since the proposed theoretical framework in this study incorporates both modernisation preconditions and Kitschelt's regime typology, the relative strength of these two factors will be assessed empirically in subsequent chapters.

Another factor that has been identified as important for long term democratisation is pre-communist experience with democracy. While all 14 countries studied have had at least some type of experiment with multi-party elections in the interwar period of the 1920s and 1930s, in Albania it lasted less than a year, while in 1918 Czechoslovakia had established a parliamentary democracy and welfare state that was put to an end only by Nazi occupation in 1938 (Berend 2001). However, how does one elaborate a causal chain that is over 100 years long? Kitschelt's regime typology starts from pre-communist experiences with democracy but develops into an argument on how communist regimes evolved and influenced politics and society until the eve of regime change. Hence previous experience with democracy is not introduced as a separate explanatory condition in the theoretical framework. Instead, Kitschelt's typology of communist regimes is assumed to capture what is left of the pre-communist democratic experience. Another argument about the importance of historical legacies for democratisation focuses on state capacity and the strength of civil society at the time of regime change as key for subsequent democratisation prospects (Ekiert 1991). Again, both of these dimensions are incorporated in Kitschelt's typology. As was described above, the two pillars of Kitschelt's typology are state capacity and the strength of opposition groups in society. In summary, Kitschelt's typology of regimes enables the aggregation of several important historical and political legacies that characterised the fourteen country cases at the moment of regime change.

To summarise this section – numerous historical legacies were identified and reviewed for their ability to illuminate democratic development in Southeast and Central Eastern Europe over the last twenty years. The analysis has shown that many of the identified dimensions overlap and can be aggregated into more complex concepts. While it has been argued that the distance from Western capitals or previous democratic experience hardly have much explanatory power on their own, the concept of modernisation which rests on economic and social development indicators on the one hand, and Kitschelt's regime typology which rests on state capacity and civil society on the other, are taken forward as two crucial structural preconditions in explaining democratisation in European post-communist countries.

State-building and war

The emergence of new nation states in post-communist Europe initially appeared 'extraordinary and undesirable to Western democracies' even though the nation state is the form within which all modern societies evolved (Lukic 2010). Territorial integrity and a clear delineation of borders have been repeatedly advocated as prerequisites for a democratic transition, which has been taken to mean that newly emerged states face increased obstacles to democratisation (Offe 1994, Linz and Stepan 1996, Rupnik 1999; quoted in Kasapović 2000).

Apart from arguing that state-building complicates democratisation, some scholars go further and say that ethnically diverse societies face permanent problems. Ethnically diverse societies are said to be worse candidates for sustained democratisation than more homogenous societies (Rabushka and Shepsle 1972, Horowitz 1985, 1993, Dahl 1998). Roeder (1999: 868) also exhibits scepticism about the sustainability of multiethnic states, arguing that crisis and instability are inherent in power sharing arrangements and that they 'contain the seed of their own destruction'. Therefore, the argument is that multiethnicity and democracy are incompatible in the long run. However, this still leaves open the question of how multiethnicity complicates democratisation. Vachudova and Snyder (1996) paint a more nuanced picture of how ethnic diversity played into democratisation in post-communist Europe. In a nutshell, their argument is that in multiethnic states, in times of poor economic performance, ethnic nationalism becomes a convenient political platform for portraying negative outcomes in zero sum logic, especially in countries with a sizeable minority where ethnic difference can be framed as a threat. According to the authors, this scenario played out in Bulgaria, Romania and Slovakia in the 1990s. Post-Yugoslav cases support this reasoning: the rise of Milošević and his ethno-nationalist rhetoric at the end of 1980s also coincided with unsuccessful economic reform and dire times for the Yugoslav economy. In the complex multinational federation where no ethnic group constituted an outright majority, playing the card of ethnic nationalism proved explosive. Once it became clear that the federation was not going to survive and the political game assumed zero sum logic, the ethnic nationalist platform was ready made and convenient for the subsequent process of state building. As a result, the secessionist states became 'entangled in a mortal embrace with their own ethnic nationalisms' (Diamandouros and Larrabee 2000: 34).

Adopting a cross country perspective, what can be made of the two arguments according to which both state-building and ethnic diversity thwart successful democratisation? Let us first examine the argument according to which the context of newly acquired statehood complicates democratisation. Of the fourteen countries studied, nine are new states, as can be seen in Table 2.1 below.

Table 2.1: New and old states in post-communist Europe

New states	Croatia, the Czech Republic, Estonia, Latvia, Lithuania, Macedonia FYR, Serbia, Slovakia, Slovenia
Old states	Albania, Bulgaria, Hungary, Poland, Romania

The label of a new state as it is used here refers to those states that in the period 1989–1991 established independence within new state borders, irrespective of whether they had flirted with independence in the interwar period of the 1920s and 1930s or not. Analogously, the label of old state refers to those countries that in the period 1989–1991 did not acquire independence and change state borders. If the two groups of states in Table 2.1 are related to democratisation data presented in Chapter 1, it is clear that both new and old states have exhibited either types of democratic trajectory. The Baltic states acquired independence at the beginning of the 1990s but they were among the fastest democratisers of the whole group of European post-communist countries. Conversely, among the so-called old states we find the successful Hungary and Poland, as well as the laggard Bulgaria, Romania and Albania. Simply establishing whether a post-communist country is a new state tells us practically nothing about whether it has successfully democratised. The fate of new states in post-communist Europe has been quite divergent and it is necessary to look for alternative ways in which state-building has affected democratisation prospects.

Similarly, while some ethnically diverse societies have experienced grave difficulties in democratisation, such as the case of former Yugoslavia, this

Table 2.2: Ethnic composition of European post-communist states

Country	Last communist census	Post-communist census (in %)	Year of census/ Estimate*
Hungary	98.5	/	1990c
Poland	98.2	/	1985e
Albania	97.9	/	1989c
Czech Republic	94.4	94.4	1983e/1991c
Romania	88.6	89.5	1985e/1992c
Slovenia	87.8	83	1991c/2002c
Slovakia	86.6	85.7	1992c
Bulgaria	[no data]	85.7	1992c
Lithuania	79.6	81.4	1989c/1996e
Croatia	78.1	89.63	1991c/2001c
Macedonia	64.6	66.6	1991c/1994c
Serbia and Montenegro	62.6	/	1991c
Estonia	61.5	64.6	1989c/1996e
Latvia	52.0	55.1	1989c/1996e
Yugoslavia	36.3	/	1985e

Sources: Roeder (1999: 859) CSB Croatia Census 2001, SB Slovenia Census 2002

Note: c stands for census, e for estimate

relationship is anything but straightforward. As Table 2.2 shows, most of the fifteen European post-communist countries have had sizeable ethnic minorities, but in spite of that they have exhibited widely divergent democratisation trajectories.

Only Hungary, Poland and Albania among the group of fourteen can claim substantially homogenous populations. In spite of that Albania did not avoid institutional breakdown and widespread violence in the late 1990s. At the other end of the continuum is former Yugoslavia, an extreme example of a federation with effectively no majority population, which experienced violent dissolution. Nevertheless, the wide majority of European post-communist countries have substantial minorities but have in spite of that managed to establish rule of law guarantees of civil rights to their citizens. This includes even the Baltic states which face large Russian minorities, coupled with troublesome inter-ethnic history and a strong kin state. At the same time, it cannot be overlooked that ethnic politics played a very prominent role across post-communist Europe, from Macedonia and Romania to Slovakia and the Baltic. Ethnicity is one of many potential sources of the fear rhetoric that can be used in political competition, and the presence of a substantial ethnic minority facilitates such divisive political strategies. However, in the absence of internal minorities, these threats can be framed as coming from economic migrants, or outside threats from other nations or organisations, as current trends in rightwing movements across Western Europe aptly demonstrate.

Overall it stands that multiethnic new states may have a harder time democratising, but whether the ethnic divide becomes an obstacle to democratisation is conditional on whether there is a dispute between the minority and the majority in a given state. In Rustow's (1970: 350) account, the only condition for democracy is a unified nation state, where national unity means that the vast majority of citizens in a polity have no reservations as to which political community they belong to. The main obstacles to achieving consolidation in plural societies arise therefore due to disputes over the boundaries of the state, its character, and the question regarding who has a right to citizenship (Linz and Stepan 1996). Linz and Stepan call this the stateness problem (ibid.). Conflicts are 'reduced when empirically almost all the residents of a state identify with one subjective idea of the nation, and that nation is virtually contiguous with the state' (ibid.: 25). The congruence between the polity and the demos is therefore one of the conditions for successful consolidation of democracy. If a significant group of people 'does not accept claims on its obedience as legitimate (…), this presents a serious problem for democratic transition and even more serious problems for democratic consolidation' (ibid.: 27). Among the nine new states in this study, some were cases of disputed statehood by internal minorities (Croatia, Macedonia and Serbia) and others by politics of territorial expansion on the part of the kin state (Serbia). In these cases minority issues spilled out of the framework of institutional conflict into violence, and in such circumstances the democratisation process was effectively derailed for a longer period of time. Croatia had gone through war with Serbia (initially Yugoslavia), which ended in 1995. The country re-established full territorial sovereignty in 1998 and after that moment two countries in post-communist Europe remained with an open stateness problem: Serbia and Macedonia.

In Serbia the national question remains open due to continuous challenges to its state borders (Zakošek 2008). Throughout the 1990s Serbia (at that time Yugoslavia) unsuccessfully led wars in Croatia, Bosnia and Kosovo – morphing into a 'defeated aggressor',[1] which had a strong negative impact on its state identity. In addition to that, it had been dealing with resistance in its Kosovo province, with Kosovar claims over time growing into demands for secession. After the 1999 NATO intervention, Serbia no longer engaged in violent conflicts but it still experienced the loss of further parts of its territory. Montenegro left the union with Serbia in 2006, while in 2008 Kosovo declared independence. Though

---

1. Author's interview with Srđa Popović. Interview No. 10, November 2010

Serbia accepted the secession of Montenegro, it still disputes the sovereignty of Kosovo. The two decades of undefined state borders have resulted in the national identity question dominating the political agenda in that country.

In Macedonia during the 1990s the Albanian minority disputed their constitutional status in the newly formed state, keeping the stateness problem open for a whole decade. After the inter-ethnic conflict was resolved through the Ohrid Agreement in 2001, the name dispute with Greece took over as the main obstacle to Macedonia's full statehood. As a result, as in Serbia, in Macedonia questions of national identity still dominate the domestic political agenda. Due to long term disputes to their statehood, in Serbia and Macedonia the ethnic question exerts strong effects on the character of political party competition and the perseverance of authoritarian parties that ground their platforms in ethno-nationalist appeals. Similarly, disputed statehood has helped strengthen authoritarian features of political culture in these countries, stifling liberal and pluralist values, respect for human rights and principles of legality. A similar dynamic had occurred in Croatia during the 1990s, but during the last decade societal dynamics and those of the party system have experienced the strengthening of pluralist democratic values.

In summary, this analysis shows that state-building on its own has not exerted a negative effect on the prospect of democracy, while multiethnicity was shown to carry potential for destabilisation. The point is that democratisation faced serious obstacles only in cases where multiethnic populations led to disputes over statehood and created violent conflicts. The fact that in post-communist Europe disputed statehood has led to war introduces the need for the next set of arguments which relate the state of war to democratisation prospects. In attempting to review literature that theorises the relationship between war and democratisation, I join Bermeo (2003) in her surprise over the fact that the democratisation literature leaves the connection to war either wholly neglected or seriously under-theorised:

> This is perplexing because so many new and renewed democracies emerge in the context of war. Of the 73 democracies founded after 1945 that still exist today, over half emerged either in the immediate aftermath of a war or as a means of bringing an ongoing war to an end. (Bermeo 2003: 159)

The few existing theoretical propositions regarding the influence of war on democratisation focus on its authoritarian nature as antithetical to democratic development. Horowitz (2003) proposes three main negative effects of war on democratisation: it distracts governments from reform agendas and provides cover for political repression and cronyism; it facilitates greater accumulation of arbitrary executive power; and it can lead to long term economic isolation and disruption. Zakošek (2008) puts forward a similar argument that focuses on the political effects of war. According to him, violent conflicts lead to authoritarian centralisation, fostering hierarchy and discipline, while thwarting deliberation, political competition and full realisation of civil and political rights. Similarly, Pridham (2000: 1) argued that 'experience until 1995 tended rather to reinforce authoritarian practices if not institutions, while flouting human rights and highlighting the breakdown of pluralist tolerance'. According to Fish (2001:

59), war may also spark democratic reversal 'since the human and material costs of war may reduce popular support for a new democratic government and the requirements of prosecuting war may lessen state officials' tolerance for dissent'. Wars may also enhance the popular appeal of antidemocratic forces, including chauvinists and nationalist extremists.

In writing more specifically about Yugoslavia, Ramet argued (1996: 215) that war 'has allowed the respective ruling parties [in Serbia and Croatia] to engage in seductive oversimplifications of complex issues, to marginalise representatives of minority interests (whether ethnic or otherwise), and to harness nationalism as a false principle of legitimation'. In addition to that, war often meant a postponement of programmes that might have enjoyed higher priority in times of peace. Like Pridham, Fish, Horowitz and Zakošek, Ramet argues that 'war has reinforced a tendency towards authoritarianism (...) and has muted political opposition (ibid.: 319). Using the example of Croatia, she argues that as a result of the war nepotism appeared, the parliament was marginalised, key media outlets were taken over, and human rights abuses of the Serbian minority were taking place. Similarly, Dvornik (2009) argues that wars across Yugoslavia stunted pluralist tendencies that emerged during the 1980s, and reinforced ethno-nationalist identification. Finally, Batt (2007) concentrates on the effect that war may have on state exploitation. She argues that war set the stage for crony capitalism which went much further than in Central Eastern Europe. While in CEE corrupt privatisations faced constraints by more robust legal and institutional checks, as well as international scrutiny, in SEE the process unfolded in the absence of almost any scrutiny (ibid.).

While these propositions that elaborate the influence of war on democratisation seem plausible and supported by anecdotal case evidence, any cross country empirical analyses that assess the effect of war against other factors influencing democratisation are very difficult to find. Since violent conflict occurred in several of the fourteen cases in this study, the condition of violently disputed statehood is included in the theoretical framework and analysed empirically in subsequent chapters.

Moving from regime type and modernisation arguments towards disputed state-building processes and the eruption of violent conflicts in Southeast Europe has already shifted the analysis of explanatory factors towards the contingency that surrounded the period of the early 1990s. In the remaining part of this chapter two other key factors are reviewed whose specific morphology during the 1990s have exerted a longlasting effect on democratisation trajectories of European post-communist countries. The first one refers to the nature of political party dynamics in the initial period after regime change, and the other introduces an international perspective to events in post-communist Europe by focusing on the influence that the European Union has exerted on democratisation prospects of the fourteen analysed cases.

Political party dynamics

The emergence of many new polities and the comprehensive reform of political, economic and social institutions that started in the early 1990s in post-communist Europe represented a vast laboratory for institutional scholars in political science. Many arguments from earlier studies of Latin America and Southern Europe regarding the effects of political institutions on democratisation gained new testing grounds. While scholars who studied regime change focused on institutional choice, those who were interested in democratisation more often observed institutions as environmental constraints on actors' choices. Such work falls within historical institutionalism, where primary emphasis is placed on institutions as sources of constraints. In this strand of the literature political institutions are conceptualised as explanatory factors, rather than outcomes to be explained (Hall and Taylor 1996). The bulk of the work in this field has been devoted to three key institutions: constitutional frameworks (presidentialism versus parliamentarianism), electoral systems and political party systems.

The presidentialism versus parliamentary debate is long and undecided. Looking for a way out of this deadlock, in his analysis of post-communist states Fish (2001) claims that the key common institutional feature among democratic laggards is power concentrated in the office of the president. He refers to such a system as a superpresidency (2001: 69). In developing this argument Fish builds on Migdal (1988), who argued that rulers possess an anti-institutional urge, disabling even the institutions that they themselves build. Strong rulers create arbitrary concentrations of power, which is detrimental to political competition and the dispersion of power which are necessary for democratic institution building. According to Fish, 'a Madisonian approach to institutions, rather than simple avoidance of presidentialism, provides the firmest basis for avoiding democratic erosion' (2001: 88). This focus on concentration of power is directly relevant for the types of power morphology outlined in Chapter 1 as happening in post-communist context. Parliamentarism, with its inbuilt division of power, contains the prerequisites for strengthening new democratic states and enabling pluralisation and democratisation, while concentration of power in the presidency has a disabling effect on emergent institutions of monitoring and mutual control.

Empirical research confirms the relationship between strong presidencies and weak democracies and the evidence from post-communist countries seems to strongly support it. Henceforth, in this analysis countries are selected by excluding political systems characterised by super-presidentialism. Political systems with this characteristic, which would include Russia and the large part of the former Soviet world, are understood as overdetermined for a slow and laggardly democratisation. European post-communist states on the other hand adopted either fully parliamentary or semi-presidential constitutional frameworks, instituting formal mechanisms for political competition and division of power as crucial components of democratic regimes. Therefore, they are considered as containing formal preconditions for the development of democracy, which then sharpens the question of why we observe such diversity with respect to democratisation advances within constitutionally similar systems. At the same time, as was argued in Chapter 1, the type of constitutional framework is treated as a scope condition, or in other words, excluding countries that exhibit the features of superpresidentialism allows for reducing the number of explanatory factors in the theoretical framework.

Studies of electoral systems have largely focused on the ways in which electoral systems affect party systems (e.g. Katz 1980, Taagepera and Shugart 1989). Lijphart focused scholars' attention on the crucial relationship between types of government, which results from electoral formulas, and the functioning of democracy (1986). Taking part in a wide debate on preferred constitutional solutions for the institutional laboratory of post-communist Europe, Lijphart (1991: 163) argued that the combination of parliamentarism with a proportional representation electoral system should be 'especially attractive to newly democratic and democratising countries'. According to him, features of the electoral system affect the makeup of the party system, the type of executive and the nature of executive-legislative relations. More specifically, PR electoral systems lead to multi-partyism, coalition governments and more equal executive-legislative relations, which are features conducive to power sharing. Similarly to Fish's (2001) argument about how avoiding a strong presidency helps establish checks and balances among branches of government, Lijphart argues that a PR electoral system divides power and that this is good for new democracies. And indeed, almost all European post-communist countries instituted proportional representation electoral systems. Of the countries included in this study, Bulgaria, Croatia, the Czech Republic, Estonia, Latvia, Macedonia, Poland, Serbia, Slovakia, Slovenia and Romania have fully PR systems, while Albania, Hungary and Lithuania have mixed systems (Birch 2005). Of the latter group, the Lithuanian electoral system is 50 per cent PR, the Hungarian 54 per cent PR, while only the Albanian system is dominantly majoritarian (ibid.). Therefore, the presented overview of constitutional frameworks and electoral systems shows that the case selection has been done in order to treat the two potential factors as scope conditions. By excluding majoritarian electoral systems and superpresidencies, the analysis focuses on fourteen country cases that had the institutional prerequisites for the development of multipartyism and of robust parliamentary opposition. Whether this indeed happened depended on the overall structural context. The following sections explore the role of political party dynamics in post-communist democratisation.

Holding free and fair elections which result in peaceful alternation of political parties in power represents a baseline for classifying a country as democratic. Bellamy (2007: 5) argues that party competition 'institutionalises a balance of power that encourages the various sides to hear and harken to each other, promoting mutual recognition through the construction of compromises'. Indeed, political parties can be thought of as central institutions of democracy (Blondel 1999) and they have an exceptional role to play in representative systems since they organise the critical citizen-elite bonds through the electoral process (Kitschelt *et al* 1999). The structure and interaction of political parties are 'the most significant variables which contribute to the consolidation or failure of the political systems of democratic polities' (Elster, Offe and Preuss 1998: 110). In addition to that, the role of political party systems is of particular significance in post-communist Europe, where democratisation occurred after a lengthy and extensive one-party mobilisation (Lewis 2001, Sitter 2002).

Perhaps the most recurrent argument in post-communist democratisation scholarship is the one about the importance of political party competition for democracy (Vachudova and Hooghe 2009). Some of the best scholarship in comparative politics has been written precisely on the relationship between party systems, EU accession and democracy in post-communist Europe (Grzymala Busse 2002, 2007, Vachudova 2005, Schimmelfennig 2005). There are several points that scholars agree on as relevant for developing political party competition in post-communist countries: the exit of the communist party from power at the first multiparty election, the existence of a strong enough democratic opposition to take its place, the prompt reform of the former communist party into a modern Social Democratic party after losing office, and the subsequent regular alternation of political parties in power (e.g. Bunce 1999, Fish 1998, Vachudova 2005, Grzymala Busse 2002, 2007). Hellman (1998) famously encapsulated the essence of the competitiveness argument: where politicians were most vulnerable to electoral pressures, countries adopted and sustained the highest level of reform. Conversely, in countries where governments were insulated from electoral pressures, there was only partial reform. The dynamic of reform was thwarted by initial winners, who drew rents from the partially reformed system. Instead of supporting reforms, 'the short-term winners have often sought to stall the economy in a partial reform equilibrium that generates concentrated rents for themselves, while imposing high costs on the rest of society' (1998: 204, also Aslund 2007). Counterintuitively, the argument goes, it was in the most competitive political systems that necessary reforms were initiated and sustained. A competitive political party system therefore seems to hold the key to strengthening the system of checks and balances, and sustaining reform efforts – which makes it a major factor in the democratisation of post-communist polities.

Two recent studies, Grzymala Busse's *Rebuilding Leviathan* (2007) and O'Dwyer's *Runaway State Building* (2006), put forward the argument according to which party system competitiveness helped curb state politicisation. Both scholars were concerned with explaining why Central Eastern European countries experienced various degrees of state exploitation, and they proposed that the more competitive the party system was, the less state abuse happened. While the two authors aim primarily to explain the influence of party system competition on state capture, their theoretical argument seems pertinent for establishing the relationship between party system dynamics and advances in democratisation as it is here conceptualised. As was argued in Chapter 1, problems of corruption and state capture may be understood as the inverse measurement of the extent to which democratic polities have succeeded in establishing functioning rule of law systems to protect their citizens' civil liberties.

The concept of political party competition refers to a party system where the incumbents are faced with a political opposition that 'offers a clear, plausible and critical governing alternative that threatens the governing coalition with replacement' (Grzymala Busse 2007: 1). A strong opposition can monitor and influence the incumbent's behaviour, and it poses a threat of replacement, which should have the effect of inducing more accountable behaviour by shifting the preference of incumbents towards strengthening formal institutions (ibid.). In other words, if a party in power can plausibly imagine being voted out of office in the forthcoming election, it will have the incentive to strengthen formal institutions so that it does not get a raw deal once out of power. Vachudova (2005) applies the logic of political competition to argue that political competition at the moment of regime change determined whether European post-communist countries embarked on a democratic trajectory. This is an extension of her earlier argument (1996, with Snyder). The quality of political competition is determined, she argues, by the presence or absence of an opposition to communism strong enough to take power at the moment of regime change, and secondly the presence or absence of a reformed communist party. This is basically the same argument that Grzymala Busse makes, but Vachudova explicates the essential link between political party competition and democratisation.

The arguments that were just reviewed emphasise the importance of the critical juncture at the moment of regime change for subsequent democratisation trajectories. Whether a new democracy sets off on a virtuous path of reform depends to an extent on whether at least two strong political alternatives start competing for power right from the first multi-party election. Their alternation in government as a source of mutual restraint is considered to have a strong positive effect on the development of democracy. Conversely, in the absence of competition at that critical juncture of the first few rounds of elections, new regimes spiralled into vicious circles of corruption, state capture and partial reform. These arguments seem to capture well the diverse fates of, for instance, Poland on the one hand or Romania on the other. However, what this argument leaves out is propositions about what should happen in cases where political competition evolved gradually, after key features of the new regime were already in place. Also, it leaves open the question about what should happen if competition was present, but it took place among nondemocratic political parties which only declaratively supported formal democratic institutions while their governance practices ran counter to the establishment of rule of law. In order to extend the explanation regarding the influence that political party systems had on democratisation in Southeast Europe, it is important to introduce the concept of political party constellation.

Schimmelfennig (2005) and Schimmelfennig, Engert and Knobel (2005, 2006) use the concept of political party constellation to capture the extent to which major parties operate within democratic principles and they explore the relationship of party system constellation with democratisation and European integration. While most political party systems, including those in Western Europe, have the experience of extremist parties with various types of undemocratic platforms (fascist, communist, ethno-nationalist etc.), historical experience shows that a democratic regime is incompatible with such parties becoming major parties; when this happened, authoritarian regimes emerged such as in interwar Germany and Italy. Now, while Schimmelfennig (2005) and Schimmelfennig, Engert and Knobel (2005, 2006) refer to these types of parties as illiberal, I prefer to call them undemocratic or authoritarian since this better reflects the empirical operationalisations of the term as it is used here. Referring to parties as undemocratic stresses two important characteristics. First of all, it points to the fact that such parties advocate a platform and rhetoric that is exclusionary and polarising, whether towards ethnic or religious minorities, or based on some other type of ideological exclusionary principle such as xenophobia (Rose and Mishler 1998). Hence such parties in principle oppose the full attainment of civil liberties for all citizens, which are here defined as a fundamental substantive aim of democracy. Secondly, and more importantly, referring to parties as undemocratic stresses the fact that their practices undermine the intended effects of formal democratic institutions. Such practices would be a disregard for the law and arbitrary exercise of power, cronyism and the abuse of state resources, electoral fraud, influencing the media or harassing the opposition. They have been referred to in Chapter 1 under the three types of post-communist power morphology: concentration of power, the conversion of political into economic power and the weakening of state capacity through a politicisation of state administration and the public sector. This typology of undemocratic or authoritarian practices enables the tracing of ways in which political parties created obstacles to the establishment of rule of law systems, hence slowing down democratisation processes. Even though they operate in a democratic institutional setting and they declaratively endorse it, when they come into power such parties undermine the foundations of a democratic regime.

The typology of party constellations considers only the major parties in a given system, in other words, the two or three political parties that are large enough to lead a government. Schimmelfennig (2005) and Schimmelfennig, Engert and Knobel (2006) propose that countries with mixed party constellations, characterised by a combination of democratic and undemocratic major political parties, experienced prolonged periods of authoritarian rule in the 1990s, which delayed their democratisation. According to, Schimmelfennig (2005) where major parties were not undemocratic, democratic regimes should quickly consolidate, countries where undemocratic parties dominated should remain far off-mark, while countries with mixed constellations should experience stalled democratisation. It is only when all major parties adopt democratic rhetoric and practices that the trajectory can become progressive. Until then there is a back and forth movement depending on which party is in power or how international pressures oscillate.

Going back to the argument regarding party competition, when authoritarian parties operated in environments that provided them with free rein to rule over regime change, they subverted the establishment of the rule of law despite at the same time introducing formal democratic institutions. Here the focus on timing becomes of crucial importance. While the general argument postulates that party competition advances democratisation, the focus on party constellation emphasises the importance of the kind of political party that dominates the regime change period. If party competition develops after an authoritarian party has established its dominance over the political system, it will not be as effective in engendering positive democratisation effects. In other words, party constellation conditions the relevance that party competitiveness has for democratisation. Party constellations without authoritarian parties as a rule engendered competitive party systems, and in such cases democratisation was fast and successful. This combination characterised Hungary, Poland and the Baltic states. Even when there was no frequent alternation in power, like in the Czech Republic and Slovenia, in the absence of authoritarian parties successful democratisation was not jeopardised. In contrast, in cases where regime change was dominated by authoritarian parties, competition among parties did not entail the mechanisms of mutual monitoring that would strengthen mutual checks and balances. Instead, in most cases they managed to secure power over several terms in office, firmly establishing their dominance over all aspects of the political system. This configuration of party dynamics characterised Bulgaria, Croatia, Macedonia, Romania, Slovakia and Serbia. Even in cases when parties competed and alternated in power, they perpetuated state capture and continued to subvert the rule of law. Such a competitive party system of authoritarian parties characterised Albania.

The length of time an authoritarian party stayed in office uninterrupted is argued to exacerbate negative effects on democratisation, but the key features here are governing practices that subvert the rule of law. If alternation in power does not bring a change to authoritarian disregard for the principle of legality, then the party competition mechanism does not carry the democratisation potential that previous scholarship argued for. Authoritarian party dominance over regime change has perpetuated detrimental practices from the period of state socialism as well as added new forms of abuse of power. It made possible the accumulation of arbitrary power in governing political parties, created a parallel web of informal networks of power and led to state capture. Secondly, it was based in a clientelist relationship between party and electorate, trading votes for various kinds of material benefits. Finally, it led to instrumentalisation of the law and subverted the division of power between branches of government.

In contexts where the emergent party system was embedded in a stronger framework of independent institutions and civil society that created pressure for democratisation, frequent alternation in power was of less consequence. Given the chance, political elites will abuse power, so this is not an argument about Slovenian elites being somehow inherently more moral than, for instance, Bulgarian ones. Instead, the key distinction is whether the societal and institutional framework is strong enough to guarantee mechanisms of control and scrutiny, which brings us back to the initial argument according to which structural preconditions of socioeconomic development draw the parameter within which political choice is exercised. The fact that in some post-communist countries the supply of parties was overwhelmingly devoted to democratic practices, while in others major political forces had strong authoritarian tendencies is the product of the level of economic and social development, as well as of previous regime legacies. More developed countries with stronger and more independent societies created better preconditions for a stand-off among two or more parties with essentially democratic agendas. Democratisation from below was stronger in such cases, where citizens demanded the upholding of their political and civil rights and created pressure for respect of rule of law. Such a context is characteristic of both the Czech Republic and Slovenia, and it might explain why the absence of alternation in power was of little consequence for their successful democratisation.

As the proposed theoretical framework unfolds, it reveals its configurational nature, in that explanatory factors offer meaningful accounts of divergent democratisation trajectories only when related to each other. Structural preconditions such as level of development and previous regime type contribute directly to contingent factors such as the supply of political parties and the character of their competition at the moment of regime change. The next sections introduce the final indispensable component of this complex picture: the influence that the EU has had on divergent democratisation trajectories of post-communist Europe.

EU as external democracy promoter

Among the international organisations that have been involved in post-communist Europe, the EU has been argued to have the most powerful set of resources for promoting democracy (Pravda 2001, Vachudova 2009), exercising 'tremendous influence on domestic politics' (Sedelmeier 2010: 519). With its potential for accepting countries as members, as the argument goes, the EU holds the stick as well as the carrot for coercing compliance with criteria it chooses to uphold. There is wide consensus in the literature that the promise of membership structures the relationship between aspiring members and the EU, and that this has acted as an important driver of democratisation in post-communist Europe (Vachudova 2005, Schimmelfennig and Sedelmeier 2005, Grabbe 2006, Schimmelfennig, Engert and Knobel 2006, Schimmelfennig 2007, 2008, Rupnik 2002, 2007, De Ridder and Kochenov 2011). While not abandoning the argument according to which the EU has exerted a positive democratisation influence in post-communist Europe, I aim to show that the relationship between countries aspiring to become EU members and the EU as external democracy promoter is multifaceted and complex, for several reasons.

First of all, with the benefit of time passed it seems fair to say that existing literature has exhibited too much optimism with respect to the effects of EU democracy promotion. Writing around the time of the first Eastern Enlargement in mid-2000s, scholars saw convergence towards successful democratisation in initially authoritarian post-communist states such as Slovakia, Bulgaria and Romania, and attributed this change of trajectory to the positive influence of EU conditionality (Vachudova 2005, Schimmelfennig, Engert and Knobel 2006, Noutcheva and Bechev 2008). Looking back, it seems that the convergence trend needs to be reconsidered. Bulgaria and Romania, though EU members, have still not reached a satisfactory level of civil rights protection and functioning rule of law. According to the European Commission's most recent CVM report (2012), neither country has produced convincing results in areas of judicial reform, fight against corruption and organised crime. Political events since the coming of Victor Ponta's government to power in 2012 have prompted President of the European Commission, José Manuel Barroso to express major concern regarding the government's respect for the rule of law.[2] The control verification mechanism (CVM) that was put in place after the two countries acceded to the EU in 2007 remains in place both for Romania and Bulgaria. In addition to that, Bulgaria's scores on the Nations in Transit dimension of judiciary framework and independence show backsliding (Figure 1.3), despite recent scholarly arguments against it (see Levitz and Pop-Eleches 2010). Similarly, while Serbia and Croatia have made important adjustments to their trajectories since 2000, opening up their membership perspective and signing up to the project of European integration, ten years later they are still struggling to establish functional rule of law systems. EU's involvement in Macedonia with respect to democratisation is anything but simple and the opinion of the European Commission issued on Albania in 2010 postponed accession negotiations for the undetermined future.

Many scholars agree that Central Eastern European states would have become consolidated democracies regardless of EU conditionality (Vachudova 2005, Schimmelfennig, Engert and Knobel 2006, Sedelmeier 2010). It is important to know that it was the CEE countries that initially raised the issue of membership and pushed the EU to commit to this goal (Schimmelfennig 2001, 2005a; Vachudova 2005). Schimmelfennig (2001, 2005b) argued that the EU's decision to enlarge could not be explained as the result of cost-benefit calculations. Instead, because the EU's legitimation rested on the ideology of a 'pan-European community of liberal democratic states' (Schimmelfennig 2001: 46), when this rhetoric was taken up by CEE states to stake their claim in the Union, the EU was rhetorically entrapped. After the CEE states adopted the EU's founding myth of pan-European liberal states to justify their interests on the grounds of a shared legitimacy, the EU conformed to its own norm and allowed for Eastern Enlargement (ibid.).

If CEE countries would have democratised anyway, then the strength of EU democratisation influence should be assessed against countries of Southeast Europe. If the test of this relationship is the extent to which these countries have managed to secure basic civil and political rights for their citizens, it seems that the EU has had only qualified success. This divergence in outcomes can be accounted for either by claiming that the EU has behaved differently towards some countries than to others; or by arguing that overall the EU has exercised the same approach, but that circumstances in recipient countries varied sufficiently to explain the resulting divergence. I contend that there is merit to both of these arguments, as I try to explain in the following paragraphs.

One way of getting at this is by applying a counterfactual analysis. Had Southeast Europe not gone through conflicts and the resulting ethnification of politics, would they have been able to join the EU together with the rest of Central Eastern Europe? Had democratisation reforms been domestically driven, as was

---

2. Statement by President Barroso following the adoption of the Cooperation and Verification Mechanism Reports for Romania and Bulgaria, July 18, 2012; available at http://europa.eu/rapid/pressReleasesAction.do?reference=SPEECH/12/565&format=HTML&aged=0&language=EN&guiLanguage=en. Last accessed August 23, 2012.

the case in CEE countries, would for instance Croatia or Macedonia have joined the EU in 2004? If we accept the argument that the EU has been reluctant to receive new members and it was due to efforts by aspiring states that they joined, it should hold that, had the determination to join the EU been as unequivocal in SEE as it had been in CEE, these countries would have equally successfully claimed their part in the project of Europe. The case of Slovenia supports this reasoning. Though a former Yugoslav republic, Slovenia managed to escape the escalation of violent conflict and ethnification of politics, pursuing unfaltering democratic reforms and European integration. As a result, it was joined with the CEE states in the first round of Eastern Enlargement. Further evidence in support of this counterfactual exercise is the fact that at the last meeting of the Yugoslav Communist Party Congress in January 1990, delegations of Croatia and Slovenia endorsed the idea of joining the European Community in a joint declaration (Caratan 2009) and that the European Community offered Yugoslavia an association agreement in May 1991 (Cviić and Sanfey 2008). However, since the signing of the Association Agreement was predicated on Yugoslavia remaining united at a moment when the dissolution of the federation was unavoidable, the deal fell through.

Nevertheless, these facts support the argument that the EU may have been fairly consistent (or reluctant) about its Eastern Enlargement across the board, but that Southeast European countries posed a different type of challenge whereby its mechanisms of political conditionality were less effective since it tried to pursue a 'one-size-fits-all' model of accession (Börzel and Risse 2004, Bicchi 2006) in a very different context. The positive sides to this uniform approach are that it supposedly treats every potential applicant the same[3] (cf. Vachudova 2005). At the same time, this model can be seen as insensitive to socioeconomic differences and cultural diversity (Börzel and Risse 2004). It reflects the prevailing orthodoxy according to which you need to put the incentives right, and the desired behaviour will follow – irrespective of context.

According to the second argument, the role of the EU as democracy promoter has not been the same over time and across the fourteen cases analysed in this study. After the decision of the Copenhagen European Council in 1993, membership criteria for joining the EU required that the candidate country must achieve 'stability of institutions guaranteeing democracy, the rule of law, human rights and respect for and protection of minorities; the existence of a functioning market economy as well as the capacity to cope with competitive pressure and market forces within the Union; the ability to take on the obligations of membership including adherence to the aims of political, economic & monetary union'.[4] The very broad formulation of political and economic criteria by the

---

3. The Luxembourg European Council (12–13 December 1997) states that all candidate countries are 'destined to join the European Union on the basis of the same criteria and [...] on an equal footing (para 10).

4. The Copenhagen Criteria as formulated by the European Council as part of the enlargement

Copenhagen Council has meant that in practice there has hardly been a 'single aspect of the functioning of the candidate countries [that] was to be regarded as immune from EU's scrutiny' (De Ridder and Kochenov 2011: 5). Such a broad and vague mandate has made it easier for the EU to develop political conditionality over time and more complicated to properly assess its reach when it comes to democratisation. To this day the underlying concept of democracy that the EU is supposed to be promoting has not been specified either by the EU or the academic literature that analyses it (Wetzel and Orbie 2011).

According to Kurki (2012) the concept of democracy that the EU promotes is dominantly liberal but deliberately fuzzy. Unlike the US, the EU has been reluctant to be ideologically openly committed to pursuing a liberal democratic agenda, so its documents and actions sometimes refer to social democratic and participatory democracy as well, echoing the European social model (ibid.). According to some views, this fuzziness reduces its effectiveness in democracy promotion – particularly since in the economic domain it has consistently promoted a liberal market model. Liberal economic reforms that have been pursued as part of European integration processes in post-communist countries clearly influence the political system and the reach of democracy in these states. Furthermore, the financial crisis that has engulfed the EU since 2008 has reinstated the debate regarding democratic controls over the market and made a serious dent in the EU's credibility as a democracy promoter (Kurki 2012).

The fuzziness of EU's democracy promotion is further complicated by a very legitimate question of whether the development of democracy can be conditioned from outside of a given society (De Ridder and Kochenov 2011). While some scholars advocate the EU as having transformative power (Grabbe 2006), others emphasise that its reach goes only as far as the domestic political context allows. If the EU's democracy promotion is defined less ambitiously, as pursuing interventions in institutional, legal and governance reforms that further political and civil liberties, the EU can be considered as a relatively successful democracy supporter (Kurki 2012). The literature on the power of EU conditionality has developed insights into the tools and types of leverage the EU has at its disposal for changing the incentives of domestic actors towards adopting the Copenhagen political and economic criteria. The relationship between the EU and a potential candidate for membership is clearly asymmetric, with the EU setting all the rules of the game, while aspirant member countries should comply (Vachudova 2005, Grabbe 2006). This relationship of asymmetric power enables the use of political conditionality, which has been defined as 'a strategy of reinforcement used by international organisations and other international actors to bring about and stabilise political change at the state level' (Schimmelfennig 2007: 127). It involves the linking of perceived benefits such as aid, trade concessions, cooperation agreements, political contacts or international organisation membership to the fulfilment of conditions

process, available at http://ec.europa.eu/bulgaria/documents/abc/72921_en.pdf. Last accessed August 23, 2012.

relating to the protection of human rights and the advancement of democratic principles (Smith 1997). If the benefits are perceived by recipient countries as large enough, conditionality can change the incentive structure for elites to trigger domestic reforms (Sedelmeier 2010). However, if domestic political adaptation costs threaten the security of the state or the survival of the regime, even the presence of credible membership incentives may fail to entice governments to comply (Schimmelfennig, Engert and Knobel 2006, Schimmelfennig 2008).

The process of European integration certainly creates enormous traction in the legislative arena and it furthers formal prerequisites of democracy, for the process to work the country in question must be willing to introduce political reforms (Schimmelfennig and Sedelmeier 2005). If this willingness is missing, the EU has limited influence. More realistically, as we have often seen in practice in Southeast Europe, governments exhort willingness, but hope to talk the talk without walking the walk (Jacoby 2002). As was already elaborated in Chapter 1, pro-democratic, at least declaratively pro-EU governments had to win domestic elections in Serbia or Croatia before the process of European integration could get underway.

To summarise, the influence of the EU on democratisation of European post-communist countries was multifaceted. On the one hand, Southeast European states posed a greater challenge for political reform, not least due to violent conflicts that emerged in former Yugoslavia and to the emergence of new states, but also due to weaker socioeconomic preconditions of countries in the region. On the other hand, the EU was also muddling through as a reluctant democratiser while balancing political interests of its member states and avoiding committing to a clear concept of its democratic agenda. As a result, the match between the EU's liberal democratic agenda and the SEE governments' mode of rule was less than perfect, to say the least. Even though these countries adopted constitutions that established them as parliamentary democracies, governance practices that emerged from authoritarian party constellations were subverting these same democratic principles. Though the EU became involved in the region early on in the 1990s and evolved into a more important actor of democratisation over time, governments in Southeast European countries faced huge hurdles in trying to square the circle over maintaining their grip on power and at the same time securing the preconditions for European integration. Having said that, further analysis rests on the premise that the EU promotes a circumscribed form of democracy which rests on an orthodox neoliberal model that focuses on elections, separation of powers, constitutionalism, rule of law and the protection of human rights (Ayers 2008), and that external democracy promotion can have only a limited reach. This is juxtaposed with authors who claim the EU should have a transformative effect in democratising states. Based on such an understanding, the EU's influence on democratisation in post-communist Europe is argued to be positive, especially in areas of human rights and rule of law, which are pertinent to this analysis.

Let me now tie together the preceding elaboration of different factors impacting on European post-communist democratisation, focusing on modernisation preconditions, communist regime types, disputed statehood, political party dynamics and the influence of the EU. These factors appeared in different configurations at the moment of regime change in the early 1990s and coalesced into recipes more or less favourable for democratisation in post-communist countries in Central Eastern and Southeast Europe. Structural preconditions in terms of socioeconomic development and previous regime legacy influenced the characteristics of political party competition at the time, while the circumstances of disputed statehood in some multinational states further complicated the transformation towards democratic regimes. How these circumstances combined in turn influenced the role that the European Union would play in each of the new democratic states. In a second step, following the logic of path dependency, the circumstances that characterised the moment of regime change are understood to have coalesced into a new legacy that helps explain the persistent stagnation of Southeast European post-communist countries.

Though this framework creates an interface between structural and contingent factors, it clearly predicates structure as conditioning contingency. The supply of political parties and their strategies is understood as the function of structural preconditions that characterise a given country. In other words, the socioeconomic context and regime legacy influence whether democratic contenders will compete for power, or whether an authoritarian party will preside over regime change – introducing formally democratic institutions but at the same time trampling over them with authoritarian politics. The democratisation outcome that emerges from this crucial nexus is further conditioned by the international environment at the moment of regime change. Those new democracies that experienced smooth transformations after the first multi-party election were also the first to initiate European integration processes. Those same new democracies under close international scrutiny from the onset of democratic reform were less likely to give in to the temptation that wholesale economic and political reform offered to elites in terms of abuse of power. In cases where violent conflicts occurred in the early 1990s, processes of international political opening and European integration were postponed. As a result, once European integration was initiated in cases such as Macedonia or Serbia, its democracy promotion toolkit faced an already petrified authoritarian rule that needed dismantling in order to further democratisation. A simplified rendering of the argument is shown in Figure 2.1.

Figure 2.1: Scheme of the theoretical framework

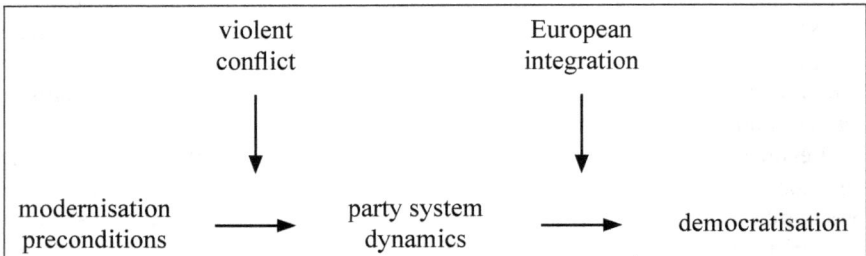

Looking at Figure 2.1, it is important to emphasise that, had there not been violent conflicts, or external democracy promotion on the part of the EU, structural preconditions would have conditioned the supply of political party alternatives, and together they would form the strongest predictors of success in democratisation. Good socioeconomic development coupled with facilitating regime legacy, leads to democratic elites and competitive party systems, influencing decisive and fast democratisation. Conversely, poor modernisation preconditions cannot engender democratic elites and hence authoritarian parties preside over regime change, making democratisation more precarious. Violent conflict occurred in only a minority of the analysed fourteen cases. In those that it did occur, conflict exacerbated an already unfavourable combination of inhibiting legacies and authoritarian elites in some cases, while in others it side-tracked an originally positive trajectory into a negative spiral. These two different scenarios will be explored in case studies of Serbia and Croatia in Chapters 5 and 6. Finally, the start of European integration is linked with the occurrence or absence of conflict. Among cases of peaceful regime change, EU integration accentuated already favourable combinations of facilitating legacies and democratic elites, while in others it helped reorient an originally wavering trajectory onto a positive spiral of democratisation.

The research question that animates this study is why democratisation in Southeast Europe has not reached levels comparable to Central Eastern Europe – and more specifically why in Southeast Europe the protection of civil liberties remains problematic well after democratic regimes were established. The conditioning effect of socioeconomic development and the resulting dominance of authoritarian parties in some European post-communist countries at the beginning of the 1990s play a crucial part in the explanation. The central argument is that the dominance of authoritarian parties over regime change has produced a mode of rule inimical to functioning rule of law as the procedural objective of democracy. Authoritarian rule is operationalised through three processes of power mutation: concentration, conversion and dispersion, as elaborated in Chapter 1. This mode of rule is the causal mechanism that connects initial authoritarian party dominance with persistent obstacles to fully functional rule of law systems, which persist even after the initial dominance of an authoritarian party over the political system has been broken. It coalesces into a fundamental feature of these democratic regimes that becomes difficult to undo.

The following chapters analyse empirically the presented arguments. Chapters 3 and 4 analyse the relationships among each of the explanatory factors and the outcome while Chapter 5 looks at ways in which these explanatory factors configured to influence democratisation trajectories by applying fuzzy set QCA. The application of fsQCA enables a search for parsimonious answers by providing causal recipes both for democratic advancement and its failure. Fourteen countries are analysed to establish which explanatory factors carry most weight, and to assess how they combined to produce diverging outcomes. Finally, the sequential logic of the proposed relationships presented here is explored in Chapters 6 and 7 through case studies of Serbia and Croatia. Case studies are used to test the findings of fsQCA in a careful tracing of causal mechanisms that converted initial configurations into lasting legacies that burden democratisation processes. Systematic process analysis is well placed to establish whether the hypothesised relationships among the explanatory factors and the outcome actually hold. At the same time, the search for causal mechanisms that integrate the framework serves the purpose of theory building. The Conclusion draws out the main implications of the implemented analyses.

chapter three | exploring structural preconditions for post-communist democratisation

In this chapter the fourteen selected cases are compared by employing the theoretical framework presented in Chapter 2, analysing ways in which long term structural factors such as socioeconomic development and previous regime legacies influenced democratisation trajectories of European post-communist countries.

How socioeconomic development influences democratisation

Though Chapter 2 quoted many theoretical and empirical studies that claim a relationship between economic development and democracy, before proceeding with further analyses it seems crucial to establish whether data for the fourteen analysed countries supports the relationship. Data used to perform this analysis are Freedom House scores for democracy and World Bank data for GDP per capita (in current US$), an indicator most often used for economic development. A simple linear regression is designed, with democracy as the dependent variable, and economic development as the independent variable:

$$democracy = a + b \times economic\ development + e$$

Data covers the twenty-one-year period from 1989 to 2009, and there are 273 observations in total. A one year lag is introduced in the dataset, assuming that a given level of economic development shows up in democracy scores the following year. The results of the regression procedure show a Pearson's R of 0.566, indicating a fairly strong relationship between economic development and democratisation, and this correlation is significant at 0.01 level. The coefficient of determination (R2) is 0.321, indicating that about 30 per cent of the variance in democracy scores is accounted for by the level of economic development. Overall this finding represents a firm confirmation that the level of economic development influences democratisation advances. Lipset's argument seems to hold in the case of post-communist Europe too, and we can use this finding as a baseline for the analysis that follows.

The history of economic development of Eastern Europe during the twentieth century reveals Eastern Europe as a relatively backward region, even though attempts were made in the nineteenth and twentieth centuries to catch up with Western Europe (Berend 1997). Through the introduction of Western institutions and joining the international trade system at the onset of the nineteenth century this region made progress, but it was not able to close the development gap relative to Western Europe. As can be seen from Table 3.1, in 1820 and 1870 Eastern European countries reached 58.1 and 48.8 per cent of Western European per capita GDP level respectively (ibid., data from Maddison 1994). After that, at the start

Table 3.1: Eastern Europe's GDP per capita as percentage of Western Europe's GDP per capita

Year	Per cent
1820	58.1
1870	48.8
1913	42
1938	44.1
1973	46.6
1980s	ca. 25

Source: Maddison 1994; quoted from Berend 1997

of the twentieth century the region declined to 42 per cent of Western European GDP per capita, and stagnated during the first half of the twentieth century. By the outbreak of the Second World War, Eastern Europe was at 44.1 per cent of the Western European GDP per capita.

During the 1950s the region achieved fastest development, growing at an average rate of 3.9 per cent between 1950 and 1973 and improving its relative position to other peripheral regions such as Latin America. Still, even during the period of its unprecedented development, the region could not advance beyond 50 per cent of development in Western European economies. After that, in the last third of the twentieth century, the catching-up endeavour failed. A period of stagnation and crisis ended in the collapse of communist regimes 1989–1991. Between 1973 and 1992, Eastern Europe had a negative growth of -0.8 per cent, while Western Europe managed to grow at a rate of 1.8 per cent during the same period (Berend 1997). As a result, the development gap between the two regions plunged from a ratio of 1:2 to a ratio of 1:4. By the end of the twentieth century, when across the region former communist regimes collapsed, European post-communist countries' relative position to Western Europe was far worse than it was in the mid-nineteenth century. At the moment of regime change the fourteen analysed countries were significantly poorer and less developed than their Western European neighbours. However, in addressing the relationship between economic development and democracy, it is not the relative position of Eastern Europe to that of the West that is crucial, but rather whether the level of development they achieved was sufficient to sustain democratic regimes.

The changing level of economic development in the period after 1989 represents another important aspect of the picture. Figure 3.1 displays change in real GDP per capita for the fourteen countries studied, over the period 1989–2009, using World Bank data.[1]

---

1. Real GDP per capita for the 20 years under study is calculated by using World Bank data on GDP

Figure 3.1: Real GDP per capita in post-communist Europe, 1989–2010

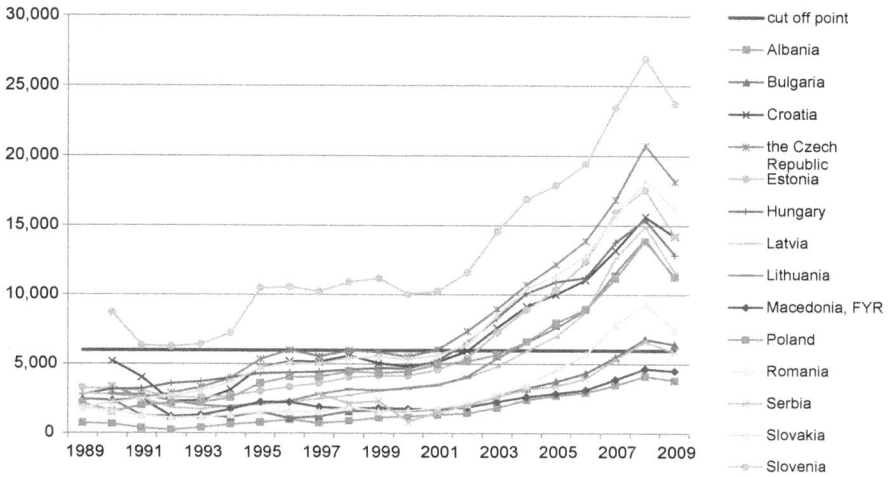

Source: World Bank Data, calculations by author

The flat line in Figure 3.1 displays a cut-off point at $6,000, representing Przeworski's cut-off point for democratic survival, or in other words the level of income above which economic development is argued to contribute positively to democratic survival and development. The only country that keeps fairly high above this cut-off point is Slovenia, falling below only in 1992, right after the dissolution of Yugoslavia. The data series for Slovenia starts in 1990, when Slovenia's GDP per capita was at $8,699 while the rest of the group was between $642 (Albania) and $5,184 (Croatia). Regarding change over time, while GDP per capita scores for the fourteen countries were fairly similar at the beginning of 1990s, in the second decade after regime change these scores diverge considerably. Before the financial crisis in 2008, the spread of GDP per capita scores was between $25,807 (Slovenia) and $3,953 (Albania). In other words, after two decades of democratic development Slovenia was at a 71 per cent of EU's GDP per capita, while Albania was at 11 per cent of EU's GDP per capita.[2] At the moment of regime change thirteen countries were below the $6,000 threshold, while in 2010 Serbia ($5,056), Macedonia ($4,201) and Albania ($3,595) remain the only ones below the threshold, with Bulgaria hovering just above the threshold at $6,129 GDP per capita. In all remaining countries the levels of economic development in the second decade after regime change have become high enough by Przeworski's

per capita in current $US and the GDP deflator also provided by the World Bank online dataset. The calculation is based on the following formula: real GDP = nom GDP / ((GDP deflator/100)+1).

2. Average GDP per capita for the European Union in 2010 was $32,365 (World Bank Data).

criteria to positively influence democratisation. However, as Figure 3.1 shows, the second decade after regime change also displays a fair amount of divergence, with mainly CEE group of countries making significant strides forward, including Croatia and Slovenia, while in the SEE group Albania, Macedonia, Serbia, Bulgaria and Romania made more modest advances in economic development since 2000.

Does economic development as displayed in Figure 3.1 help us understand how democratisation progressed over the twenty year period? In the initial period 1989–1995, no country except Slovenia had crossed the democracy threshold of $6,000. Even Slovenia could be added to the indeterminate group since between 1991 and 1993 its real GDP per capita was below $6,000. At the same time, if we look at data for 1990, the difference between $642 GDP per capita in Albania and $5,184 GDP per capita in Croatia is certainly not trivial. To establish whether these levels of economic development were varied enough to account for differences in subsequent democratisation, these findings are first compared to other development indicators, then correlated with democratisation outcomes. Back when Lipset (1959) posited the famous relationship between economic development and democracy, apart from looking at levels of wealth in the given countries, he also examined levels of urbanisation, education and industrialisation. Since the aim is to establish as detailed as possible a development context for the early 1990s, many data sources have been mined for information. Table 3.2 shows a number of key indicators of modernisation for the fourteen countries. Countries are sorted by first indicator, GDP per capita, descending from highest to lowest.

Assembling this dataset was a challenge, as can be seen from the long list of sources that were used. While data for the CEE group of countries as well as Bulgaria and Romania is fairly accessible, data on former Yugoslav republics has proven difficult to obtain, especially in the case of Serbia (the Federal Republic of Yugoslavia in the 1990s). As a result, Table 3.2 is an amalgam of various data sources, as is indicated in the reference list. The first six columns of the table show indicators of wealth, per cent of rural population, life expectancy, telephone lines per hundred inhabitants and gross enrolment ratios for basic and tertiary education in 1990. The next column to the right, which shows HDI rankings, serves to separate data from the moment of regime change in 1990 from historical data on literacy and urbanisation prior to communism in these countries. Finally, the last column shows civil society sustainability scores, but for a later period since this USAID index is only available since the end of the 1990s.

Sources: a World Bank Dataset Online: http://data.worldbank.org/, b EBRD Life in Transition Report 1999, c World Bank GER data document, d Darden and Grzymala Busse 2006, e Human Development Reports of the UN, http://hdr.undp.org/en/reports/, f USAID CFO sustainability index, http://www.usaid.gov/locations/europe_eurasia/dem_gov/ngoindex/index.htm, g data on Serbia's GDP per capita in 1990 was not available from any international dataset, so I use data quoted by Fink-Hafner (2000) on GDP per capita in Yugoslav republics in 1986 to calculate the ratio of Serbia's GDP per capita to Croatia's, and then apply that ratio to the 1990 World Bank data; h data from former Yugoslav republics are from Fink-Hafner (2000), for 1986; i data for Serbia is from a UNICEF 2001 report 'Primary Education in the Federal Republic of Yugoslavia', j data is for 1991, k data is for 2003.

Table 3.2: Development indicators for post-communist European countries, 1990

Country Name	a 1990 real GDP per capita	a 1990 % of rural population	a 1991 life expectancy at birth	b 1990 telephone lines per 100 inhabitants	b 1990 basic school enrolment ratio (%)	c 1990 tertiary education enrolment ratio	c 1990 HDI rank	d literacy rate at onset of communism	d pre-communist urban-isation	f CSO sustain-ability 2000
Slovenia	8699.17	49.6	73.35	h 26	97.1	19.3	high	91	9.3	k 3.4
Croatia	5184.55	46	72.19	h 18	94.0	j 13.9	high	68	9.3	4.3
Serbia	g 4250.00	49.6	71.49	h 18	i 99.1	16.9	high	35	9.3	4.5
Czech Republic	3365.82	24.8	71.90	16	98.6	13.6	high	99	25	2.4
Lithuania	2841.18	32.4	70.36	21	93.0	17.2	high	77	15	3.1
Hungary	2535.64	34.2	69.38	10	99.2	14.2	high	96	42.5	2.3
Estonia	2388.97	28.9	69.47	20	94.9	14.2	high	99	33	2.4
Macedonia, FYR	2342.07	42.2	71.45	h 13	89.4	j 14.4	high	30	9.3	4.6
Latvia	2246.25	30.7	69.03	23	96.4	15.5	high	93	36	2.8
Slovakia	2075.46	43.5	70.88	14	97.2	13.8	high	92	15	1.9
Bulgaria	1884.03	33.6	71.56	24	98.6	18.8	high	69	21	3.7
Poland	1547.16	38.7	70.59	9	97.5	12.4	high	79	20	2.1
Romania	1452.76	46.8	69.78	11	89.5	10.1	high	57	21	4.1
Albania	641.90	63.6	71.90	1	90.7	5.8	medium	20	13	4.6

In assembling this data the first guiding principle was to include all relevant indicators for which it was possible to locate data for the fourteen cases. The real GDP per capita data in the first column are the same as used in Figure 3.1, and this information is used to sort the cases from highest to lowest GDP per capita in 1990. Here the interesting finding is that three constituent republics of former Yugoslavia had higher GDP per capita in 1990 than any country in CEE. While data for Serbia is not as reliable as the rest in the dataset, and too much should not be read into one data point in a given year, it seems safe to say that when looking narrowly at economic wealth preconditions of democratisation, Slovenia and Croatia were in as good a position as the Czech Republic or Hungary. Looking solely at this indicator, it is not possible to group the fourteen country cases into two regions of SEE and CEE. But let us relate this indicator to the others in the table.

The second column shows the percentage of rural population in 1990. This indicator shows a clear distinction between the more industrialised Baltic states and Central Eastern Europe on the one hand, and Southeast European states on the other, which had higher percentages of rural population. For instance, in 1990 the Czech Republic had only 24.8 per cent rural population, while Serbia had 49.6 per cent and Albania 63.6 per cent. Life expectancy, shown in column three, was fairly homogenous across the region, ranging between 69 years of age in Latvia and 73.35 in Slovenia. Though this indicator shows some variance, again it does not separate countries into geographic regions of SEE and CEE; so Serbia for instance had longer life expectancy than the Czech Republic. Data for phone lines per a hundred inhabitants again group Slovenia, Croatia and Serbia with the more developed CEE states. When it comes to education indicators, Macedonia and Romania performed most poorly with respect to basic school enrolment ratio, while Hungary's basic enrolment ratio was 99.2 per cent. Overall this indicator confirms Fish's (1998) claim that communist regimes established fairly well educated societies. Tertiary enrolment ratio for the analysed countries ranges from 5.8 per cent in Albania and 19.3 in Slovenia – once again confirming developmental reasons that separated Slovenia from the SEE group.

Though this analysis is focused on establishing grounds for diversity among analysed cases, it is important to keep in mind that the presented differences are not very large and should not be overestimated. When taking a more global perspective on the region of post-communist Europe, as the HDI[3] scores do, all analysed cases except Albania are countries exhibiting high development, while Albania is in the medium development group. In order to explore the differences among countries a bit further, another set of indicators was introduced, focusing on the pre-communist period.

Two indicators from Darden and Grzymala Busse's (2006) study on the relationship between pre-communist literacy and communist parties losing the

---

3. The Human Development Index is UNDP's measurement that combines indicators of life expectancy, education and income into a composite index. More information about this index is available at http://hdr.undp.org/en/statistics/hdi/. Last accessed August 23, 2012.

first multi-party elections are included in the table: the pre-communist literacy rate and pre-communist level of urbanisation. While their urbanisation data does not discriminate among former Yugoslav republics and hence blurs the picture somewhat, the difference between Central Eastern and Southeast Europe is clearly visible. While former Yugoslavia had only around 9 per cent urban population before the 1940s, the per cent of urban population in Hungary at the time was already at 43.5 per cent and in the Czech Republic it was 25 per cent. As for the literacy rate before communism, it shows an even larger spread, between 20 per cent literate population in Albania, 30 per cent in Macedonia or 35 per cent in Serbia on the one hand, and 99 per cent literate population in Czech Republic and Estonia on the other. This data testifies to a difference among countries of Central Eastern Europe and Southeast Europe with respect to inheritance of an educated urban population from pre-communist times. The communist modernisation project has been described as authoritarian, bringing infrastructure, education and industry but without engendering individualist value orientations (Dahrendorf 1990, Elster, Offe and Preuss 1998). Though state socialist regimes significantly modernised their societies, this modernisation was partial. The data on urbanisation and literacy from the pre-communist period indicate potentially stronger roots of modernity in these countries, supporting the argument according to which CEE countries had better structural preconditions for engendering democratisation pressure from below. This argument is further supported by the USAID data on sustainability of civil society, shown in the last column of Table 3.2. The CSO index aims to provide a measure of viability and sustainability of a given country's civil society, analysing components such as the legal environment, organisational capacity, financial viability, advocacy, public image, service provision, and the infrastructure of non-governmental organisations.[4] As is visible from Table 3.2, this indicator neatly separates Central from Southeast European countries.

Historical legacies of communist regimes

Moving towards an assessment of historical regime legacies, Kitschelt *et al*'s (1999) typology of communist regime types seems empirically verified by the data presented in Table 3.2. According to that typology, socioeconomic structure and resulting state capacity during the interwar period of the twentieth century determined the key features of communist regimes across Europe. The explanatory potential of modernisation theory is linked to the types of communist regimes that characterised post-communist Europe up to the moment of regime change in that Kitschelt *et al*'s (1999) typology relies on the modernisation argument about the movement from an agrarian to an industrial society. The classification into three types of communist regimes is based on two key characteristics: the socioeconomic features of society and state capacity. Where society was economically stronger

---

4. More information on the CSO index is available at http://transition.usaid.gov/locations/europe_ eurasia/dem_gov/ngoindex/. Last accessed August 23, 2012.

and better educated, a reservoir of opposition to communism was maintained throughout the decades of communist rule, representing the social base for opposition to communism and the nucleus for political pluralism at the moment of regime change. At the same time, in more modernised societies the state possessed stronger bureaucratic autonomy, which prevented the politicisation of the state. These characteristics form the bureaucratic-authoritarian communist regime.

At the other end of the continuum is the patrimonial communist regime, with both weak state capacity leading to party-state rule, and a less economically developed society which has meant effectively no organised opposition to the communist party. Finally, national-accommodative communist regimes were characterised by a degree of professionalisation of the bureaucracy and hence some separation between state and party, as well as some degree of political opposition to communism. Being such an in-between category, its distinguishing characteristic seems to have been the nature of relations between the communist party and the opposition. In national accommodative communist regimes the communist party was trying to accommodate appeals to national autonomy and square the circle between national demands on the one hand and the official communist ideology on the other. This feature is especially relevant in the case of Yugoslavia, where Croatia and Slovenia had strong national movements that strived for more independence and decentralisation of the Yugoslav state.

Kitschelt *et al* (1999) classified all post-communist countries within this typology of regimes, including the fourteen countries included in this study. Table 3.3 shows the classification of cases along the three regime types and their combinations.

According to the authors, only the Czech Republic exhibits all the features of bureaucratic-authoritarian communism, while Poland shared some features of bureaucratic-authoritarian and some features of national-accommodative communism. The reason for this could be that Poland had a larger rural population and a less industrialised society, as well as less developed central bureaucracy.

Table 3.3: Classification of countries into Kitschelt's communist regime types

Bureaucratic-authoritarian communism (3)	Mix (2.5)	National-accommodative communism (2)	Mix (1.5)	Patrimonial communism (1)
Czech Republic	Poland	Hungary, Slovenia, Croatia	Slovakia, Estonia, Latvia, Lithuania, Serbia	Bulgaria, Romania, Macedonia, Albania

Source: Kitschelt *et al*, 1999: 39

The next group of countries are Hungary, Slovenia and Croatia, which belong to the national-accommodative regime type, followed by the Baltic states, Slovakia and Serbia which share some features of the national-accommodative type of communism with some patrimonial features. Finally, Bulgaria, Romania, Macedonia and Albania are, according to this typology, patrimonial communist regimes, with the least developed state bureaucracies and the least social and political opposition to communism. Romania, for instance, had virtually no organised opposition to the extremely oppressive form of communism that evolved under the dictatorship of Nicolai Ceauşescu (Vachudova 2005). Similarly, Albania under Enver Hoxha was an isolationist communist dictatorship and the least economically developed country in Europe (Elbasani 2004).

An interesting feature of this typology is that the authors do not treat then-existent federative states as units of analysis, but rather classify pre-communist nation states into groups. As a result, former Yugoslav states are grouped into three different categories, with Croatia and Slovenia belonging to national-accommodative communist regimes, Macedonia to patrimonial communism, and Serbia in an in-between category. Similarly, while the Czech Republic belongs to bureaucratic-authoritarianism, Slovakia is classified in the same group as Serbia. Following the findings regarding economic and social development of these countries shown in previous sections, this approach seems well founded. While it takes apart the current political division into two regions of Central Eastern and Southeast Europe, it seems to do a much better job in capturing key differences among them.

Having established the regime types of all fourteen cases, next we explore the bivariate relationship between communist regime type and the level of democracy to determine whether there is association. The level of democracy is measured by again using reversed Freedom House Democracy scores. The 2010 Freedom House Democracy score is correlated with Kitschelt's typology. In order to do this, the regime typology is converted into an ordinal scale following a procedure very similar to that used by Pop-Eleches (2007). Bureaucratic-authoritarian communism is accorded the maximum score of three, national-accommodative communism is accorded the score of two, patrimonial communism the score of one, and mixed types score 2.5 and 1.5 respectively. The dataset is displayed in the Appendix. The resulting correlation between communist regime type and the level of democracy in 2010 across the fourteen cases is fairly strong, at 0.69, and it is significant at 0.01 level. A correlation of 0.69 suggests a strong association between the two phenomena, confirming empirically the relevance of Kitschelt's typology to explaining success in subsequent democratisation.

Demand for democracy from below

All the analyses so far have looked at macro and aggregate indicators of socioeconomic development and regime legacies while the preceding theoretical discussion in Chapter 2 has also elaborated the micro foundations of democratisation, in terms of citizens' value orientations. It would therefore be fruitful to analyse survey data on populations in these countries and engage with what citizens think about democracy, political and civil liberties. Unfortunately, no such comparative survey for the beginning of the 1990s exists for the analysed countries. The first international survey to include all fourteen cases was the World Values Survey 1995 Wave (WVS 1995), which was effectively conducted on the ground in the late 1990s. Since the aim is to reconstruct the social and economic conditions at the period of regime change between 1989 and 1991, this dataset is not a perfect match. On the other hand, since value dispositions are known to change slowly, an analysis of democratic values as recorded in the late 1990s might nevertheless provide valuable insights into citizens' preferences at the time of regime change.

In using survey data to say anything about democracy one must be careful not to rely on questions that ask respondents to declaratively state their positions regarding democracy, tolerance, and so forth. Overt support of democracy in analyses of political culture has been shown to reflect superficial motives that do not indicate intrinsic support of values inherent to democracy (Inglehart and Norris 2003, Inglehart and Welzel 2005, Welzel 2006). This is the chief problem, for instance, with the 'Consolidation of democracy in Central and Eastern Europe 1990–2001' survey conducted at the beginning of the 1990s. It has two drawbacks for application in this analysis. Firstly, it includes only nine of the fourteen countries: no former Yugoslav countries, or Latvia. Secondly and more importantly, available survey questions do not include items that would allow for a sophisticated analysis of value dimensions argued to be relevant for democratisation. Instead the survey asked questions such as the one presented in Table 3.4, on whether respondents thought that 'in democracy the problems of our country will be solved'.

As can be seen from Table 3.4, in 1990 the greatest confidence in democracy to solve societal problems was displayed by citizens in Bulgaria and Romania, at 74 and 63 per cent respectively, while respondents from Slovenia, Slovakia and Hungary that exhibited such a belief were in the minority – at 46.9, 44.3 and 37.3 per cent respectively. When these country averages are linked to the economic and social data shown previously, it turns out that faith in democracy was stronger among the more rural, less educated and poorer nations, whose subsequent democratisation was more protracted and tenuous. This therefore reconfirms the need to be careful in the interpretation of such survey findings. Instead of concluding that these results indicate widespread social support for democracy in Bulgaria and Romania, it might be wiser to assume that the citizens of more developed countries were more realistic about the democratic prospects of their countries.

To avoid such interpretative problems, I follow Inglehart and Welzel (2005) in analysing the presence of democratic values by relating the spread of self-expression values in a society with democratisation advances. Operationalisations are formulated so as to enable empirical analysis using question items in the WVS. The aim is to establish empirical grounds for judging to what extent democratic pressure from below may have influenced democratisation in each of the fourteen cases. The empirical analysis is based on the 1995 round of the World Values Survey, which is the only comparative survey from the 1990s in which all fourteen countries were present.

In order to analyse differences in self-expression values across countries,

*Table 3.4: Agreement with statement that 'In democracy problems will be solved',
by country*

Country	% agrees
Bulgaria	73.60
Romania	63.00
Lithuania	59.40
Estonia	57.00
Poland	53.20
Czech Rep	50.90
Slovenia	46.90
Slovakia	44.30
Hungary	37.30

Source: Consolidation of Democracy Dataset 1990–1991, (author's calculations)

Inglehart and Welzel (2005) extracted question items that best capture this concept, which they link explicitly with advances in democracy. The five dimensions of the survival – self-expression value cluster are materialist versus post-materialist values, life satisfaction, sexual liberalism, protest potential and interpersonal trust. My analysis uses the same value cluster as Inglehart and Welzel (2005), with the difference that on some dimensions I used more question items from the survey to construct composite variables. For the dimension that pertains to sexual liberalism, I do not use only the item regarding homosexuality, but instead I create a composite variable that also includes attitudes towards abortion and divorce. Similarly, with respect to the dimension of protest potential, Inglehart and Welzel (ibid.) use only the item regarding willingness of respondents to sign petitions, while I create a composite variable that includes attitudes towards attending demonstrations, supporting boycotts and so forth. In summary, three of the five operationalisations are identical to those used in Inglehart and Welzel (2005), while the remaining two operationalisations are based on a larger number of question items that, arguably, better capture the value dimensions identified as drivers of democratisation. The operationalisations of concepts and analyses are presented next.

In a recent contribution that emphasises the importance of citizens' attitudes, Welzel (2006) argued for the importance of liberty aspirations in the population as a particularly important ingredient of democratisation. According to him, progress in democratisation, or its absence, is directly related to 'the shrinkage and growth of civil and political freedom' (2006: 875). Civil and political freedoms represent the emancipative essence of democracy (Dahl 1971) and the perspective of human development is the only appropriate way to deal with democracy (Sen 1999), since human development is itself an emancipative concept, focusing on the societal conditions that promote human freedom and choice (Welzel 2003, Welzel *et al.* 2003). 'More than any other supposedly pro-democratic attitude, liberty aspirations (i.e. aspirations for decision making freedom) are targeted at democracy's core human achievement: civil and political rights' (Welzel 2006: 876). Like Inglehart and Norris (2003), he criticises the use of overt support of democracy in analyses of political culture because it can reflect superficial motives that do not indicate intrinsic support of the values inherent to democracy (Inglehart & Welzel 2005, Welzel 2006). Liberty aspirations, by contrast, 'reflect an intrinsic valuation of the essence of democracy: decision-making freedom' (Welzel 2006: 890).

Having developed this argument about liberty aspirations, Welzel (2006) uses Inglehart's scale of materialist – post-materialist values, constructed out of several questions in the World Values Survey. Welzel, in essence, provided another potential interpretation of Inglehart's scale of post-materialism, claiming that it says important things about the democratisation potential of given populations. Using the dataset from WVS 1995, I replicate almost the same procedure as in Welzel (2006).[5] In the WVS 1995, respondents were given the following four choices, and asked to determine the first and second most important: maintain order in a nation, give people more say in decisions regarding government, fight rising prices, and protect freedom of speech. According to Inglehart and Welzel (2005), options two and four represent post-materialist values, or liberty aspirations according to Welzel's (2006) subsequent interpretation. I recoded the two question items (V106 and V107 in WVS 1995) so that respondents who chose post-materialist values as their first and second preference are identified in opposition to those choosing the other two options. The two questions are combined into a summed index variable, where the value of one stands for Post-Materialists, two for Moderates, and three for Materialists.[6] Figure 3.2 shows the means for the fourteen countries; a lower score standing for a population with stronger demand for civil and political rights. Countries are sorted from lowest (post-materialist) to highest (materialist) score.

Figure 3.2 displays interesting results according to which citizens of Slovenia and Croatia showed the highest demand for decision-making freedom, followed by the Czech Republic and Latvia and Poland. These findings echo earlier analyses of socioeconomic indicators, where Slovenia and Croatia also clustered with the Czech Republic and some Baltic states on several dimensions. Among countries with a lower average of post-materialist values are Bulgaria, Albania, Serbia and, surprisingly, Hungary. However, it is important not to read too much into any individual result since survey data are not always reliable. Instead, the purpose of

---

5. The difference is that Welzel worked with three items, while I work with two since only two are available in the 1995 round of the World Values Survey.

6. Hansen and Tol did essentially the same procedure in terms of coding in their working paper from 2003 (in biblio). They set the boundaries from 1 (Materialist choosing a) and c) from the Four item index) to 3 (Post-materialist, choosing b) and d) from the Four item index), while 2 means the Mixed Type (choosing either a) and c) or b) and d)).

Figure 3.2: Materialist values in countries of post-communist Europe

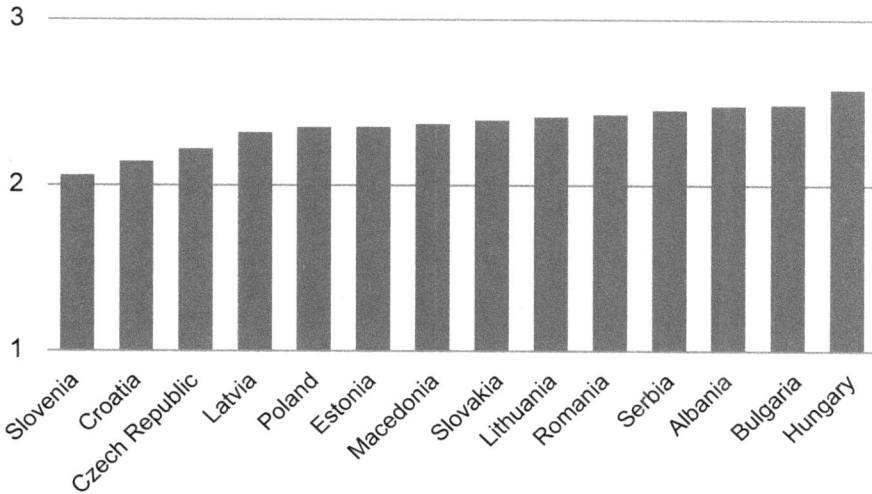

Source: World Values Survey 1995 dataset, calculations by author

comparative analyses in this chapter is to juxtapose various data sources in order to establish a fairly reliable pattern.

Life satisfaction is the second part of the survival – self-expression cluster. Figure 3.3 overleaf shows respondents' attitudes towards life satisfaction, ranging between the score of one, representing complete dissatisfaction, and ten, representing full satisfaction.

The mean sample for the fourteen countries taken together is displayed as a chequered bar to distinguish it from country scores. It can be taken as the dividing line between countries which show lower than average life satisfaction and those with higher than average life satisfaction. Considering the range of the scale, answers above the score of five can be taken as indicative of a satisfactory life. Data shows that more countries are in this group than in the unsatisfied one. Counterintuitively, respondents from countries undergoing political upheaval and crisis at the time the survey – Croatia, Serbia or Macedonia – are on average fairly satisfied with life. It is known from existing literature that life satisfaction judgments depend on the standards individuals have set for themselves and that individuals who are in similar objective circumstances may judge their lives to be more or less satisfying. Measures of life satisfaction have also been criticised as contaminated by mood, immediate context, cultural frames of reference, order in which questions are presented, as well as a person's income (Forgeard *et al* 2011). It has been shown that GDP per capita explains more than 50 per cent of inter-country variation in life satisfaction, and that the estimated relationship is linear (Economist Intelligence Unit Report 2005). In twenty-four out of twenty-eight countries surveyed by Eurobarometer, material wellbeing is identified as the most

Figure 3.3: Life satisfaction among citizens of post-communist Europe

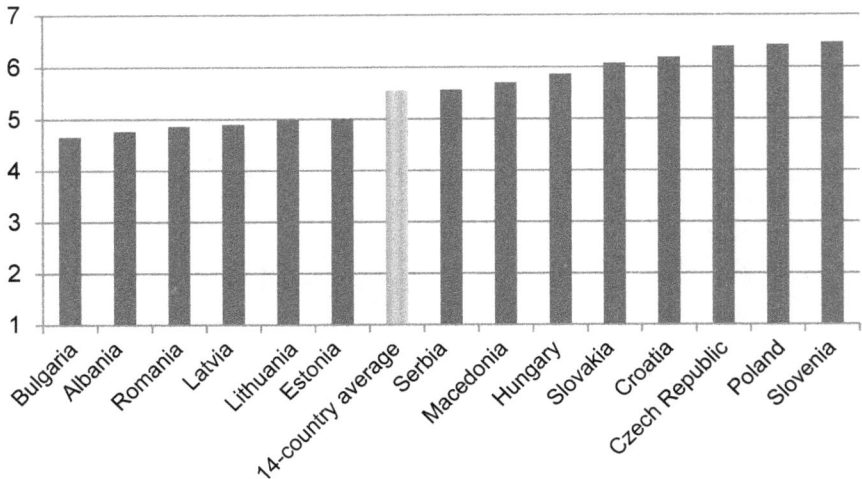

Source: World Values Survey 1995, calculations by author

important criterion for life satisfaction (ibid.). Though not much should be read into one item in a survey, this research suggests that the unexpected findings from Figure 3.3 might in part be attributed to the fact that international surveys such as the WVS tend to include a disproportionate share of better off respondents, who are more satisfied with life than their less well-to-do compatriots.

A society's commitment to sexual liberalisation 'proves time and again to be the most reliable indicator of how strongly that society supports principles of tolerance and egalitarianism' (Inglehart and Norris 2003: 65). Attitudes towards sexual liberalisation are measured using WVS items regarding attitudes towards homosexuality, abortion and divorce. The survey respondents were asked to say whether each of the three phenomena could always be justified, never be justified, or something in between – choosing on a scale of one to ten. Factor analysis revealed an underlying factor for the three items, with KMO of 0.66 and Cronbach's Alpha of 0.74. These statistics establish sufficient reliability for creating a composite index of sexual liberalism. Figure 3.4 shows the means for the fourteen countries in the study, from lowest to highest tolerance of sexual liberalism. Attitudes range from the opinion that divorce, abortion and homosexuality can never be justified (score of one) to the opinion that they can always be justified (score of ten).

Almost all countries' mean scores are below five, which signals that overall, the populations of post-communist Europe are sexually conservative. This is to be expected, since in most of these countries the majority of respondents characterised themselves as religious. The most sexually liberal populations were in the Czech Republic and Croatia, while the populations of Lithuania and Macedonia were the

Figure 3.4: Sexual liberalisation attitudes in post-communist Europe, 1995

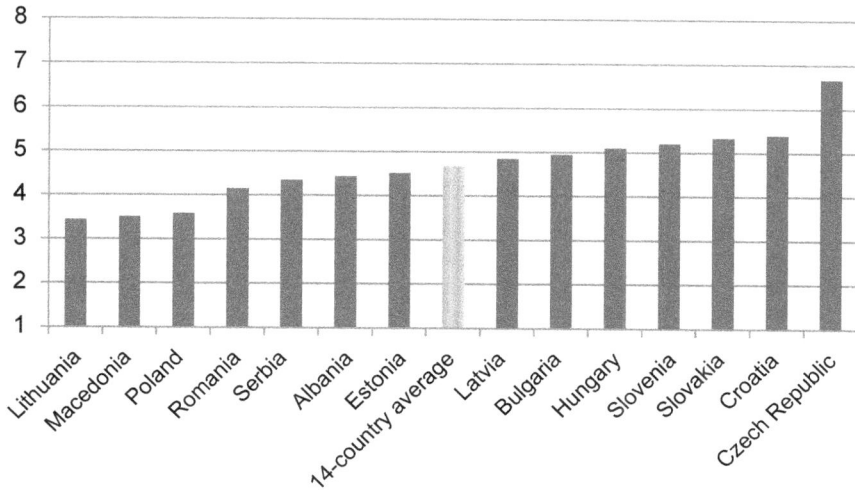

Source: World Values Survey 1995 dataset, calculations by author

most sexually conservative. As in the analysis of previous dimensions, countries do not group according to geographic regions, so Poland and Lithuania join Macedonia, Romania and Serbia in the more conservative group.

With respect to protest potential, I follow the conceptualisation of Dalton and Van Sickle (2005) to create a composite variable. Testing theories of protest derived from relative deprivation theory, political opportunity structures and political culture, they found that 'the primary sources of protest reflect the existing of resources and political opportunities to engage in protest activity. People protest not because they are frustrated and excluded from politics, but because they can protest and they expect governments to respond to their actions' (2005: 1). Therefore, one way to capture the presence of democratic culture in a society is to look at its protest potential. Engaging in protest activities is part of the democratic repertoire of citizenship – and political participation represents a key motor in democratisation. Protest activities create a bottom-up pressure on governments and political institutions, demanding accountability and enabling citizens' voice.

Protest potential is analysed by creating a composite variable from several question items in the WVS 1995. Factor analysis showed that five question items capturing respondents' attitudes towards attending demonstrations, joining boycotts and unofficial strikes, signing petitions and occupying buildings have a strong underlying factor. The values of KMO at 0.85, and Cronbach's Alpha at 0.77 allow sufficient reliability for the creation of a composite variable, 'protest potential'. In the composite variable, values still range between one and three, with lower scores signifying stronger protest potential or, in other words, a greater ratio of a country's population that is prepared to engage in protest activities. Figure 3.5 shows the means for the fourteen analysed country cases.

Figure 3.5 shows nearly homogenous results for the fourteen countries, capturing only very small differences among them. Croatia and the Czech Republic lead the group of countries with higher protest potential, while Poland and Bulgaria are at the end of the lower protest potential group. After analysing four separate dimensions of the self-expression – survival value cluster, regularities across countries are becoming evident by now. For instance, respondents from the Czech Republic and Croatia regularly appear at the more democratic end of the value spectrum, while respondents from Bulgaria and Albania repeatedly exhibit less democratisation potential. But, before drawing any conclusions, let's have a look at the final dimension, which relates to interpersonal trust.

Features of interpersonal trust and cooperation are important for democratic culture because they reduce incentives to free-ride and cheat, they reduce uncertainty and engender virtuous circles of future cooperation. By extension, high reported levels of interpersonal trust indicate a well-established culture of general reciprocity and civic engagement (Putnam 1993). Question V27 in the WVS 1995 was formulated so that respondents were asked to choose between agreeing that most people can be trusted (score of one), or that overall, one must be careful in trusting people (score of two). Figure 3.6 shows the results.

First of all, the differences are fairly small, ranging from an average country score of 1.7 to 1.92. Since this is a dichotomous question, mean scores above 1.5 could be interpreted as standing for a population that is, on average, suspicious of its fellow citizens, which applies to all fourteen countries. Among the differences

Figure 3.5: Protest potential in post-communist Europe

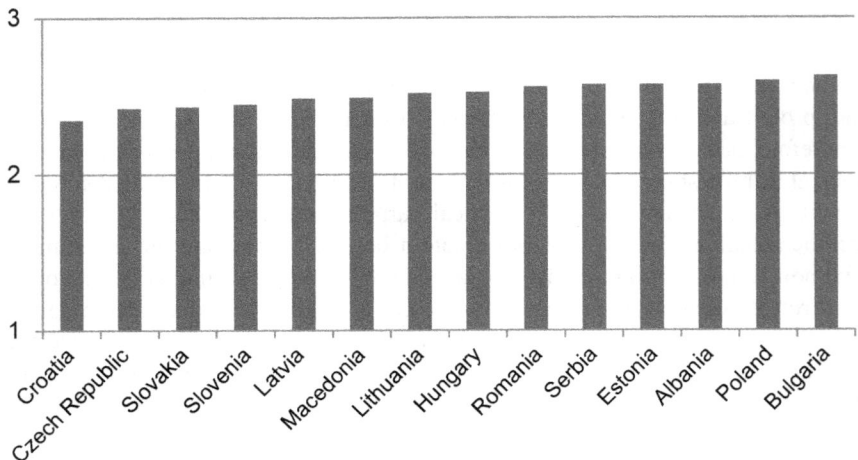

Source: World Values Survey 1995 dataset, calculations by author

Figure 3.6: Trust among citizens of post-communist Europe

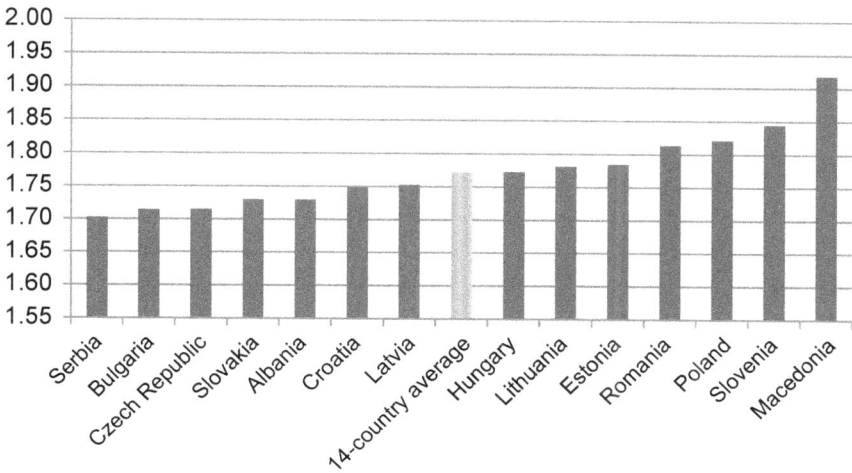

Source: World Values Survey 1995 dataset, calculations by author

that do exist, Serbia, surprisingly, exhibits the highest level of interpersonal trust. As was the case in the four previous dimensions, Croatia and the Czech Republic are again in the group of countries with higher democratic potential. Macedonia and – surprisingly – Slovenia, lead the group of countries whose citizens are least trustful of their fellow citizens. Overall, however, in the late 1990s, citizens in post-communist European countries were distrustful. This finding echoes other research which has shown that citizens of post-communist Europe rely on family and private friendship networks, they are distrustful of civil society organisations and disappointed with the political elite (Howard 2003).

After reviewing each of the five dimensions of the survival – self-expression value cluster, the next analysis brings these dimensions together, and relates them to democratisation outcomes. In order to create a mean value for each country across the five dimensions, each variable is rescaled into a zero to one scale, and some of them are reversed so that for each dimension a higher value stands for more liberal democratic values. The resulting dataset is shown in Table 3.5.

Values in the last column represent the new composite variable that stands for Inglehart and Welzel's (2005) value cluster of survival – self-expression orientations. The higher this value the more, on average, a population of a country exhibits self-expression orientations, which is taken to stand for democratic potential in the population. Data shows that all values are below 0.5 on a scale from zero to one, which can be interpreted to say that in all fourteen cases the populations are, on average, characterised by survival values rather than self-expression values, which push for effective democratisation of a society. This finding

Table 3.5: Survival – self-expression value cluster dataset

Country	Post-materi-alism	Sexual liberalism	Inter-personal trust	Protest potential	Life sat-isfaction	Demo-cratic potential
Albania	0.26	0.38	0.27	0.21	0.42	0.31
Bulgaria	0.26	0.44	0.29	0.19	0.41	0.31
Croatia	0.43	0.49	0.25	0.33	0.58	0.41
Czech Republic	0.39	0.63	0.29	0.29	0.60	0.44
Estonia	0.32	0.39	0.22	0.21	0.44	0.32
Hungary	0.21	0.46	0.23	0.24	0.54	0.33
Latvia	0.34	0.43	0.25	0.26	0.43	0.34
Lithuania	0.29	0.27	0.22	0.24	0.44	0.29
Mac-edonia	0.31	0.28	0.08	0.26	0.52	0.29
Poland	0.33	0.29	0.18	0.20	0.60	0.32
Romania	0.29	0.35	0.19	0.22	0.43	0.29
Serbia	0.27	0.37	0.30	0.21	0.51	0.33
Slovakia	0.30	0.48	0.27	0.29	0.56	0.38
Slovenia	0.47	0.47	0.16	0.28	0.61	0.40

Source: WVS 1995, calculations by author

echoes Inglehart's research according to which the political culture of Eastern Europe is characterised by survival rather than self-expression values, which he attributes to the fact that these societies' experience of the collapse of communism 'shattered their economic, political, and social systems, and brought a pervasive sense of insecurity' (2006: 73). At the same time, Inglehart (2006) stressed that irrespective of the fact that all these countries underwent communist regimes, their cultural heritage seems to play a significant role, since important differences persist among value systems of historically Catholic or Protestant societies on the one hand and Orthodox societies on the other. This fact might suggest one reason why, throughout this chapter, country level analysis fails to group countries into contemporary political regions of Central Eastern and Southeast Europe.

Taking all this on board, it is important to establish whether citizens' value orientations and democratic outcomes are related. The assumption is that higher extent of average self-expression values should be associated with better democratic outcomes. In order to perform this analysis, composite scores from Table 3.5 are used, together with reversed Freedom House democracy scores for 2010. The dataset is displayed in the Appendix. The correlation between these two variables is 0.463, and the relationship is significant at the 0.1 level. This result confirms the argument that relates the two phenomena, pointing to a moderately strong relationship between citizens' value orientations and subsequent success at democratisation.

Summarising the discussion so far, several findings stand out. First of all, whether looking at economic development, education, regime type or values in the population, the fourteen countries do not group under the political regions of Central Eastern and Southeast Europe. While the names for the two regions are often used as conventional placeholders, this analysis reconfirms the need for analysts to remember that they hide a lot of diversity and that their usefulness is therefore limited. Secondly, while the analysis revealed interesting aspects of diversity, it has also testified to an overall level of homogeneity among countries in the region. Maintaining such a contradiction is possible as long as we are able to look at post-communist Europe from different levels of abstraction. When looked at from a global perspective, the region does not exhibit vast differences in wealth, socioeconomic development or predominant values in the population – which is in part a testimony to the homogenising effect of the communist rule and another confirmation of the need to incorporate communist regime types in seeking explanations for divergent democratisation trajectories. At the same time, if the region is looked upon from a smaller distance, important differences emerge, which can in part be attributed to long term cultural legacies of Orthodoxy and Catholicism, as well as to the fact that the communist regimes across Europe exhibited important differences in the extent to which they brought modernisation to these countries. Finally, empirical findings discussed in this chapter have confirmed the theoretical predictions according to which the levels of socioeconomic development, communist regime type and citizens' value orientations are important factors of subsequent democratisation.

Apart from arguing that structural conditions influenced democratisation, I have also stressed the fact that the particular trajectory democratisation would take in a given country depends on how environmental factors combine with political choice. This is the topic of Chapter 4.

chapter four | the impact of political choice

While in the previous chapters the focus has been on structural preconditions, in the following analyses the focus moves to the role that political choice played in democratisation. The quality of political elites represents the scope of choice that citizens have in a democracy, and here this crucial supply of elites is understood as the function of environmental factors just discussed.

Authoritarian parties dominating regime change

Authoritarian parties that dominated over regime change at the beginning of the 1990s are a crucial ingredient in explaining divergence in post-communist democratisation. Their dominance over periods of regime change after 1989 produced governance practices that were inimical to functioning rule of law systems and this mode of rule coalesced into a fundamental feature of these democratic regimes. The main analytical categories advanced here are competitiveness and constellation, while their interrelationship is assumed to affect the strength of authoritarian party dominance. The concept of political party competition relies on the importance of parliamentary opposition, which is argued to influence democratisation through the mechanisms of mutual monitoring and threat of replacement. However, in addition to that I argue that the dynamic of alternation in power that results from competitive elections is crucial for conceptualising party system competitiveness. Two recent studies that focused on the effect that party competition has on state exploitation, one by O'Dwyer (2006) and the other by Grzymala Busse (2007), provide measures for operationalising the concept of party competition, but they define and measure political competition differently. While I build on both scholars' theoretical insights about party system competitiveness, I decided against using Grzymala Busse's measures of party system competitiveness, and I use a modified version of O'Dwyer's measures. Let me elaborate the reasons behind this decision.

Grzymala Busse (2007) proposed an index of competitiveness that consists of three elements. The first element refers to the extent to which the former communist party reformed after regime change, and the scale ranges from full reform, across partial reform and ends with no reform. The second element in the index is the share of seats in parliament of plausible parties. This measure counts parties which are not ostracised and unable to enter any coalitions and aims to capture the range of plausible governing alternatives as an important aspect of competition. Finally, since Grzymala Busse (2007) argues that there can hardly be robust competition if the opposition is not vociferous in monitoring the government, she introduces the third measure of average number of questions asked per Member of Parliament coming from the opposition. Based on the data that Grzymala Busse supplies, the three measures co-vary, seemingly indeed capturing important characteristics of political party competition. A closer examination of this empirical strategy, however, reveals a number of problems. In order to calculate the index, Grzymala Busse used average values over the first fifteen years of democracy for the nine countries that she studied. Since during the 1990s political party systems were still evolving in post-communist countries, this averaging of scores across the observed time period wipes away a lot of variance. Instead of that, the index could have been calculated after each election, and then aggregated for up to and after the initial three rounds of elections. Since studies have shown that across the post-communist region, party systems stabilised during the first three rounds of elections (Dawisha and Deets 2006), such a periodisation might have been more appropriate and it would have captured more variation.

The second element of Grzymala Busse's index is the seat share of plausible parties in parliament, which is a measure she takes from Ferejohn (1986). This measure aims to capture the extent of plausible governing alternatives or, in other words, the space taken up by parties ostracised from any coalitions. The logic of the argument is that 'the more seats held by plausible opponents, the greater the number of potential alternative coalitions' (2007: 12). This measure does capture some aspect of the theoretical argument, even though it is a rather indirect measure for assessing the mechanisms of mutual monitoring or threat of replacement. However, the problem with this measure is that it singles out those parties which are ostracised by everyone else, while it does not account for the presence of bloc politics, i.e. the fact that only some combinations have coalition potential, which actually constrains competition to a much greater extent. More importantly, the measure shows little or no variation across European post-communist cases. It fits the Czech case very well because the Czech Republic has had an unreconstructed communist party with an important parliamentary presence throughout the period under study, but in this aspect the Czech case is an exception. Communist parties, where they exist among European post-communist countries, are tiny non-parliamentary parties. A communist anti-system party of comparable strength did not exist anywhere else in post-communist Europe and hence this component of the index seems to be a convenient measure for capturing Czech particularities, but carries little value when the analysis is expanded to other cases.

Finally, the third element of Grzymala Busse's index of competitiveness aims to capture the parliamentary arena of party politics and, more precisely, the extent to which opposition parties are performing their main function. On a theoretical level it is a good measure for the described mechanism of mutual monitoring, with opposition parties imposing important constraints on government power, as well as informing and enabling the wider public to demand accountability and participatory governance. However, since it is notoriously difficult to obtain comparable data on parliamentary behaviour of parties, and since this is further compounded by the fact that formal rules of parliamentary debate affect the behaviour of the opposition parties, Grzymala Busse opted for a rather roundabout proxy. She uses the yearly average number of questions posed by MPs (any MP), and then applies the assumption that around eighty per cent of those were posed by opposition MPs. Setting aside the mentioned differences in parliamentary rules across countries which probably affect opposition MPs' behaviour, this measure leaves too much to assumption, especially given the context of new democracies with emergent party systems and emergent parliamentary practices.

Connor O'Dwyer (2006) studied ways in which the absence of robust party competition influences the strengthening of patronage politics in the Czech Republic, Poland and Slovakia. While I do not employ all the measurements he proposes – O'Dwyer was able to analyse three cases in more detail than I am able with fourteen – I draw on several aspects of his analysis. I consider his emphasis on the presence of a dominant party and of alternation in government especially important, as well as his measurement of the effectiveness of parliamentary opposition. Competitive party systems with balanced political forces that alternate in government have been shown as most successful in sustaining democratic institutions and ensuring more equitable policy outcomes. Where one political faction or constellation of political parties has ruled for long periods of time and controlled organs of the state, the trend has been towards greater authoritarianism and greater corruption (Ekiert, Kubik and Vachudova 2007). In addition, whether or not communists lost the first election turned out to be crucial for subsequent democratisation prospects (Fish 1998, Ganev 2007).

O'Dwyer (2006) considers the absence of a Sartori-type predominant party an important characteristic of party system competitiveness. I rely on the same logic in emphasising the importance of alternation in power, and in identifying dominant parties that have in some cases ruled over regime change in post-communist Europe. Carothers (2002) has also argued that dominant power politics, where one political grouping – a party, movement or single leader – dominates over the political system leads countries into the grey zone in between democracy and authoritarianism. According to Huntington's (1991) two-turnover test, it is only after the opposition wins and then loses office to the pro-regime party that we can claim a stabilisation of the democratic regime. Lijphart (1999) would say that this alternation argument is biased toward majoritarian democracies since in consensual democracies governments are usually coalitions and most alternations in power are partial. Germany or Switzerland in the period 1940s to 1990s, Lijphart argues, fail Huntington's two-turnover test of democratic consolidation. Taking Lijphart's argument on board, I argue that in consensual democracies we can still speak of significant turnovers in power. Huntington's concept of a turnover states that a political party or group of parties loses power and is replaced with another party or group. Whether it is two single parties or two blocs of parties that switch in office does not change the most important implication of the causal mechanism: that alternation in office prevents one party from becoming dominant and abusing power. Furthermore, in three-to-five multiparty systems, which are typical in post-communist countries, two parties are usually large and their alternation in power does represent a significant political change. At the same time, cases of Germany or Switzerland reinstate the relevance of establishing the political party constellation when assessing the influence of party system dynamics on democratisation. I argue that the party system constellation conditions the effect that party system competitiveness will have on democratisation. In the following sections party system competitiveness is operationalised by using concepts of communist exit, fractionalisation of the opposition, the two-turnover test, and the presence of party dominance. After that, the concept of party system constellation is operationalised by identifying and analysing key political parties in SEE with authoritarian party platforms. Finally, the dimensions of party system competition and constellation are combined into an argument about the influence of authoritarian party dominance on democratisation in post-communist Europe.

The exit of communist parties from power in the first democratic election was crucial for providing the initial impetus for political and economic democratic reforms (Fish 1998). In all CEE countries the former communist party lost the first multiparty elections to anti-communist opposition, providing impetus for immediate political reforms. In contrast to that scenario, among the six Southeast European cases, the former communist party lost the first multiparty election only in Croatia while in Albania, Bulgaria, Macedonia, Romania and Serbia the former communist party stayed in power. In Albania the Democratic Party defeated the Socialist Party in the 1992 election, but lost office in the 1997 election, so Albania has had a competitive system since the moment of regime change with two strong parties alternating in office. However, neither party had credible democratic credentials but instead perpetuated authoritarian rule inimical to the strengthening of the rule of law and furthering democratisation. As was shown in Chapter 3, Albania initiated regime change under the most adverse preconditions for democracy, characterised by 'Stalinism and almost half a century of self-imposed isolation' (Szajkowski 1992: 157). As a result, in the 1990s Albania had no real counter-elite to speak of, with both parties emerging from the former communist elite and having no democratic tradition to draw from (Elbasani 2004). During the 1996–1998 period, which was characterised by democratic breakthroughs among its neighbours, Albania was experiencing a political and societal meltdown (Szajkowski 2003, Batt 2007). State power disintegrated, law and order broke down, while tribalism and organised crime took over the power vacuum (Elbasani 2004). Therefore, while the competitive characteristics of the Albanian party system should be beneficial to advancing democracy, the constellation argument together with the political context of Albania in the 1990s help explain why this has not been the case. While the leader of the Democratic Party, Sali Berisha, was not a communist, he was no democrat either (ibid.). Upon assuming power in 1992 the Democratic Party thoroughly politicised the state and feudalised the state administration with party loyalists, while Berisha ruled authoritatively, ignoring the legislature and judiciary (ibid.). Therefore, by the early 1990s it was already clear that both major parties were authoritarian, and that political competition in this context could not bring about democratic reform as predicted by theory.

In four SEE cases former communists stayed in power through the period of regime change, the initial elections and for the best part of the 1990s: Bulgaria, Macedonia, Serbia and Romania, signalling weakness of the opposition and creating a period of authoritarian party dominance. The case of Croatia is different in that the former communist party was in opposition during the 1990s, creating the potential for a stronger monitoring mechanism within parliamentary politics. On the other hand, the feature that connects all Southeast European cases is the dominance of authoritarian parties over the political system throughout the 1990s: the Socialists in Bulgaria, Macedonia, Serbia and Romania, the nationalist rightwing Croatian Democratic Union in Croatia, and both Socialists and Democrats in Albania. In order to more formally assess the comparative strength of political party opposition in the period after regime change, O'Dwyer's measure of fractionalisation of the opposition is used. This is a modified version of the Laakso-Taagepera's number of effective parties (1979), where the calculation is made only for political parties in opposition:

$$Fo = 1/\sum pi2$$

In this formula Fo stands for fractionalisation of the opposition, while pi is the fraction of parliamentary seats in the overall opposition bloc won by the i-th opposition party (2006: 39). The downside of this measure is that it does not capture the actual behaviour of opposition parties, but only its potential that stems from structural determinants. Nevertheless, it is a measure that can provide a quantified assessment of the effectiveness of parliamentary opposition based on the assumption that less fragmented opposition is more effective in monitoring those in power. Figure 4.1 shows the fractionalisation index, averaged for the period 1991–2000. The focus is on this period because it encompasses the first three parliamentary elections during which, typically, the emergent regimes consolidated major features of the party system (Dawisha and Deets 2006). Smaller scores indicate less fractionalised parliamentary opposition.

Figure 4.1: Effectiveness of parliamentary opposition, 1991–2000 average

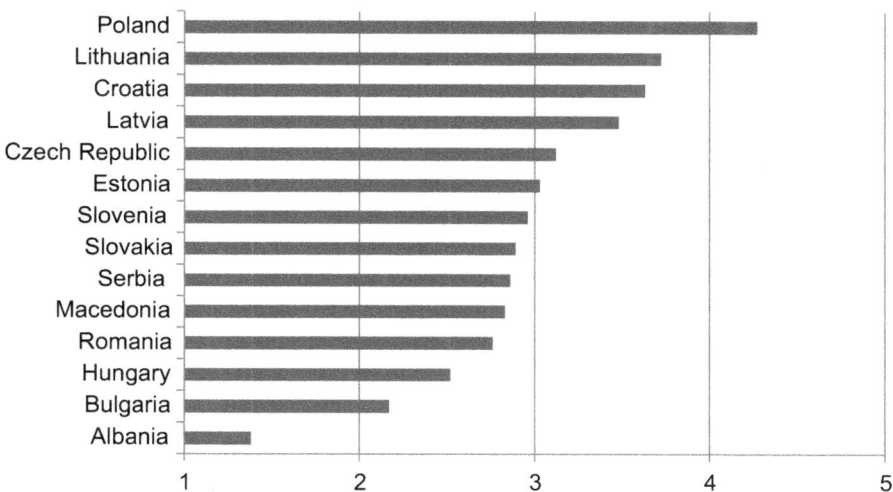

Source: author's calculations

It is well known that in the initial period of 1989 to 1993 Poland had a notoriously fractionalised party system, inspiring some scholars to describe it as a 'kaleidoscopic mosaic' (Millard 1994). After the first fully competitive election in 1991, deputies from twenty-nine electoral committees took seats in the Sejm (ibid.). Though a stable and in Mair's (1997) conception, a 'closed' party system is normally considered a prerequisite of democratic consolidation, Poland has not developed such a system. Poland continues to exhibit high levels of electoral volatility and a fluctuating party landscape, with parties lacking strong roots in societies and having few members (Millard 2009). At the same time, in the first decade after regime change Poland managed to develop a democratic regime that protects political and civil liberties. Albania, on the other hand, shows low fractionalisation, which signals a strongly unified parliamentary opposition, but this finding bears little correspondence with successful democratisation. Also when looking at the overall ranking of countries according to this indicator, it does not seem to cohere well with subsequent democratisation trajectories. Overall it seems that this measure of oppositional strength corresponds poorly with subsequent democratisation trajectories. Part of the problem probably lies in the fact that it does not capture actual oppositional strength, but only its structural potential – which seems to have little purchase during the first decade of regime change that was characterised by emergent political parties and fledging political pluralism.

Huntington's two-turnover test states that, 'a democracy may be viewed as consolidated if the party or group that takes power in the initial election at the time of transition loses a subsequent election and turns over power to those election winners, and if those election winners then peacefully turn over power to the winners of a later election' (1991: 267). Applying the two-turnover test allows us not only to establish when a country entered a period of consolidated democracy, but also helps create a comparative, easily readable visual of the length of rule of political parties in post-communist European countries. Figure 4.2 shows moments of first and second turnover for the fourteen countries under study. Countries are sorted according to the year of first turnover, from earliest on the left hand side of the graph, to most recent year of first turnover in the right hand side of the graph.

According to Huntington, the first turnover usually has great symbolic significance, signalling the functioning of elections as the cornerstone of democracy (ibid.). Looking at Figure 4.2, interesting patterns emerge. Setting aside Albania, countries that have subsequently established a more positive democratisation trajectory were those where the first turnover happened early: Estonia, Lithuania, Latvia, Poland, Hungary, and Slovenia. Among this group Slovenia stands out due to a subsequently quite long period of Liberal Democracy of Slovenia (LDS) party rule (though in different coalition permutations), from 1992 until 2004. However, the LDS did not come to power in the first, but rather in the second election. Both this, and the fact that LDS was a credible democratic party, makes the Slovenian case different from countries in the SEE group. Therefore, six CEE countries experienced the first turnover by 1994, with only the Czech Republic and Slovakia crossing that threshold in 1998. Slovakia resembles countries from Southeast Europe since there the first turnover in 1998 also brought democratic

Figure 4.2: Two-turnovers in post-communist Europe

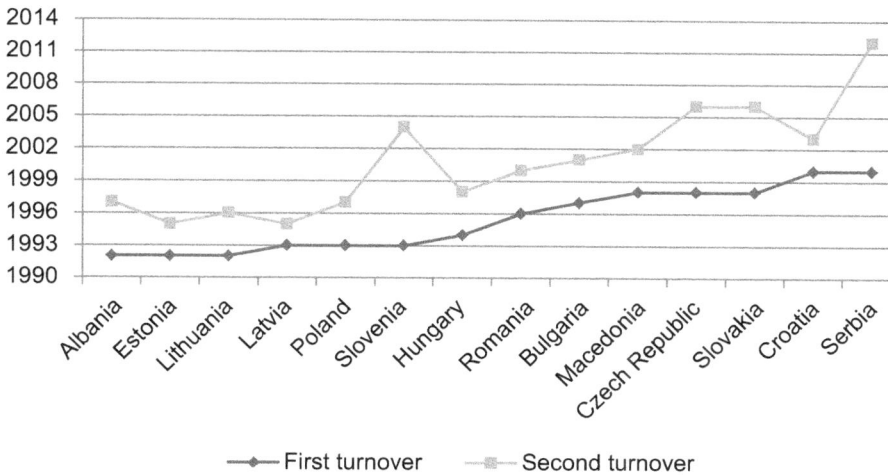

Note: election data was compiled from several sources, listed in the References.
Main sources are Berglund *et al* (2004) and Rose and Munro (2009).

turn elections after Vladimir Mečiar's Movement for a Democratic Slovakia (HZDS) had ruled over a long period after regime change.

Figure 4.2 shows a group of countries where the party that won the initial elections stayed in power for six to ten years: Romania, Bulgaria, Macedonia, the Czech Republic, Slovakia, Croatia and Serbia. The last two countries of that group did not pass the first turnover test until 2000. Even though, from today's perspective, the Czech Republic and Slovakia are comparatively better democratic reformers than countries in the SEE group, in the 1990s they were also marked by a long period in which one party was able to consolidate power over the entire political and economic spectrum. What differentiates the two cases is that in the Czech Republic the dominant party espoused credible democratic practices, while in Slovakia it had strong authoritarian tendencies. The difference in political party constellation seems to show up in how successful the two countries have been in democratisation. According to the Nations in Transit report (2010), Slovakia has the worst scores for judiciary independence and corruption among countries in the CEE group. On the other hand, in the Czech Republic, like in Slovenia, one-party dominance occurred in a more robust democratic setting, where no major party espoused ethno-nationalist, exclusivist rhetoric and the political context was more conducive to democratisation, as shown in Chapter 3.

Authoritarian party dominance in countries of Southeast Europe seems to have had strong long term impact on the democratisation prospects of these countries. Looking back at Figure 4.2, in countries of SEE the first turnover carried the added importance of bringing to power democratic governments after a longer period in which authoritarian parties headed governments (everywhere except

Albania): 1996 in Romania, 1997 in Bulgaria, 1998 Macedonia and 2000 in Croatia and Serbia (cf. Vachudova 2005, Schimmelfennig 2005). The same is true of Slovakia in 1998, when Vladimir Mečiar's HZDS was removed from power. Until this first turnover in power, in all these cases nationalist parties dominated the first decade after regime change. It was only after these nationalist parties lost power that cycles of alternation in power started. In Bulgaria and Macedonia these late 1990s reform governments were also the first governments to survive entire terms in office.

With respect to the second turnover in power, all fourteen countries have crossed it, though Serbia stands out as the case where this occurred only in 2012. Between 2000, when the coalition Democratic Opposition of Serbia (DOS) came to office and the most recent parliamentary election in 2012, all governments were composed from the DOS coalition – Democratic Party (DP) and the Democratic Party of Serbia (DPS). In other words, since the seminal October 2000 election that ousted Milošević from power the two main parties of the Milošević regime – the Socialist Party of Serbia (SPS) and the Serbian Radical Party (SRS), have not led governments until the most recent election in 2012. The SRS became a junior partner in the 2008 DP government, while the second turnover that occurred in June 2012 brought the Serbian Progressive Party (SPP) to power, with Ivica Dačić from the SRS becoming Prime Minister. Since SPP is a splinter party from the Serbian Radical Party and SRS the party that ruled over Serbia throughout the 1990s, a significant alternation of power has occurred in Serbia. The new government has only recently entered office, so it remains to be seen whether it will pull Serbia back into some form of hybrid regime (Pavlović and Antonić 2007) or whether the two parties will moderate upon resuming power, following the dynamic that happened elsewhere in post-communist Europe.

If we focus on long periods of domination whereby one party successively headed either majority or coalition governments as an important dimension that remains hidden in the two-turnover test, such an analytical focus singles out all SEE cases except Albania, and adds the Czech Republic, Slovakia and Slovenia from the CEE group. The comparison between the Czech Republic and Slovakia illustrates a key point to be kept in mind. While the two countries passed the test at identical points in time, their democratisation trajectories have differed. This was due primarily to the fact that in the period up to 1998 Slovakia was governed by Mečiar's HZDS party, which based its political practice on an ethno-nationalist platform 'that served to enable the party to carry out an authoritarian concentration of power' (Vachudova 2005: 44). As a result, during the 1990s Slovakia deviated from established norms of democratic practice, jeopardising its international standing and the process of European integration. At the same time, the fact that the Civic Democratic Party (ODS) was the dominant party in the Czech Republic until 1998, as was the LDS in Slovenia, did not derail successful democratisation processes since both countries were characterised by parties with democratic rhetoric and practice which operated in a political context favourable for democratisation. Albania, as was shown, represents the opposite example where competition did not have the assumed positive effect on democratisation because it took place among authoritarian parties that disregarded democratic principles, in a political environment not conducive to democratisation. This analysis confirms the pre-eminence of the character of party constellations in explaining the effects of party system competitiveness. Table 4.3 summarises the findings of the analysis so far.

Table 4.1: European post-communist party systems in the early 1990s

	Democratic party system constellation	Mixed or authoritarian party system constellation
One-party dominance	Slovenia, Czech Republic	Croatia, Serbia, Slovakia, Bulgaria, Romania, Macedonia
Regular alternation in power	Hungary, Poland, Estonia, Latvia, Lithuania	Albania

As can be seen from Table 4.1, there is a significant overlap between one-party dominance and mixed-party constellations, identifying cases of Bulgaria, Croatia, Macedonia, Serbia, Slovakia and Romania as the group of countries that were characterised by a combination of two negative characteristics: absence of alternation in power, and a mixed-party system constellation. Albania is a rather different case, where competition was somewhat stronger, but since the party constellation was inimical to democratisation, political party competitiveness did not produce expected positive effects. In the next section the focus is on identifying the most prominent political party offenders to democratic practice in Southeast Europe.

In Schimmelfennig, Engert and Knobel (2006) authoritarian parties are defined as seeking legitimacy in exclusionary ideologies and authoritarian practices. I have further specified these practices as concentration of power in the executive branch, different forms of conversion of political into economic power and weakening state capacity through a politicisation of state administration and the public sector. This redefinition enables a clearer focus on the causal mechanisms which link the rule of authoritarian parties with obstacles to the establishment of rule of law systems. State socialist regimes were often characterised as a symbiosis of party and state (Linz and Stepan 1996, Bunce 1999a, Ekiert and Kubik 1999, Ganev 2007). Having this in mind, the key transformation that needed to take place for democratisation to advance was the 'devolution of power from a group of people to a set of rules' (Przeworski 1991). In authoritarian regimes the rule of law serves primarily to legitimise a ruler's preferences and is operational as long as it is in tune with his preferences (O'Donnell 2004). In other words in authoritarian regimes power is arbitrary (Przeworski 1995) and the law is used instrumentally (Fish 2005). In state socialist regimes where the leader and party-state 'create both policy and plan, there is no space for a legal system to constrain or bind the leader or the party-state' (Linz and Stepan 1996: 248). Therefore, in such regimes there is effectively no rule of law (Ekiert and Kubik 1999), creating an obstacle to democratisation (Fishman 1990). In the process of transformation towards a democratic regime, establishing an effective rule of law proves to be the most demanding task. It is therefore reasonable to expect that in cases where an authoritarian party dominated the political system in the period after regime change, the development of rule of law was more tenuous and protracted, resulting in the reduced extent of civil liberties.

Many comparative studies of party systems focus on Central Eastern Europe, sometimes including Baltic countries, and occasionally Bulgaria and Romania. This is in large part due to the fact that research in post-communist political institutions has been driven by the European integration agenda, as well as interests of US specialists in the former communist region. As a result, studies on Visegrad countries are most numerous apart from those on Russia, while the Baltics, Slovakia, Bulgaria and Romania were studied by a smaller but still substantial number of authors (see for instance: Gallagher 1996, Karasimeonov 1996, Tismaneanu 2007, Ganev 2001, 2007, Vachudova 2005, Fisher 2006). The political party systems of former Yugoslav states have received much less attention, while much of what exists is captured either in single case studies or country reports by international organisations such as the Freedom House, International Crisis Group and others. Due to wars on Yugoslav territory, comparative analyses of democratisation processes largely excluded these countries (Džihić and Segert 2012). However, notwithstanding these gaps in existing literature, major parties whose profile substantially falls outside democratic practice have been identified. In Central Eastern Europe the party that received most attention was Mečiar's HZDS, which dominated Slovakia in the 1990s (Fisher 2006). Outside of Slovakia, overall the party space in CEE has been dominated by democratic parties of various guises while extremist parties have been kept on the margins of political competition.

In countries of Southeast Europe the phenomenon of dominant authoritarian parties heading governments has been more widespread, with stronger and more lasting consequences. In the first decade after regime change, Bulgaria and Romania both had large former communist parties on the left, while the political right was fragmented.[1] Although the Bulgarian Socialist Party (BSP) officially governed only during 1990–1991 and 1994–1997, it was also the major supporter of the government in the interim period 1991–1994. Its support and influence eroded only gradually, and it never experienced any major rifts during the early 1990s (Karasimeonov 1996: 258). According to Ganev (2007), the period of regime change in Bulgaria did not bring about a successful separation of party

---

1. In the cases of Bulgaria and Romania the concepts of political left and right only partially conform to Western patterns since a party such as the Bulgarian Socialist Party is classified as left due to its economic policies but is at the same time traditionalist and authoritarian, while parties classified as right are both more economically liberal and more cosmopolitan in their cultural outlook (see Vachudova and Hooghe 2009).

and state. Since the separation of party from state was prolonged beyond the first election, the 'damage inflicted on the institutional edifice of the state becomes more serious' (2007: 35), arguably creating a lasting effect on democratisation. In Bulgaria the former Communist party, which had dubious democratic credentials, exerted a hegemonic position both on the national and local level until 1997. The BSP implemented three structural changes to the Bulgarian state after the 1990 election that had lasting negative effects on democratisation: dismantling of control mechanisms, informalisation of discretion and deinstitutionalisation of information (ibid.: 47).

The first process refers to the abolishment of various government institutions charged with monitoring and oversight over state-run enterprises. The second process refers to privatised executive power within the bureaucracy, which was directed through a closed system of informal connections, and used for economic gain in a time of massive transfer of state owned assets to private hands – leading to a *de facto* 'selective privatisation' (p.50). Finally, the third process refers to disabling access to large state repositories of information and statistical data, including, for instance, data on the operation of offshore companies and foreign subsidiaries of Bulgarian firms. As Ganev (2007: 53) explains, 'existing institutions were abolished, assets were transferred to new legal entities, but the information stored at the "centre" vanished'. Party loyalists were strategically placed within state institutions in order to increase informal power networks and extract resources from the state, coupled with instrumental reforms that severely crippled state capacity for control and monitoring. Hence, once the BSP finally left office, severe defects in state mechanisms of control and monitoring remained, creating a lasting negative legacy for the process of democratisation.

It is reasonable to assume that when the democratic opposition eventually won office, it found it very difficult to dismantle the authoritarian practices that structured economic and political relations. The temptation to extract resources from the state and dominate the economic sphere meant that features of the same mode of rule might have easily survived changes in governments, helping to explain why party competition did not have the presumed effect on democratisation. While these assertions are only fully explored in the case studies in Chapters 6 and 7, Ganev's work is very important in delineating the specific modalities which, in the case of Bulgaria, brought about a mode of rule inimical to rule of law. While work comparable to Ganev's does not exist for other SEE countries, analogous patterns of authoritarian practices of dominant parties and accompanying structural factors substantiate the assumption that similar dynamics took place. This is further explored by examining the cases of Serbia and Croatia in Chapters 6 and 7, while the rest of this section introduces the main authoritarian parties in countries of Southeast Europe.

As in Bulgaria, in Romania the first multiparty election did not lead to communist exit. Instead the former communist party declaratively morphed into a socialist party, won elections and took a long while to embark on more substantial reforms (Vachudova 2005, Schimmelfennig 2005). In both countries these authoritarian parties had free rein to exploit the high contingency surrounding simultaneous political and economic reform (Vachudova 2009). The evolution of multi-partyism against the background of patrimonial regimes and low modernisation levels created new 'feuds' based on family and local ties, creating favourable circumstances for a corrupt and uncontrolled political elite (Karasimeonov 1996). While in Bulgaria the BSP faced an anti-communist opposition, though it was weak, the end of 1989 in Romania was actually a clash of two sets of authoritarian values (Gallagher 1995, 1996). At the onset of the 1990s Romania was leaving the extremely oppressive form of communism that evolved under the dictatorship of Nicolai Ceauşescu (Vachudova 2005, Mungiu-Pippidi 2006). Regime change was made possible by the consent of Ceauşescu's army and secret police (Mungiu-Pippidi 2006), a circumstance repeated in Serbia with the ousting of Milošević in 2000. On the one hand there were orthodox communists and some Gorbachev-style reformers while the other side has been characterised as 'doctrinaire personal communism associated with Ceauşescu' (Gallagher 1996: 213). Romania's power struggle within the communist establishment was won by the least authoritarian faction, but their commitment to genuine pluralism was doubtful. Gallagher (1996) argues that Iliescu and his supporters were sceptical democrats who preferred a plebiscitary autocracy, developing a mode of rule that manipulated institutions to restrict political competition. A comparable weakness of any democratic opposition to that in Romania was also characteristic of Albania and Macedonia. As was argued in Chapter 3, in all these cases competitive elections were organised in a context of low socioeconomic preconditions, within regimes that emerged from patrimonial communism.

In the cases of Bulgaria and Romania the initial period of regime change in the 1990s was dominated by cosmetically reformed former communist parties and faced with disorganised and weak oppositions. After the so-called democratic turn elections in which these parties left office, their transformation process ensued, securing some advancement in democratisation (Vachudova 2005). In Bulgaria after the 1997 election, the former communist party adopted a 'pro-European stance' (Kuzio 2008). In Romania the Partidul Social Democrat (PSD), led by hardline nationalist Iliescu, also made attempts to convince the public and the European Union that they had reinvented themselves as democratic champions (Downs and Miller 2006). At the same time, both parties had trouble shedding the spectre of the old regime, as well as initiating substantial economic and political reform, which led to a postponement of the two countries' accession process to the EU (ibid.).

With respect to democratic credentials of major parties, in Albania neither of the two major parties – the Democratic Party and the Socialist Party – had them. These two political parties dominated the party system, while others barely managed to enter parliament. When the rest of the Southeast European cases experienced a democratic turn in the late 1990s, Albania experienced a meltdown (ICG Balkans Report N° 87, 2000), followed by 'several months of near anarchy' (Szajkowski 2003: 361). Not only has Sali Berisha's rule in the 1990s been described as 'increasingly dictatorial and authoritarian' (ICG Balkans Report N° 87, 2000), but the more recent 2001 and 2005 elections were also characterised by fraud, irregularities and violations of democratic standards (Szajkowski 2003, 2007). Even in the 2009 elections irregularities were still reported, though the election process was more peaceful (Hashimoto 2009). Judging by available data and reports, violations to democratic practice in Albania extend even further than the concept of authoritarian party dominance is able to capture.

As in Albania where no anti-communist movement was in place at the time of regime change, democracy in Macedonia was instituted mainly as a result of changes in the external environment following the dissolution of Yugoslavia (Engström 2009: 110). Two major parties emerged in the first multi-party elections: the former communist SDSM and the VMRO-DPMNE. As in the cases of Bulgaria and Romania, the former communists (SDSM) won the first election and then ruled Macedonia for most of the 1990s. The country was dominated by President Kiro Gligorov of the SDSM while the old political establishment continued to dominate the country after it left Yugoslavia (Szajkowski 2000). The acronym VMRO-DPMNE stands for Internal Macedonian Revolutionary Organisation – Democratic Party for Macedonian National Unity, and it alludes to the 1893 heritage when VMRO was founded as a political movement to liberate Macedonia from Ottoman rule (ibid). The party was re-established in 1990 as a rightwing nationalist party, and it won the 1998 parliamentary election in Macedonia.

The Albanian minority in Macedonia represents 23 per cent of the population (Daskalovski 2004) and after the introduction of competitive elections the party system in Macedonia became structured along ethnic lines. The issue of group rights for the Albanian minority has dominated Macedonian politics ever since independence, and the resulting ethnification of politics has kept questions of democratic accountability and corruption permanently in the background. During the 1990s major political parties of the two ethnic groups clashed over the basic concept of the state (Daskalovski 2004). The precarious balance of peace between ethnic communities was shattered after the crisis in Kosovo spilled over to Macedonia, erupting in violence between Macedonians and Albanians in 2001. The crisis ended with the adoption of the Ohrid Agreement under the auspices of the international community, which gave the Albanian minority more extensive rights. However, almost a decade after the signing of the Ohrid Agreement, ethnicity remained highly politicised and the dynamic of party competition encourages parties to radicalise their appeals (NIT Report 2010). According to Engström (2009: 132), although the 2001 Ohrid Agreement was designed to address ethnic strife by instituting power sharing, it might have produced the opposite: 'the development of a bi-national state'. The state of Macedonia seems to have institutionalised a lasting challenge to its national unity, with ethnic group rights permanently dominating the political agenda at the expense of further democratisation.

Fairly recently, during the 2008 parliamentary elections, rioting erupted and the electoral process was marred by irregularities. In several villages with an Albanian majority shootings occurred on election sites, including shots fired from the offices of Albanian DUI party. In police raids after the incidents cars loaded with guns and ammunition were found, and eleven people were arrested, mostly

DUI activists.[2] Since 2009 the Albanian party DPA had been boycotting sessions of parliament (NIT Report 2010). In January 2011 the oppositional party Social Democrats also started boycotting parliament, protesting the VMRO-DPMNE decision to freeze the account of the A1 television broadcasting company, which is critical of the government. The extremely polarised situation between the two major parties provoked an early election, held in June 2011.[3] No alternation in power ensued, however. VMRO-DPMNE won the election and Nikola Gruevski formed the new government, again with DUI as the junior partner. Gruevski has been PM since 2006, while DUI has been junior partner in government since 2008.[4] In the 2011 election the Social Democrats managed to double their seats in parliament from 19 to 43, but they have not succeeded in replacing VMRO-DPMNE in office (ibid.). The first session of the newly elected parliament took place amid street protests, provoked by the death of a man beaten by the police on election day.[5] Similarly, in April 2012, five ethnic Macedonian men were shot dead under unclear circumstances, provoking a new wave of interethnic tensions.[6]

The international environment has further exacerbated interethnic tensions in Macedonia. The most pressing problem has been the name dispute with Greece, which has led to a block of Macedonia's NATO membership in 2008 and a *de facto* blocked process of European integration ever since. In addition to that, Bulgaria is disputing aspects of Macedonia's statehood, most notably its language and its claim to a separate ethnic identity. As a result, Macedonian nationalism, which is voiced primarily by the ruling VMRO-DMPNE, is nurtured by the continued challenge to the country's statehood and national identity. According to the NIT 2010 Report, 'additional delay of the Europeanisation of Macedonia risks further antagonising interethnic relations (...) nationalism could become a dominant force in a country that already once experienced a warlike conflict in 2001' (p. 347). Similarly, in April 2011 the European Parliament adopted

2. B92 web portal: 'In Macedonia: Incidents during election day', June 1, 2008, http://www.b92.net/info/vesti/index.php?yyyy=2008&mm=06&dd=01&nav_id=301387. Last accessed August 23, 2012.

3. 'Macedonia Opposition Accepts Call for Early Election', *Balkan Insight*, February 21, 2011. Available at http://www.balkaninsight.com/en/article/macedonia-opposition-greets-early-elections. Last accessed August 23, 2012.

4. 'Government Talks Expected to Start in Macedonia', *Balkan Insight*, June 14, 2011. Available at http://www.balkaninsight.com/en/article/government-talks-expected-to-start-in-macedonia. Last accessed August 23, 2012.

5. 'Macedonian Parliament Holds First Session Amid Protests', *Balkan Insight*, June 27, 2011. Available at http://www.balkaninsight.com/en/article/macedonian-parliament-holds-first-session-amid-protests. Last accessed August 23, 2012.

6. 'Macedonia Police Halt Attack on Albanians', *Balkan Insight*, April 16, 2011. Available at http://www.balkaninsight.com/en/article/macedonia-police-clash-with-protesters. Last accessed August 23, 2012.

a non-legislative resolution expressing regret that the name dispute with Greece was causing deadlock, and voicing 'concern over the growing interethnic tensions in the country, as well as corruption and recent attacks on freedom of the media and civil society representatives'.[7] Having reviewed the current political context and features of political competition in Macedonia, it seems safe to say that the political situation is inimical to further democratisation.

Finally, the cases of Serbia and Croatia were often compared during the 1990s with respect to Milošević's and Tuđman's authoritarian rule. While case studies in Chapters 6 and 7 carefully delineate the mode of rule that developed in the early 1990s in each of the cases, the following sections provide brief sketches of the major parties and inter-party dynamics in these two countries. Dominant parties in both countries were ethno-nationalist, even though the Croatian Democratic Union (CDU) was an anti-communist party, while Milošević's Socialist Party of Serbia was the successor of the Communist party of Serbia. However, this is where similarities between the two countries' party systems end. While in Croatia the CDU was the only major party to espouse ethno-nationalism, in Serbia Milošević's Socialist Party of Serbia (SPS) had an even more extreme wingman in the Serbian Radical Party (SRP). In the early 1990s the SRP provided parliamentary support to Milošević's SPS by implementing a radical ethno-nationalist platform through which Serbia resisted the dissolution of Yugoslavia and attempted to acquire territories in Bosnia and Herzegovina and Croatia. During the first decade of regime change these two extremist parties dominated Serbia's political space.

In Croatia the CDU emerged in 1990 as the national movement for independence and developed into a charismatic-clientelist type of political party, centred on the image of its leader (Kasapović 2001). All governments from 1990 to 2000 were majority CDU governments (Kasapović 2005). The year 2000 is the first time that the CDU was removed from power, and a centre-left coalition came into power led by the Social Democratic Party (SDP). The 2000 election was a democratic turning point (Schimmelfennig 2005, Čular 2005). It was in 2001, after Tuđman's death and the removal of the CDU from power that Croatia moved from a semi-free to a free country according to Freedom House ratings. The new party leader after Tuđman's death, Ivo Sanader, initiated the transformation of an ethno-nationalist organisation into a Christian Democratic party (Zakošek 2002, Fish and Krickovic 2002, Dolenec 2008, 2009). By the 2007 parliamentary election the CDU shed its image as an extremist nationalist party and reformed into a centre-right Christian Democratic party, further strengthening the direction of gradual political moderation and democratisation that began in 2000 (Zakošek 2007). However, the course of events since 2007 in Croatia cast a long shadow over the depth of this transformation since many international and domestic assessments emphasised Croatia's persistent problems with the rule of law and corruption that

---

7.   European Parliament Press Release, April 7, 2011. Available at http://www.europarl.europa.eu/en/
      pressroom/content/20110407IPR17166/html/Accession-talks-with-former-Yugoslav-Republic-
      of-Macedonia-should-start-now. Last accessed August 23, 2012.

occurred under the rule of Ivo Sanader and the CDU. This is explored in detail in the case study of Croatia in Chapter 6.

While Croatia has been characterised by a marked stability of political party supply, Serbia has experienced some reconfigurations in the political party arena. For the large part of the analysed period major parties in Serbia could be classified into extremist nationalists and a tentatively defined democratic bloc. In the extremist bloc were the Socialists, Radicals and the Serbian Renewal Movement (SRM), while the democratic opposition consisted primarily of the Democratic Party (DP) and the Democratic Party of Serbia (DPS), joined by the Liberal Democratic Party (LDP), G17 Plus and the New Serbia party in more recent times. While this has become the standard way of classifying parties in Serbia, a more detailed analysis of party system dynamics in Serbia in Chapter 7 shows that this division into two blocs only partially holds true since the democratic credentials of these parties were relatively weak.

From 1997 until 2008 (the exception being the pro-democratic 2000 election) the Radical Party won the largest number of seats in Serbian parliament. Party leader Vojislav Šešelj, one of the chief executors of the Serbian aggression in Croatia and Bosnia and Herzegovina, is currently standing trial before the ICTY in the Hague, where he is facing charges for persecution, deportation, crimes against humanity, murder, torture, cruel treatment, destruction, devastation, and wilful damage to institutions and plunder of public and private property (ICTY Case Information sheet 2009). At the same time, since his incarceration in 2003 he has remained the Radical Party leader and managed to win between 27 and 29.5 per cent of the popular vote in Serbian parliamentary elections in 2003, 2006 and 2008. According to some estimates, in 2008 the Radicals had around two million faithful supporters.[8] However, the appearance of its splinter party, the Serbian Progressive Party, in 2008 spelled the end of the Serbian Radical Party; in the 2012 parliamentary election the SRS failed to win enough votes to enter parliament.

While extremist and authoritarian political parties undoubtedly dominated Serbia's politics during the 1990s, more recent times have brought important changes to their prominence. This is especially true for the period after the 2008 parliamentary election, after which the Socialist Party of Serbia entered government as a junior partner and broke off its alliance with the Radicals, signalling important reshuffling in party space. Under the leadership of Ivan Dačić the Socialists began rebranding themselves as Social Democrats – leaving the extremist nationalist field now populated only by the Radicals. Soon after that, the Radicals suffered an internal split, where the 'regent' leadership ran by Šešelj from prison in The Hague left the party over the parliamentary vote for Serbia's ratification of the Stabilisation and Association Agreement with the EU.[9] The splinter group established the Serbian Progressive Party (SPP) a month later, announcing more

---

8.   Serbian news portal *Oslobođenje*, September 10, 2008

9.   As reported in the Serbian news magazine *Novosti,* on September 12, 2008

moderate nationalist politics.[10] As a result of this split and the Socialists' makeover, after that election Bochsler predicted that the Radicals would lose some of their appeal with the voters and the formerly extremist parties would moderate their appeals (2009). This is exactly what happened in the most recent parliamentary election in Serbia, held in May 2012.

Under the leadership of Tomislav Nikolić the SPP won 29.2 per cent of seats in parliament, followed by Boris Tadić's DP (26.8 per cent), Ivica Dačić's Socialist Party of Serbia (17.6 per cent) and Vojislav Koštunica's DPS (8.4 per cent).[11] This is a significant reshuffling of party power – while most of the protagonists are the same as in the early 1990s, their stated objectives have changed markedly. In the presidential election that was held at the same time, Tomislav Nikolić defeated Boris Tadić from the Democratic Party. As a result, the 2012 elections represent a strong defeat for the Democratic Party, who has lost both the seat of president, and the majority in parliament. The new government also represents an important alternation in power, being composed of SPP, SPS and another smaller party, with Ivica Dačić of the SPS serving as Prime Minister. During the 1990s Ivica Dačić was a spokesperson for Slobodan Milošević, but he managed to distance himself from that past while serving as a Minister of Interior in the 2008–2012 government led by the Democratic Party. Overall, however, this overview of political party dynamics highlights the fact that since regime change in the early 1990s, extremist non-democratic parties played very prominent roles in Serbia's politics and that this has begun to change only very recently.

This analysis identified six cases in Southeast Europe as characterised by authoritarian party dominance during the early 1990s: Bulgaria, Croatia, Macedonia, Serbia, Slovakia and Romania. Out of the six, in four countries party systems have since then transformed into more credibly democratic constellations – Bulgaria, Croatia, Slovakia and Romania. In the two remaining countries, Serbia and Macedonia, authoritarian parties remain today but the most recent developments in Serbia signal a moderation of its political party space. Nevertheless, all six cases share authoritarian party dominance in the 1990s and they all exhibit lasting difficulties in establishing the rule of law and, as a result, democratic stagnation. This finding offers tentative confirmation of the importance of critical junctures: authoritarian party dominance over the initial period of regime change has produced lasting negative effects on democratic progress. In addition to that, examples of the Czech Republic and Slovenia on the one hand, and Albania on the other, asserted the need to hold on to the distinction between democratic and authoritarian party dominance. In the next section these variables are operationalised to analyse the relationship between party system dynamics and democratisation outcomes. Table 4.2 summarises the presented discussion by showing dates of the first multiparty election, the election that led to a turnover of

10. As reported on the Serbian news portal *Blic online*, October 21, 2008

11. Election results published in the Official Gazette of the Republic of Serbia, No. 48/12

party in power, the length of one-party dominance over the initial period of regime change and the resulting party constellation.

Table 4.2: Party system dynamics during regime change

Country	First election	First turnover	Length of one-party dominance, in months	Political party constellation
Albania	Apr 1991	Mar 1992	10	authoritarian
Bulgaria	Jun 1990	Apr 1997	81	mixed
Croatia	Apr 1990	Jan 2000	115	mixed
Czech Republic	Jun 1990	Jun 1998	95	democratic
Estonia	Mar 1990	Sep 1992	17	democratic
Hungary	Mar–Apr 1990	May 1994	48	democratic
Latvia	Mar–Apr 1990	Jun 1993	13	democratic
Lithuania	Feb 1990	Oct–Nov 1992	20	democratic
Macedonia	Dec 1990	Oct–Nov 1998	93	mixed
Poland	Jun1989	Sep 1993	38	democratic
Romania	May 1990	Nov 1996	77	mixed
Serbia	Dec 1990	Oct 2000	117	mixed
Slovakia	Jun 1990	Oct 1998	99	mixed
Slovenia	Apr 1990 / Dec 1992	Dec 1992 / Oct 2004	31 / 141	democratic

Sources: Berglund *et al* (2004), Rose and Munro (2009), Parties and Elections website, http://www.parties-and-elections.de/index.html, author's calculations.

Before attempting to combine the constellation and competition dimensions into a composite variable, each dimension is analysed separately to look for association with the outcome of interest, democratic progress. Party dominance is operationalised by measuring the length of authoritarian party rule in months, as shown in column four in Table 4.2. In a second step, in order to create a numeric ordinal variable, the properties of party constellation are transformed into three values; one for democratic, two for mixed and three for authoritarian party constellations. These party system variables are the correlated against the most recent Freedom House scores for democracy, and the scores for Freedom House Nations in Transit rule of law. As argued in Chapter 1, the Freedom House Nations in Transit 'judiciary framework' variable stands for success at establishing the rule of law, the component of the democratic regime hypothesised to be most influenced by one-party dominance. The dataset is shown in the Appendix. After doing that, both variables are analysed for strength of association with the outcome of interest. Table 4.3 shows the resulting correlations.

Table 4.3: Correlations of party system variables with democratisation outcomes

	Overall democracy progress	**Judiciary independence**
Party system competitiveness	-0.08 / not a significant relationship	-0.58 / significant at 0.05 level
Party system constellation	-0.75 / significant at 0.01 level	-0.86 / significant at 0.01 level

Source: author's calculations

As can be seen from Table 4.3, all relationships are negative as expected. Longer one-party dominance results in lower democracy scores, and authoritarian constellations result in lower democracy scores. However, the party constellation dimension shows markedly stronger association with the outcome than is the case with the competitiveness variable. Party system competitiveness operationalised as absence of alternation in power does not exhibit a significant relationship with the overall progress in democratisation. However, it does show a moderately strong negative relationship with the rule of law dimension pertaining to the functioning of the judiciary. The correlation is -0.58, significant at the 0.05 level. Political party constellation on the other hand shows high association with both the overall democracy outcome (-0.75 correlation), and with the success in establishing a rule of law (-0.86), both relationships significant at the 0.01 level. In a direct showdown between these two party system characteristics, party system constellation seems to carry more weight in explaining subsequent democratisation trajectories. This analysis confirms the argument according to which party system constellation conditions the strength of the effect that party system competitiveness will have on democratisation prospects.

Nevertheless, since both dimensions contribute to the overall explanation, a composite of the two variables is also analysed, labelled 'authoritarian party dominance'. The length of party in rule is first transformed into a nominal variable, carrying the value of one if the party stayed in office for one term only, two if it stayed in office longer than one term. The length in office of 48 months is taken as the dividing line. The ordinal scale for party constellation is kept the same, and the composite is created by multiplying the two dimensions. The resulting dataset is shown in the Appendix. When the new composite variable is correlated with the two Freedom House measures for the outcome, results show significant relationships. In the case of overall democratisation outcome the correlation is moderate, at -0.55 and significant at the 0.05 level, while in the case of successful establishment of rule of law the correlation is very high, at 0.85 and significant at the 0.01 level. These results point to a very strong association between authoritarian party dominance and the difficulties in establishing rule of law in the post-communist context. The argument according to which the features of party interaction plays a key role in explaining lasting rule of law deficiencies has been substantiated by empirical findings. Next the analysis moves towards the international environment of post-communist democratisation in Europe.

Influence of EU integration on democratisation

In the case of countries in Central Eastern Europe, satisfying EU conditionality criteria and progressing towards EU membership was a domestically driven political project. Long before the EU considered admitting countries from former communist Eastern Europe, Czechoslovakia, Hungary and Poland were knocking on its door and demanding entry. The speed of accession of these countries to the EU was determined by the EU's willingness and capacity to take them in, rather than their readiness and compatibility with democratic standards. These countries were characterised, as shown in the previous sections, with democratic and competitive party systems, combined with comparatively good modernisation preconditions to take on the challenges of political and economic transformation. They would have become democracies with or without the EU's conditionality (Vachudova 2005).

In countries of Southeast Europe the situation is markedly different. Though Bulgaria and Romania were incorporated into the initial enlargement package, democratisation in these cases has been more limited. The two countries became EU member states in 2007 but they still fail to secure functioning rule of law systems. However, as previous analysis in Chapter 3 has shown, compared to CEE states Bulgaria and Romania had considerably less favourable socioeconomic conditions and historical regime legacies. The process of European integration positively influenced democratisation reforms in these two countries, but both structural preconditions and initial political choices were watering down reform resolve (Noutcheva and Bechev 2008). Similarly, though the EU has been involved as external democracy promoter in the Western Balkans for over 15 years, progress has been patchy and diverged considerably among countries in the region.

While around the year 2000 scholars were claiming evidence of convergence of these states towards the CEE model of democratisation, this convergence has essentially failed to materialise, with the EU currently maintaining bilateral relations with countries in the region that are at very different stages of the EU integration process.

As was argued in Chapter 2, a stabilised democratic regime based in the rule of law represents one of the end purposes of EU conditionality, but its attainment depends on the outcomes of domestic political struggles. According to the theoretical framework that I have proposed, the influence of European integration in countries of Southeast Europe is complex, both from the side of the Southeast countries themselves where history unfolded much greater challenges, and from the side of the EU through its evolving political conditionality in the region. The following sections outline a brief history of challenges posed before external democratisation in this region, and the evolution of the EU's political conditionality.

In the early 1990s Western Balkan countries were not accorded the EU membership perspective. Instead, EU foreign policy towards the region was framed within conflict resolution initiatives and restoring security in Europe's neighbourhood. This refers especially to the period from June 1991 when the first Peace Conference on Yugoslavia was held in The Hague, until the signing of the Dayton Peace Accord in 1995 which ended the war in Bosnia and Herzegovina. During the early 1990s, regimes in the Western Balkans were consolidating under new circumstances without the EU and other international actors closely scrutinising the implementation of democratic reforms. When people are getting killed, not much else grabs anybody's attention. The authoritarian governance practices that developed in Western Balkan countries therefore had a five-year grace period in which they went about their business largely undisturbed by outside influences. The fact that emergent regimes had time to consolidate undemocratic practices and various forms of authoritarian politics before EU political conditionality came into force explains in part why EU influence was less effective in the Western Balkans. It seems plausible to expect that newly established regimes in countries of CEE, which were building their constitutional framework both on stronger modernisation preconditions and under close international scrutiny, had fewer opportunities for abuse of power while at the same time they were incentivised to pursue democratic reform. Apart from not benefiting from such a domestic and international context, those states in the Western Balkans that had gone through violent conflicts posed additional challenges for external democracy promotion.

Formal relations between the EU and the countries of SEE region started in February 1996, when the EU adopted the Regional Approach towards countries of Southeast Europe.[12] In the Council conclusions, the EU welcomed the peace process on the territory of former Yugoslavia, and offered the perspective of association in tentative language: 'neighbouring countries which so wish should

---

12. Chronology available at the European Commission Enlargement website
   http://ec.europa.eu/enlargement/index_en.htm. Last accessed August 23, 2012.

be able to be associated in the cooperation by appropriate means' (Conclusions of the General Affairs Council of 29 April 1997). Apart from adhering to signed peace treaties, re-establishing economic and other relations among countries in the region were set as explicit conditions for entering into association agreements with the EU. Being an organisation founded on the idea of healing war wounds through trade, the EU made closer contractual ties to itself, conditional to these countries' willingness to cooperate among themselves. Regionalism was elevated into an element of EU conditionality, and the countries were required to cooperate in areas of return of refugees as well as with the Hague-based International Criminal Tribunal for former Yugoslavia (Bechev 2006).

The launch of the Stability Pact in 1999[13] marked the start of more intensive EU involvement in the region. During 1998 the conflict between Serbian military and police forces and Kosovar Albanian forces in Kosovo resulted in the deaths of over 1,500 Kosovar Albanians and forced 400,000 people from their homes. Despite attempts by NATO and the UN to put an end to fighting in Kosovo,[14] the crisis escalated in 1999. After US Ambassador Holbrooke failed to persuade Milošević to stop attacking Kosovar Albanians, on March 23, 1999 NATO air strikes were authorised. The strikes lasted 77 days, stopping only after Serbian forces began withdrawing from Kosovo. The UN Security Council mandated a security force KFOR, which was deployed to Kosovo in parallel with the departure of Serb forces, and the Security Council Resolution 1244 established the United Nations Interim Administration Mission in Kosovo (UNMIK). Kosovo remains under UNMIK administration today.

After the Kosovo conflict the EU realised that development cooperation will not be enough to stabilise this region which was so close to the EU border (Börzel and Risse 2004). The 1999 NATO intervention strengthened international political resolve for preventive action in the region, and the Stability Pact involved not only the EU, but NATO, the UN, the Council of Europe, as well as international financial institutions such as the World Bank, the IMF and others. While the Stability Pact was formally under the auspices of the OSCE, Southeast European governments saw it as an EU instrument and 'judged its performance not only by looking at how much fresh money it was drawing to the region, but also how much it advanced political and economic ties with the EU' (Bechev 2006: 35).

In the Operational Conclusions of May 26, 1999, the Commission proposed the creation of a Stabilisation and Association Process (SAP) for the Western Balkan countries.[15] Drawing on its changed assessment of stability prospects

---

13. Information in this section is from the official website of the Stability Pact: http://www.stabilitypact.org/about/default.asp. Last accessed August 23, 2012.

14. Data from NATO website, information about the Kosovo campaign: http://www.nato.int/kosovo/history.htm#B. Last accessed August 23, 2012.

15. Information on the SAP available on the European commission Enlargement website http://ec.europa.eu/enlargement/policy/glossary/terms/sap_en.htm. Last accessed August 23, 2012.

in the region, the EU offered the prospect of EU integration for the first time, marking a turning point in relations between Western Balkan countries and the EU. Incidentally, this is when the term Western Balkans was introduced, to refer to the region of Southeast Europe without Bulgaria and Romania. SAP was intended to establish and deepen contractual relations with the individual Western Balkan states and it was explicitly based on the principle of conditionality. The EU offered association deals modelled on the Europe Agreements of the 1990s to reward democratic and market reforms in the individual countries (Bechev 2006). Another key SAP instrument that was opened in 1999 was the CARDS programme package of €4.9 billion for priorities like institution building, infrastructure and economic development for Albania, Bosnia and Herzegovina, Croatia, the Federal Republic of Yugoslavia and the Former Yugoslav Republic of Macedonia (Council Regulation (EC) No 2666/2000).[16]

The Kosovo crisis in 1999 had therefore been the turning point in EU policy towards the region. Absorbing the security implications of the Kosovo crisis, the EU discursively shifted towards advocating an inclusive enlargement which would encompass all Southeast European states (Börzel and Risse 2004, Vachudova 2005). This commitment was formalised at the European Council meeting in Santa Maria da Feira on 19 and 20 June 2000, when the EU gave countries of the Western Balkans EU membership perspective. The electoral defeat of CDU in Croatia and the end of the Milošević regime in Serbia in 2000 further reorganised Balkan equations because from that moment onwards reform-minded governments were in power in all capitals across the region (Bechev 2006). This positive mood set the background for the Zagreb Summit in 2000 that launched the Stabilisation and Association Process (SAP) for five Western Balkan countries: Albania, Macedonia, Bosnia, Croatia and then-Yugoslavia.

However, in 2001 a new security challenge for Europe erupted in Macedonia. The 1999 Kosovo crises had first spilled over into Macedonia in the form of a refugee crisis. The question of how to handle a quarter of a million Albanian refugees strained relations between political parties in Macedonia (Daskalovski 2004). In addition to that, the fact that Kosovar Albanians seemed to successfully pursue autonomy gave impetus to Albanian demands in Macedonia and the emergent conflict was spurred on by the radicalisation that happened in Kosovo (Hislope 2003, Daskalovski 2004, Engström 2009). Led by former Kosovo Liberation Army fighters from Kosovo and Macedonia, Albanian insurgents from Southeast Serbian regions entered Macedonia, joined with Albanian radicals and nationalists, and undertook a seven-month armed insurrection against the government in the first half of 2001.

---

16. Ibid., available at http://ec.europa.eu/enlargement/pdf/financial_assistance/cards/general/2666_00_en.pdf. Last accessed August 23, 2012.

Back in 1995 Misha Glenny wrote about the importance of avoiding a war in Macedonia. He stressed its geostrategic importance because it lay on territory where the 'Balkan mountains can be traversed from north to south, from Belgrade to Thessaloniki, and west to east, from Durres to Istanbul' (1995: 99). As a result, if a conflict erupted there, at least three states would be urged to intervene: Greece, Bulgaria and Serbia. Perhaps due to this realisation, as well as the ten-year history of attempts to mitigate conflicts in the region, the international community quickly intervened in the conflict in Macedonia. The EU, NATO and US actors applied sufficient pressure to convince Albanian and Macedonian elites that their best interests lie in a negotiated settlement (Hislope 2003). The EU urged Macedonia to sign the Stabilisation and Association Agreement and become the first post-Yugoslav country to enjoy preferential trade relations with the EU. In return it asked for Macedonia to promise to pass reforms that would benefit Albanians (Whyte 2001 and Border 2001; quoted in Hislope 2003). According to Hislope, while the Albanian rebels were at first invariably charged as terrorists and blamed for the escalation of violence, over time the international community started applying increasing pressure on the Macedonian state to provide concessions to the Albanians (2003). The Ohrid Agreement was concluded on April 13, 2001. According to some analysts, though it was designed to transform Macedonia into a civic multiethnic state, it might have actually produced a bi-national state whose lasting stability remains in question (Adamson and Jović 2003, Engström 2009).

More recently a new source of instability in Macedonia emerged, with Greece blocking Macedonia's accession to NATO and the EU over the name dispute. Macedonia was granted candidacy status to the EU in 2005, but has not been able to open accession negotiations due to Greek veto on the name issue. At the NATO summit in Bucharest in April 2008 it was expected that Albania, Croatia and Macedonia would be invited to join the Alliance. Instead, Macedonia was withheld this invitation until a 'mutually acceptable solution to the name issue is reached' with Greece.[17] During 2008 parliamentary elections rioting erupted and the electoral process was marred by irregularities. Since the summer of 2009, the Albanian party DPA has boycotted sessions of parliament (Nations in Transit Report 2010). According to the Nations in Transit Report for 2010, delays in the European integration of Macedonia risk exacerbating interethnic tensions in the country.

In summary, after the creation of the Stabilisation and Association Process for the countries of the Western Balkans, the EU took centre stage as external democracy promoter in this region. Starting in 1999, the EU began applying its full arsenal of conditionality instruments in pursuit of democratic and market reforms. In 2003 at the Thessaloniki Summit the EU reiterated its support for the European perspective of the Western Balkans. However, even though large-scale conflicts in the region had ceased by 1999, security challenges remained in Kosovo and Macedonia (as well as in Bosnia and Herzegovina) – creating a far more complex

---

17. Information from NATO, http://www.nato.int. Last accessed August 23, 2012.

context for democracy promotion than the EU had faced in countries of Central Eastern Europe. Political strategies aimed at restoring stability are not necessarily compatible with democracy promotion, as the most recent involvement of the West in the Arab states reminds us. In its peacebuilding efforts the EU negotiated with and sometimes helped Slobodan Milošević, Ali Ahmeti and the like to hold on to power. In addition to that, large quantities of aid have been transferred to the region, often into the hands of deeply corrupt, irresponsible and undemocratic governments.[18] In its relations with governments in the Western Balkans, the EU sometimes relied on the very elites who could be expected to undermine its policies (Ivanov 2010).

This analysis of challenges to democratisation on the one hand, and the growing and multifaceted involvement of the EU in the Western Balkans on the other attempted to provide arguments for why the EU's influence would be weaker in Southeast Europe. It suggested that the first reason might be timing: the fact that regimes in SEE had time to coalesce before being subjected to rigorous international scrutiny might help explain why, subsequently, EU influence was less effective. The second part of the explanation was sought in the security challenges in the region, which surely complicate and perhaps weaken EU democracy promotion strategies. Finally, the third part of the explanation aimed to show that not only was democratisation in this region more complex, but that the EU's involvement in the Western Balkans was more reluctant and wavering, focusing on democratisation reforms only in more recent times while failing to prop up democratisation reforms in the early 1990s when such external incentives would have been more effective. The overall influence of European integration has been positive, especially in the area of human rights protection and establishing the rule of law, but it only came as a delayed effort after authoritarian rule had already taken root in the newly established democratic institutions in the region.

While the discussion so far was based on case evidence, there is also some benefit in attempting to directly measure EU influence on democratisation in post-communist Europe. Since the Europe Agreements in CEE and Stabilisation and Association Agreements in SEE represent the first instance of a structured relationship between the EU and an aspiring member country, a timeline of the signing of these agreements might be a way to establish the length of EU influence. However, since the signing of these agreements was already subject to EU political conditionality, it is better to use the timeline of when such agreements were offered by the EU to each of the countries (Schimmelfennig 2008). For instance, Europe Agreements with Bulgaria and Romania, signed in 1993, contained a clause that made them conditional on respect for human rights, democratic principles, principles of the market economy and respect for minority rights.

---

18. Smith mentions Slovakia in a similar context: while the EU delivered two demarches to Slovakia in 1994 and 1995, reiterating that its relations with the EU depended on democratic reforms, Slovakia was still receiving PHARE aid, and its Europe Agreement was not altered (1997).

Also, using the timeline of when the association agreements were offered avoids endogeneity problems that stem from the fact that the signing of an association agreement in itself represents a measure of progress in democratisation. The moment in which the EU offered a third country the possibility to negotiate an association agreement, on the other hand, simply marks the beginning of structured bilateral relations. These agreements were essentially trade agreements, requiring legal adjustments to align regulation with the EU's internal market while favouring EU member states' producer interests (Vachudova 2005). In the Western Balkans the Stabilisation and Association Agreements included a number of political obligations on human rights, democracy, rule of law and full cooperation with the ICTY. In addition, the ICTY was established in 1993 and the policy of cooperation with The Hague Tribunal was part of the political criteria for Croatia and Serbia from the very onset of their European integration processes (Maki 2008).

Table 4.4 shows dates when Europe Agreements were offered to CEE countries, and Stabilisation and Association Agreements to SEE countries, ranked from earliest to latest year.

Table 4.4: Year when the EU offered Europe or Stabilisation and Association Agreements

Czech Rep	1990
Hungary	1990
Poland	1990
Slovakia	1990
Bulgaria	1992
Romania	1992
Estonia	1994
Latvia	1994
Lithuania	1994
Slovenia	1995
Croatia	2000
Macedonia	2000
Albania	2003
Serbia	2005

Source: Schimmelfennig 2008

Note: The 1990 date for Czech Republic and Slovakia is the date when Czechoslovakia was offered the Europe Agreement. After dissolution, individual countries were offered these agreements in 1993.

Table 4.4 shows that there was a time span of fifteen years between when the EU offered first association agreements to the Visegrad states, and the last SAA offered to Serbia. In order to explore the bivariate relationship between EU influence and democratisation progress, the dates of each country's signing of the agreement are converted into the number of years until 2010, creating the variable length of EU influence. This variable is then correlated with Freedom House data for democracy and for judicial framework and independence. The dataset is shown in the Appendix. The correlation analysis of the relationship between EU influence and progress in democracy returns significant results both for overall democracy scores and those for judiciary independence. In both cases the correlation is 0.66, and significant at the 0.05 level. The results suggest that the process of EU integration represents an important part of the explanation for divergent democratisation trajectories in post-communist Europe. While this measurement cannot confirm or disconfirm the second hypothesis according to which the complexity of challenges in SEE and the EU's evolving approach to the region may have weakened its influence, it does confirm the hypothesis according to which timing, i.e. length of EU influence, relates positively to successful democratisation trajectories. However, since the correlation is not very strong, this suggests that we should look for ways in which EU influence combined with other factors to encourage democratic progress.

From disputed statehood to war

According to the argument I am advancing, state-building has accompanied regime change processes in nine of the fourteen countries analysed in this study. In the overwhelming number of cases state-building unravelled within a peaceful institutional framework, and while it made the transformation of political and economic spheres more complex, it left no long term negative effect on the democratisation prospects of these countries. In a majority of cases state-building has not disabled the evolution of democratic regimes with functioning rule of law. In a few cases however, state-building was disputed, and in some cases it deteriorated into war and a period of international isolation.

Having this in mind, the final explanatory factor in the theoretical framework of post-communist democratisation in Europe is violent conflict. According to Pridham (2000: 18), 'in the belligerent states the process of democratisation was effectively stalled'. Of the fourteen countries in this study, three went through several violent conflicts which were characterised differently by the international community. Conflicts in Croatia and Bosnia, both of which Serbia (Yugoslavia at the time) was involved in, have been characterised as wars. The war in Croatia ended in 1995, while the war in Bosnia and Herzegovina ended in 1996 through the mediation of the international community and the signing of the Dayton Accords. Serbia was also involved in violent disputes in Kosovo in 1998–1999, while as a spillover of these events violence erupted between minority Albanians and majority Macedonians in Macedonia in 2001. However, outbursts of violence in Kosovo and Macedonia have not been labelled as wars. In these two instances the international community also played an active role, first through NATO intervention in Serbia in 1999, and then the Ohrid Agreement in 2001. Finally, outbursts of violence in Albania in 1991 and again in 1997 have been described as a 'state of chaos' and a breakdown of the state, resembling mostly widespread street unrest and not following the pattern of ethnically motivated violence that occurred in the former Yugoslav states.

While the claim that violent conflict is inimical to democratisation is fairly trivial, the discussion of existing relevant scholarship in Chapter 2 showed that little has been said as to why this is so. Identified arguments could be summarised as saying that war thwarts the development of pluralism, civil liberties, political competition and economic reforms, while strengthening arbitrary executive power and authoritarian tendencies in the political sphere (Pridham 2000, Horowitz 2003). The focus on executive power and the person of the political leader strengthens hierarchy and lessens tolerance to dissent, which is often accompanied by a marginalisation of other branches of government, the judiciary and the parliament. A reduced tolerance to dissent can take the form of muting the opposition, instrumentalising the media (Ramet 1996) and engaging in various forms of political repression, as Levitsky and Way have argued (2002). Conflicts create circumstances for illegal government activities due to economic embargoes (Szajkowski 2000), which can help spur criminal networks and corruption as well as further weaken constraints on corrupt privatisations, while strengthening clientelism and cronyism as prevailing social ties (Horowitz 2003, Batt 2007). In addition to that, enduring political legacies of war are a mistrust of politicians and systematic evasion of the state, undermining efforts of reinstating political legitimacy (Batt 2007). Finally, since wars lessen tolerance to dissent and pluralism, this also entails severe limitations to political and civil rights (Zakošek 2008), which are of central importance to this analysis. Wars allowed political elites to 'seductively oversimplify complex issues' as well as marginalise minorities and use nationalism as a principle of legitimation (Ramet 1996: 215, Fish 2001). During the 1990s the lives of many people in former Yugoslav states were directly in danger, while for numerous others human security was jeopardised due to devastating economic circumstances (Dvornik 2009).

While these effects seem reasonable to assume, the literature does not tell us how they actually take place. The explanatory chain of arguments that looks at how war influenced democratisation is missing from existing work, as are more specific causal mechanisms that unpack the link between war and the resulting character of political institutions. To my knowledge these links have not been explored at all in the context of post-communist democratisation in Europe. Therefore, case studies in Chapters 6 and 7 are devoted to studying the effect that war has had on democratisation in European post-communist countries, and to looking at how these effects combined with other key factors proposed in this theoretical framework. The assumption is that governing in wartime circumstances left a specific imprint on the functioning of the rule of law, contributing to an authoritarian mode of rule that is proving difficult to dismantle. In addition to that, war is argued to have had different effects in Croatia and Serbia. Croatia fought a war on its territory, which means all other political processes were relegated to the background in the period

1991–1995, with serious consequences for the fledgling democracy. Nevertheless, once it reinstated its territorial autonomy in 1995, Croatia had the opportunity to move forward fast. Serbia on the other hand was involved in several conflicts throughout 1990s, both outside its territory and within, and its statehood remains disputed until this day. Violence and the wartime economy remain fresh in the minds of Serbian citizens, while democratisation remains uncertain. In addition to that, the legacy of communist regimes provided the institutional architecture and political experience for political elites that were in charge of regime change in 1990. Adding to this legacy, one-party dominance could have served as a vehicle for continuation of institutional legacies from communist regimes. This seems particularly plausible in the case of Serbia, where the former communist party was in charge of regime change and subsequent institutional reform. War would have only amplified the party-state legacy. Therefore the legacy of communist party-state centralisation of arbitrary power should be more pronounced in the case of Serbia.

If some of the main effects of war on democratisation were the centralisation and arbitrary character of political power, the stifling of pluralism and the curtailment of human rights, then the weakening of wartime legacies should manifest itself primarily through the strengthening of pluralism, more political competition, the assertion of individual rights and civil society more broadly, as well as the strengthening of horizontal accountability and media independence. As well as charting wartime legacies in the cases of Croatia and Serbia, Chapters 6 and 7 also trace the gradual evolution of these signs of democratisation. However, before delving into case study analysis, in Chapter 5 I apply a fuzzy set QCA in order to explore the interrelationships of all explanatory factors introduced so far. While Chapters 3 and 4 dealt with bivariate relationships between explanatory factors and the outcome of interest – post-communist democratisation – the application of QCA in the following chapter allows for an examination of the relative strength of the proposed explanatory factors against each other.

chapter five | applying fuzzy-set QCA to explain divergent democratisation trajectories

Five years after the moment of regime change, authoritarian trajectories of change had already been established in several of the analysed countries in post-communist Europe. In 1995 Romania, Bulgaria, Macedonia and Serbia were governed by unreconstructed communists, Slovakia and Croatia by nationalists and Albania by the authoritarian Democratic Party. At the same time, in Estonia and Latvia centrist coalitions were in power, centre-right ODS and LDS were in power in the Czech Republic and Slovenia, while Lithuania, Poland and Hungary were ruled by Social Democratic parties. Sarajevo was under siege, while Serbia and Croatia were considered 'the pariahs of Europe' (Vachudova 2005: 105). When authoritarian parties lost power in 1996 in Romania, in 1997 in Bulgaria, in 1998 in Slovakia and then in 2000 in Serbia and Croatia – hope arose that these countries would experience democratic breakthroughs that Visegrad countries underwent back in 1990. After these pro-democratic elections everyone was expecting convergence of Southeast European countries towards democratisation trajectories of Central Eastern European countries.

However, a decade later the process of convergence looks much less certain; if it is happening at all, it is taking much longer than initially expected. The chief distinction that separates democracies in SEE from those in CEE is the extent to which these new democracies managed to secure the rule of law. The main research question explored in this study is why fragile rule of law systems and pervasive corruption remain the weakest links in post-communist democratisation processes. The rule of law characterises political systems where the legal system is fair, competent and efficient, judges are impartial, independent and not subject to political manipulation and the government is embedded in a legal framework which is accepted by government officials (Carothers 1998). In a post-communist setting establishing the rule of law requires a deliberate effort on the part of the ruling class whereby they deny themselves non-institutionalised power of arbitrary rule (Dvornik 2009). As long as laws are regularly trampled upon by political elites, it is impossible to secure civil rights for citizens, which represent the foundation of democratic regimes. Weak rule of law systems have had particularly devastating consequences due to the fact that in the period of regime change post-communist states were simultaneously rewriting political and economic rules of the game. The process of privatisation created favourable conditions for abuse of power, insider deals and rampant corruption across the post-communist world. The extent to which post-communist societies had domestic and external resources for monitoring, control and pressure to draw from in order to curb corruption and strengthen the rule of law is understood as the chief explanation for enduring differences in their democratisation trajectories. Clearly, this points in the direction of analysing the political parties that presided over regime change as well as the broader socioeconomic environment. The preceding analysis has indeed established authoritarian party dominance as the centrepiece of a theoretical framework that links structural and contingent factors in an account of divergent trajectories of post-communist democratisation.

This chapter explores this main assertion and its component conditions by using fsQCA. Qualitative Comparative Analysis (QCA) is a method suited to medium range theorising in social research, where the researcher is neither explaining world systems, nor dealing with individual level variables but rather with comparable macro units such as countries, which makes it highly compatible with the methodology of this study. It enables the systematic comparison of cases, which means that it is replicable, transparent and eliminates vagueness in conceptualisation and empirical analysis. It is designed to handle and analyse rigorously a larger number of cases than usual comparative designs without applying statistical, regression based techniques (Schimmelfennig, Engert and Knobel 2006). According to some scholars, it offers a more appropriate estimation technique for analysing complex causality than standard statistics (Schmitter 2009). This is because, in contrast to standard statistical tools, it deals with a limited number of complex cases in a configurational way – meaning that each case is considered as a complex combination of properties (Rihoux and Ragin 2009). The method relies on Boolean algebra, a type of sentential calculus based on logical operations. Allowing for configurational causation means that different constellations of factors are conceptualised as potentially leading to the same result – a phenomenon called equifinality. Therefore, the researcher is not urged to specify a single causal model; instead QCA is as a method 'geared toward diversity' (ibid), whereby different causal recipes may account for positive and negative instances of a phenomenon, and may vary across analysed cases. The analysis that follows in this chapter illustrates these features of QCA very well.

The basic crisp set QCA analysis is discriminate, which requires the coding of causal conditions and the outcome as binary variables or in other words deciding for each analysed case whether a given condition and the outcome are present or absent. The use of categorical data produces a correspondence between categories and sets (Ragin 1987). While such an analysis yields a more straightforward interpretation, many potential explanatory factors in empirical political science research are difficult to conceptualise as dichotomies. In the presented theoretical framework this is specifically true for modernisation preconditions, but also for the outcome of interest – the extent to which a given country has established a functioning rule of law. Similarly, other factors such as the extent to which a political party dominated the regime change period, or the length of the EU's role as democracy promoter seem better operationalised as continuous variables.

For all these reasons fuzzy set QCA analysis is chosen, since it enables analysis of data that are not categorical in nature. Fuzzy set QCA enables the analyst to capture both differences in kind and differences in degree, and in this respect the method is very amenable to the study of diversity (Ragin 2000). The main task of the researcher is careful calibration of the data so that it mirrors closely the conceptualisation: 'a fuzzy set is a continuous set that has been carefully calibrated to indicate the degree of membership' (2000: 154). Based on case knowledge and operationalisation of concepts, it is necessary to specify 'zero' and 'one' points, which indicate values on a given condition that are 'fully out' and 'fully in' of a given set. The second step is to indicate a 0.5 threshold for values of the condition that are neither fully in or fully out of the given set. After that it is possible to specify further calibrations on a five-point or a seven-point scale. Practically though, in applying the method it is wise to avoid 0.5 scores since in the calculation they are fully indeterminate, which means that the given case cannot be assigned to any of the applied categories. Instead it is better to decide either for 0.4 or 0.6 scores (Ragin 2011). The most important thing is that the specification of qualitative anchors should be made based on explicit rationale of the researcher and on substantive and theoretical knowledge (Ragin 2000). Qualitative anchors may be understood as distinguishing between relevant and irrelevant variation, and the process of coding fuzzy membership scores should be understood as a dialogue between ideas and evidence (ibid.).

With respect to analysis once the dataset is prepared, fuzzy set QCA relies on Boolean algebra just like crisp set analysis, but applying fuzzy algebra implies some qualifications in interpretation and a few exceptions to algebraic rules that apply in binary variable analysis. The property space in the fuzzy set approach is best understood as a multidimensional vector space with 2k corners, where k stands for the number of conditions that are included in the analysis. Each empirical case's degree of membership in a corner can be interpreted as its degree of conformity with an ideal type (ibid.).

Like crisp set analysis, fuzzy set QCA cannot avoid the problem of limited diversity. This problem stems from the 'confounded nature of social phenomena' (2000: 81), which tend to occur in syndrome-like clumps. Charles Ragin, the scholar who first applied and developed the QCA method, uses the example of overlapping inequalities, where, for instance, low educational attainment, poverty, early pregnancy and various health risks usually cluster together in a case, rather than spreading out in different combinations to make it easier for the researcher to determine their independent effects. Similarly, in this study, cases that exhibit poorer modernisation preconditions are likely to have had a less facilitating regime type during communism and to exhibit authoritarian party dominance during the period of regime change. As a result, an analysis that includes four possible explanatory factors and which therefore allows for sixteen (2⁴) possible combinations of factors will have empirical cases in only a minority of these combinations. QCA analysis, either crisp or fuzzy set variant, requires that the researcher deals with this problem explicitly. While the software used for computations produces the complex and the parsimonious solution, which treat all empirically non-represented combinations as negative and positive[1] respectively, the researcher is expected

---

1. To be even more precise, parsimonious solutions treat only the remainders that help produce

to provide assumptions for the provision of an intermediary solution. Based on available empirical information and theoretical knowledge the researcher is invited to 'solve' combinations which involve easy counterfactuals. Other features of the fsQCA method important for the interpretation of findings are explained as I proceed with the analysis while the next sections introduce the data and specify the calibrations for creating the fsQCA dataset.

As summarised at the beginning of this chapter, weak rule of law systems and the presence of corruption are conceptualised as representing two sides of the same coin. Chapter 1 presented data on both of these dimensions, showing that indeed an individual country's trajectory regarding rule of law is complementary to its trajectory of success or failure in the fight against corruption. Fuzzy set QCA enables a more explicit analysis of the relationship between these two dimensions. An analytical procedure called set coincidence enables us to establish the degree to which two sets overlap or in other words to what extent they represent one and the same set (Ragin 2011). Ragin uses the example of establishing to what degree the set 'surviving third wave democracies' is the same as 'parliamentary third wave democracies': this is determined by establishing the degree to which cases that have both of these traits embrace the set of cases with either trait (2011). In set theoretic terms, set coincidence is the number of cases found in the intersection of two sets, expressed relative to the number of cases found in their union:

(# of cases in intersection)/(# of cases in union)

This procedure is applied to the two dimensions that operationally capture the variance in democratisation trajectories: rule of law and corruption. Set coincidence analysis can establish whether indeed these two dimensions capture the same phenomenon. In addition to that, since World Bank Governance Indicators data is available across time, a temporal dimension is introduced to this analysis to establish whether congruence between these two dimensions grew or diminished over time. Though Freedom House scores of democracy have been used in previous chapters, for this analysis World Bank measurements are used since the scores are more nuanced and hence capture more detail. The two datasets of World Bank and Freedom House have a very high correlation, so using either dataset arguably captures the same phenomenon and should not prejudice the results one way or another.[2] In the analysis of set coincidence World Bank rule of law and corruption scores are used for three points in time: 1996, 2002 and 2008. The dataset is shown in the Appendix.

The full range of World Bank Governance scores goes from 2.5 to -2.5, with a midpoint at zero, allowing for fairly straightforward calibration into fuzzy set scores. However, since the fourteen countries do not exhibit the full variance from -2.5 to 2.5 scores, measures of spread for the dataset are used when creating

---

a more parsimonious solution as positive.

2.   The correlation for Freedom House Nations in Transit score for judiciary independence and World Bank Governance Indicator for Rule of Law in the period 2002–2008 is 0.9.

Table 5.1: Measures of spread for WBGI rule of law and corruption variables

	rol96	corr96	rol02	corr02	rol08	corr08	AVERAGE
Mean	-0.16	-0.08	0.17	0.08	0.32	0.23	0.09
Standard deviation	0.56	0.67	0.64	0.56	0.55	0.41	0.56
Range	1.87	2.20	1.89	1.77	1.65	1.40	1.79
Min	-1.0	-1.10	-0.90	-0.90	-0.60	-0.45	-0.83
Max	0.87	1.10	0.99	0.87	1.05	0.95	0.97

Source: author's calculations

calibrations. Table 5.1 shows the measures of spread for each of the variables, and the last column to the right averages the values across the variables.

Looking at the measures of spread for the two variables in three points of time, mean values show how over time generally scores on both variables have somewhat improved, moving the mean from negative towards positive values. Overall, however, measures of spread show stability, with standard deviation averaging at around 0.56 and the range at around 1.8. Since one standard deviation to the right and to the left of the mean covers around 68 per cent of the variation, this measure is taken to determine thresholds for full membership in the given set and full non-membership in the given set. Applying two standard deviations would have covered 95 per cent of the scores, but would have produced high fuzziness (many indeterminate scores for cases). Therefore one standard deviation is applied to the averaged mean of 0.09 to produce the score of 0.65, indicating full membership in the set 'functioning rule of law' and the same for 'low corruption', and -0.47 indicating full non-membership in these sets.

Applying the set coincidence procedure requires calculating the set union for rule of law and corruption scores separately for the three points in time, then calculating the degree of set coincidence between the two dimensions separately for three points in time: 1996, 2002 and 2008. Table 5.2 shows the results.

Table 5.2: Set coincidence between 'functioning rule of law' and 'low level of corruption'

1996	0.69
2002	0.85
2008	0.85

Source: author's calculations

As Table 5.2 shows, in 1996 set coincidence between 'functioning rule of law' and 'low level of corruption' was at 0.69, which is perhaps not high enough to consider the two dimensions capturing the same phenomenon. However, since 2002 set coincidence between the two dimensions grew to 0.85, indicating high overlap between memberships of cases in both of these sets. In addition, it is stable over time, showing the same score in 2002 and 2008. This analysis confirms the theoretical connection between difficulties in establishing the rule of law on the one hand, and the extensive prevalence of corruption on the other. The imperfect set coincidence might be explained by assuming that corruption captures a subset of anomalies related to weak rule of law, which also encompasses political influence over the judiciary, legal uncertainty, human rights violations and other problems.

After analysing the phenomenon that is the subject of our investigation, the next section presents the dataset with the explanatory conditions used in the fsQCA. Table 5.3 shows the dataset. The fourteen countries are ranked alphabetically in the first column; columns two to seven represent data on explanatory factors, and column eight displays data on the outcome – Freedom House Nations in Transit data on judicial framework and independence for 2010.

Table 5.3: Fourteen countries dataset

Country	GDP per capita 1990	Pre-comm. literacy	Comm. regime type	Authoritarian party dominance	Conflict	Length of EU influence	FH judiciary 2010
Albania	0.00	20	1	3	0.4	8	2.75
Bulgaria	0.15	69	1	4	0	19	4
Croatia	0.56	68	2	4	1	11	2.75
Czech Rep	0.34	99	3	2	0	21	5
Estonia	0.22	99	1.5	1	0	17	5.5
Hungary	0.24	96	2	1	0	21	5
Latvia	0.20	93	1.5	1	0	17	5.25
Lithuania	0.27	77	1.5	1	0	17	5.25
Macedonia	0.21	30	1	4	0.6	11	3
Poland	0.11	79	2.5	1	0	21	4.25
Romania	0.10	57	1	4	0	19	3
Serbia	0.45	35	1.5	4	1	6	2.5
Slovakia	0.18	92	1.5	4	0	21	4
Slovenia	1.00	91	2	1	0	16	5.25

Sources: World Bank, Freedom House, Darden and Grzymala Busse (2006), Kitschelt *et al* (1999), author's calculations

Data in Table 5.3 is the same as that used in Chapters 3 and 4 where bivariate relationships between explanatory factors and the outcome were explored. Data on GDP per capita is from the World Bank, but in this table it has been rescaled to a zero-to-one scale in order to more easily determine the spread of values, which is important for the procedure of calibration. Data on pre-communist literacy rates is from Darden and Grzymala Busse (2006), the same as used in Chapter 3. The ordinal scale of previous regime type in column five is based on Kitschelt's typology, while the variables of authoritarian party dominance and the length of EU influence are also carried over from earlier empirical analyses. Empirical analyses in Chapters 3 and 4 discussed many aspects of the analysed phenomena, but since QCA demands a manageable number of explanatory factors in order to produce meaningful results, in this analysis the number of variables is reduced, focusing only on quantifiable composite variables.

The experience of conflict, shown in column six in Table 5.3, is neither an ordinal nor a continuous variable, and any numerical representation of this factor forces the concept into a radical simplification. I have decided to code the experience of conflict into three categories. The dichotomous outcome is noncontroversial: there are countries that went through war (value of one) and those that did not (value of zero). However there are two cases where institutional conflict did spill out into violence – Albania and Macedonia – but where the extent was considerably smaller in comparison with conflicts in Croatia and Serbia. The conflict in Macedonia was interethnic, which makes it more similar to conflicts in Serbia and Croatia. At the same time this was not a full-scale war, and neither was the conflict in Albania. In contrast with Macedonia, the conflict in Albania was not interethnic and it had a different dynamic from conflicts in former Yugoslav republics. As was elaborated in Chapter 4, violence in Albania had the character of state breakdown. For these reasons I decide to code the conflict in Macedonia as 0.6 and the one in Albania as 0.4. This is justified by considering interethnic violence as the more detrimental type of conflict for long term democratisation, while at the same time arguing that any violent conflict will have negative consequences for establishing the rule of law. That is why the scores are set to be close, but Macedonia's is higher. Building on case knowledge and empirical data collected, I believe this is theoretically the most appropriate way of operationalising this condition.

After assembling the dataset, the next step in the analysis is to calibrate this data in order to produce a fuzzy set dataset. As was mentioned with respect to set coincidence analysis, QCA has the property of being asymmetric. The researcher needs to specify the direction of the outcome she is interested in and calibrate causal conditions accordingly, as well as analyse positive and negative instances of the outcome separately. Since the research question that animates this study is the explanation for persistently weak rule of law systems in some European post-communist countries, the analysed outcome variable is 'weak rule of law', measured in 2010. The related causal conditions are lower levels of GDP per capita, lower levels of pre-communist literacy, inhibiting regime legacy, the extent of authoritarian party dominance, the extent of conflict, and the length of EU influence. Table 5.4 shows fuzzy scores for these causal conditions and the outcome, while the sections that follow explain the calibrations.

Table 5.4: Fuzzy set dataset

Country	Lower GDP per capita	Lower level of pre-comm. literacy	Inhib-iting regime legacy	Extent of authoritar-ian party dominance	Strength of conflict	Shorter EU influ-ence	Weak rule of law
Albania	0.97	1,0	0,95	0,99	0,35	0,99	0,93
Bulgaria	0.84	0,55	0,95	1	0,05	0,14	0,55
Croatia	0.04	0,6	0,5	1	0,95	0,95	0,93
Czech Republic	0.35	0,0	0,05	0,82	0,05	0,05	0,13
Estonia	0.7	0,0	0,82	0,05	0,05	0,35	0,05
Hungary	0.65	0,0	0,5	0,05	0,05	0,05	0,13
Latvia	0.75	0,0	0,82	0,05	0,05	0,35	0,08
Lithuania	0.56	0,11	0,82	0,05	0,05	0,35	0,08
Macedonia	0.72	1,0	0,95	1	0,65	0,95	0,89
Poland	0.9	0,06	0,18	0,05	0,05	0,05	0,42
Romania	0.91	0,93	0,95	1	0,05	0,14	0,89
Serbia	0.13	1,0	0,82	1	0,95	1	0,95
Slovakia	0.79	0,0	0,82	1	0,05	0,05	0,55
Slovenia	0	0,0	0,5	0,05	0,05	0,5	0,08

Source: author's calculations

The fuzzy scores of the indicators shown in Table 5.4 are the result of calibration. The process of calibration is explained for each condition in turn. With respect to GDP per capita, the guideline for setting membership scores was drawn from the distribution of the data by examining measures of spread. Based on the mean value of 0.29 and standard deviation of 0.25, full membership in 'low GDP per capita' is set at 0.04, the threshold at 0.29 and full non-membership in the set 'low GDP per capita' at 0.54. Regarding literacy levels, the spread of values would not yield meaningful categories, so instead calibration is made using knowledge of historical context. By the mid-twentieth century, the literacy rate in Western Europe was over 80 per cent, in Austria and Hungary over 70 per cent, while in Portugal and the Eastern Orthodox countries literacy rates were not above 25 per cent (UNESCO 2006). It was only after 1945 that mass literacy characterised

European countries (ibid.). Based on this historical data, a literacy rate of 80 per cent before 1945 can certainly be taken as high, or in other words, may be used to denote full non-membership in the set 'low literacy rate'. Following data for central Europe (Austria and Hungary) the threshold is set at 70 per cent, while scores considered full members of the set 'low literacy rate' are set from 55 per cent downwards.

Kitschelt's typology of previous regimes was in Chapter 3 transformed into an ordinal variable and when dealing with such a typology calibrations are made using qualitative anchors. Since for the purpose of this analysis the causal factor is coded as 'inhibiting regime legacy', type one (patrimonial regime) is calibrated as full member in the set, while type three is calibrated as full non-member in the given set. The intermediate category is set at two, guided by the logic that the national accommodative regime will have the most indeterminate effect on democratisation outcomes. Similarly, authoritarian party dominance is an ordinal variable capturing a three-part typology and calibrations are made using qualitative anchors. Cases of democratic party dominance (value of one) are calibrated as full non-members of the set 'authoritarian party dominance', and since only this category is argued not to have a negative effect on democratisation, the threshold is set at 1.5. To capture both mixed and authoritarian party constellations, the threshold for full membership in the set 'authoritarian party dominance' is set at 2.5. With respect to the extent of EU influence as democracy promoter, since this is an interval variable the distribution of values and measures of spread are taken into consideration. Based on the mean value of 16.1 and standard deviation of 5.1, the 'length of EU influence' factor is calibrated by setting eleven as the threshold for full membership, sixteen for indeterminate membership and twenty-one for full non-membership in the set.

Finally, the outcome variable is calibrated based on qualitative anchors and measures of spread. As shown in Chapter 1, various indicators such as Freedom House, World Bank Governance Indicators, the Bertelsmann Transformation Index and others identify a gap among Central Eastern and Southeast European countries with respect to democratisation outcomes – in particular with respect to the functioning of rule of law. Freedom House data on the functioning of rule of law displayed in Table 5.3 show that the values range from 2.5 to 5.5, higher values representing better functioning rule of law systems. Even though the original scale ranges from 1 to 7, to avoid excessive fuzziness the minimum and maximum values of this dataset are set as full membership and non-membership in the set 'weak rule of law'. The lower end value of 2.5 is set as full membership in the set, and the maximum value of 5.5 as full non-membership in that set. The key decision involves the setting of the threshold of indeterminacy. To avoid suspicion that I might have chosen the threshold in order to get the preferred results, measures of spread are used. Both the mean and the median for this distribution of values are 4.1, and hence this is where the threshold of indeterminacy is set.

After the fuzzy set dataset is assembled, it is possible to conduct various types of analyses using QCA techniques. I use fsQCA software developed by Charles Ragin, which is available on his website.

Analysis of necessity and sufficiency[3]

Set-theoretical logic that QCA is based upon requires the explication of relationships between explanatory factors and the outcome in terms of necessity and sufficiency. The relations of necessity and sufficiency can only be assessed within a comparative framework that includes more than one case because they require the researcher to establish whether: a given condition always precedes the outcome but that condition does not invariably lead to the outcome (necessity),

cause	outcome
1	1
1	0

or whether a given condition always gives rise to the outcome, though the outcome may come about by different means (sufficiency).

cause	outcome
1	1
0	1

To assess necessity the researcher has to work backward from instances of the outcome to identification of causes, and if she finds that a given cause always precedes the outcome then she has established necessity (Ragin 2000). If an outcome is recorded without the cause preceding it, then it is not a necessary cause. Conversely, the relationship of sufficiency is established by working forward from causes to outcomes. If the researcher establishes that the given cause always produces the outcome in question, then the given cause is sufficient for the outcome to occur (ibid.). The outcome may occur as a result of some other cause or causal recipe, but for the relationship of sufficiency it is important that there is no case where the cause is present but the outcome is absent.

Theoretically a condition may exhibit both sufficiency and necessity to an outcome, but that is rare. Even relationships of necessity or sufficiency on their own are rather rare in the social world. Instead, the researcher is often looking for INUS conditions: insufficient but non-redundant parts of a condition which is itself unnecessary but sufficient for the occurrence of the outcome (Mackie 1988, quoted by Ragin 2011). Put in more friendly language, this means that often only a combination of several factors is sufficient for an outcome to occur, though it may not necessarily lead to the given outcome. In the following sections the relationship between each causal factor and the outcome is analysed in order to

---

3. Conducting this analysis with World Bank Governance Data produces virtually the same results, confirming the interchangeability of these datasets, as well as suggesting that they are capturing the same phenomenon. I also conducted the analysis with a different calibration of the Freedom House variable (2.5, 4.5, 5.5), only to receive very similar results.

uncover possible relationships of necessity or sufficiency. This is important to get a fuller picture of how well the findings conform to predicted relationships, since some relationships between factors may be eliminated from the parsimonious solution that the fsQCA provides in the configurational analysis. In addition to that, these findings can reinforce or put in question results obtained from analyses conducted in Chapters 3 and 4.

Drawing on theoretical arguments and empirical evidence from previous chapters, it is assumed that violent conflict in contexts of disputed statehood should exhibit properties of a necessary condition. Since QCA is asymmetric, the cases that exhibit the positive outcome (functioning rule of law) versus those that exhibit the negative outcome (weak rule of law) are examined separately. In an analysis of cases where rule of law was successfully established, the absence of conflict is indeed the factor that comes closest to being a necessary condition. It has a 0.997 consistency score as a necessary condition, covering 69 per cent sum of memberships in the outcome.[4] This relationship of necessity may be described as the causal condition being a superset of the outcome, as shown in Figure 5.1. In almost every case where functioning rule of law was established, an absence of conflict preceded this outcome. Moving in the opposite direction, an absence of conflict of itself is not sufficient to bring about a functioning rule of law.

Figure 5.1: Absence of conflict as a superset of cases that successfully established rule of law

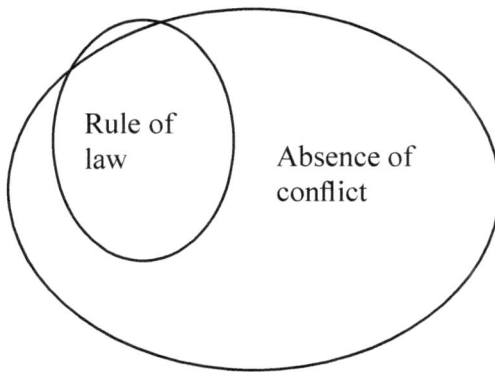

---

4. In crisp set QCA coverage may be interpreted as relating to the percentage of cases covered. Since in fuzzy set algebra all cases exhibit various degrees of membership in a set, coverage cannot be said to refer to the percentage of cases in or out of the solution. Nevertheless, the intuitive interpretation is largely the same. Coverage may also be understood as having a similar interpretation as R2, indicating how much variance is covered by a given solution.

Next the negative outcome, weak rule of law, is examined. When the relationship between conflict and weak rule of law is examined, analysis shows that the consistency score for sufficiency is 0.99, with a coverage of 51 per cent. This indicates clearly that undergoing conflict is a sufficient condition for long term difficulties in establishing the rule of law. This finding relates to cases of Croatia and Serbia in the first instance, but also Macedonia, which has been characterised by disputed statehood, and Albania, where violence spilled over from institutional conflict in 1997. The limited coverage of 51 per cent indicates that other combinations of conditions also may lead to weak rule of law, which is only to be expected. This finding is substantiated by the experiences of Bulgaria and Romania, which did not undergo conflict but exhibit weak rule of law systems.

From the assembled dataset some indicators may be combined in order to better capture theoretically defined explanatory factors or to reduce the number of explanatory factors in a given analysis. In fsQCA this is possible through the construction of macro conditions – i.e. composite variables of related indicators. In Table 5.4, data on real GDP per capita and pre-communist literacy both represent indicators of modernisation. Among the available techniques for creating a macro condition, taking the average of the two indicators seems most appropriate since it keeps information carried in each of the indicators. The macro condition 'poor modernisation preconditions' is thus created by averaging the values of 'low GDP per capita' factor and 'low pre-communist literacy' factor.

Building on the findings from Chapter 3 where regression results revealed a strong relationship between modernisation preconditions and subsequent democratisation, this causal factor is analysed next. When low modernisation preconditions are related to weak rule of law outcomes, the consistency for necessity is 0.81, covering 79 per cent of the sum of memberships in the outcome. These results suggest that by establishing whether a country is beset with weak rule of law it could be surmised with a fair amount of certainty that the country had inhibiting economic and social conditions at the onset of regime change. If however the relationship between a positive outcome, functioning rule of law, and good modernisation preconditions is examined, a relationship of sufficiency emerges. The consistency score for favourable modernisation conditions being a sufficient condition for functioning of rule of law is 0.82, with 81 per cent coverage. These results suggest that favourable modernisation preconditions have very often led to successful democratisation outcomes. When these results are related to those presented in Chapter 3, all examined evidence points to modernisation preconditions exerting a strong influence on subsequent democratisation outcomes.

Still examining the role of legacies and structural factors, the relationship between inhibiting regime legacy and weak rule of law systems shows consistency with necessity of 0.87. The coverage, however, is at 60 per cent, which means that this explanation is somewhat less relevant. These findings reconfirm those from Chapter 3 where a fairly strong relationship between regime types and democratisation was established. However, while correlation can only establish association, QCA can establish subset and superset relationships and hence determine whether they are characterised by properties of necessity or sufficiency.

In this relationship, inhibiting regime legacies are a superset of the analysed outcome, regimes with weak rule of law. When an instance of such a regime is empirically confirmed, it is highly likely that it was preceded by an inhibiting regime legacy. Starting from establishing the causal condition, in this instance patrimonial communist regime, is not sufficient for bringing about regimes with weak rule of law. This analysis nicely brings out the asymmetric nature of QCA and shows how it enables the researcher to differentiate causes relevant for negative outcomes as opposed to positive outcomes, something that was not possible when applying correlation analysis in Chapter 3.

The following section examines the relationship between party dominance and rule of law outcomes. The extent of authoritarian party dominance shows a consistency with necessity of 0.92 and 76 per cent coverage in leading to the weak rule of law outcome. However, when the positive outcome of a functioning rule of law is examined, an equally strong relationship emerges. Absence of authoritarian party dominance shows a consistency of 0.91 with being a sufficient condition, with 73 per cent coverage. With both high consistency and high coverage, this relationship is the strongest of those established so far. As was the case with structural factors, here fsQCA reconfirms a relationship established in Chapter 4 but adds another dimension by establishing authoritarian party systems as a necessary condition for weak rule of law systems.

Finally, let us relate the length of EU influence to democratisation outcomes. When shorter EU influence is related to weak rule of law outcomes, the relationship of sufficiency emerges, with a consistency of 0.76 and coverage of 67 per cent. However, when longer EU influence is related to successful establishment of rule of law, a stronger relationship of necessity emerges, with a consistency score of 0.80, and 73 per cent coverage. These results may be interpreted to suggest that the EU was more influential in cases of successful democratisation than in countries where democratisation had stalled, which confirms theoretical expectations.

Since undertaking QCA analysis with five conditions and only fourteen cases poses challenges in terms of limited diversity, the aim is to reduce the number of causal conditions to four before undertaking configurational analysis. The only two conditions that theoretically permit a merger into a more abstract concept are modernisation preconditions and regime legacy. Both factors represent structural conditions or in other words historical legacies from before the early 1990s. Also, the analysis has shown that both factors exhibit properties of necessary conditions, which means they have a delimiting effect on possible outcomes. In order to establish how these two factors could be combined, a set coincidence analysis is performed. Establishing the extent to which these two sets overlap helps determine the procedure for creating a macro condition. An analysis of set coincidence returns a score of 0.63, meaning that while the two sets do overlap, both conditions carry some independent weight in contributing to the outcome. Hence in the construction of a macro condition the compensatory approach is adopted, by averaging the membership scores. This creates a more inclusive but still reliable measure of legacies. The downside of this procedure is that averaging tends to produce maximum fuzziness i.e. a lot of middle range scores (Ragin

2011). The dataset for the component conditions and the resulting macro condition 'inhibiting legacy' is shown in the Appendix.

Historical legacies exhibit a rather strong relationship with subsequent democratisation trajectories. When inhibiting legacies are related to weak rule of law outcomes, the consistency for necessity is 0.87, with coverage of 70 per cent. Conversely, when facilitating legacies are related to functioning rule of law outcomes the relationship of sufficiency emerges, though a slightly weaker one (consistency score is 0.85, coverage is 67 per cent). These symmetric results for the two outcomes mean that by knowing how successful countries have been in establishing the rule of law we might surmise with quite a lot of certainty the historical legacies of individual post-communist states. The relationship of 'almost sufficiency' should be read as meaning that favourable legacies have often preceded the successful establishment of rule of law.

Having examined individual conditions' relationships to more and less successfully established rule of law, fsQCA configurational analysis is conducted next.

Configurational analysis

The configurational analysis has four causal conditions: historical legacies, conflict, the extent of EU influence and the extent of authoritarian party dominance in the first decade after regime change. The observed outcome is establishing the rule of law, analysed separately for positive and negative instances of the outcome.

After the outcome variable and the causal conditions are specified, calibrated and entered into a dataset, the fsQCA software produces the complex and parsimonious solutions. As was mentioned before, in an analysis with four causal factors, sixteen combinations of conditions are possible, and only a minority of available combinations is covered with empirical cases. This is known as the problem of limited diversity. The complex solution is calculated by not involving any counterfactuals or in other words using only those configurations of factors that have empirical cases attached to them. This makes the complex solution rather descriptive and fairly limited in reach. In order to overcome this problem, the fsQCA software calculates the parsimonious solution as well, in which logical remainders (i.e. combinations of causal factors without empirical cases) are treated as if the outcome was present if they contribute to simplifying the solution. Since this might involve a rather big theoretical leap from what we know to what we assume, there is also the third option where the researcher can specify assumptions about conditions that should lead to the observed outcome. This is called the intermediary solution of the analysis. In specifying conditions for the intermediary solution cues are taken from analyses of necessity and sufficiency in the previous section as well as empirical analyses conducted in previous chapters.

Since the main research question of this study aims to account for weak rule of law regimes in Southeast Europe, first an analysis of the negative outcome is conducted. Referring to the results of analysis in the previous section, the specified assumptions for the intermediary solution are that authoritarian party dominance, inhibiting legacies, conflict and weaker EU influence should lead to weaker rule of law. Table 9.9 in the Appendix shows detailed results of the configurational analysis, including the complex, parsimonious and intermediary solutions. In the following sections I focus on the most relevant findings.

The complex solution for the negative outcome consists of two paths, and can be factored as follows:[5]

weak rule of law = extent of authoritarian party dominance *
(inhibiting legacy * ~ conflict + brief EU influence * conflict)

This solution suggests that dominance of an authoritarian party over the period of regime change always preceded the development of weak rule of law regimes. Authoritarian party dominance is here a necessary condition, though not sufficient to produce the outcome on its own. The part of the recipe in brackets stands for two possible solutions, divided by the OR sign ('+'). In the first solution authoritarian party dominance is combined with inhibiting legacies and the absence of conflict, encompassing cases of Albania, Bulgaria, Romania and Slovakia. In the second solution authoritarian party dominance is combined with violent conflict and shorter EU influence, covering cases of Croatia, Macedonia and Serbia.

The parsimonious solution did not produce a simple causal recipe in this analysis, so the intermediary solution is analysed next. With consistency of 0.92 and 93 per cent coverage it represents the best fit of the three solutions. In addition to that, it somewhat simplified the complex solution. After factoring it can be represented as follows:

weak rule of law = authoritarian party dominance *
(inhibiting legacy + conflict * brief EU influence)

Authoritarian party dominance over the period of regime change is present in both paths to the solution, specifying the causal condition that links all cases that experienced difficulties in establishing the rule of law. In the first path this causal factor is combined with inhibiting historical legacies in the form of lower economic development and unfavourable previous regime type, specifying causal recipes for Albania, Bulgaria, Macedonia, Romania, Slovakia and Serbia. In the second path authoritarian party dominance is combined with the occurrence of conflict and a shorter time span of EU influence. These two are obviously related, since the eruption of conflict was the reason for postponed European integration. This path encompasses cases of Croatia, Macedonia and Serbia.

The intermediate solution is an improvement on the complex solution in two ways. First of all, it has better scores for coverage and consistency, signalling more confidence in the results. Secondly, it is an improvement in that it correctly identifies that inhibiting legacies were also characteristic of the democratisation trajectories of Macedonia and Serbia. Applying a counterfactual, these results can

---

5. In configurational fsQCA, the multiplication sign '*' stands for AND, the addition sign '+' stands for OR, while the tilde sign, '~' is used to denote the absence of a condition.

be read to suggest that even had Macedonia and Serbia avoided violent conflicts, their inhibiting structural preconditions might have trapped them into a protracted progress towards democratisation. By contrast, had Croatia escaped the war at the beginning of the 1990s, it might have pursued a trajectory similar to that of Slovenia or other countries in Central Eastern Europe.

The analysis of causal recipes that account for weak rule of law outcomes has clearly emphasised authoritarian party dominance as the causal factor connecting all configurations leading to slower democratisation. The dividing context is one of disputed statehood. Where democratisation was peaceful but nonetheless fraught with weak rule of law, it can be traced back to inhibiting historical legacies. In cases where conflicts erupted, the later initiation of a European integration process seems to have contributed to the negative outcome. Next the analysis of positive outcome is presented. Table 9.10 in the Appendix shows detailed results of the configurational analysis, discussed in the following sections. Since calibrations and names of variables in this chapter were tailored towards the negative outcome (weak rule of law), the following analysis is characterised by the inversion of these conditions, i.e. its opposites: functioning rule of law, facilitating legacies, competitive party systems, absence of conflict and long influence of the EU.

The parsimonious solution produces a three-path solution which does not represent a simplification, and therefore the interpretation is based on the complex and intermediary solutions, which produce the same causal recipe:

functioning rule of law = absence of conflict * early EU influence
* (no authoritarian party dom. + facilitating legacies)

According to the results of the configurational analysis, successful establishment of rule of law was preceded by absence of conflict and early EU integration. In the first path this is combined with democratic competitive party systems, in the second with good structural preconditions in terms of economic development and previous regime type. The causal recipe involving facilitating structural preconditions refers to cases of Hungary, Poland and the Czech Republic, while democratic competitive party systems were important in the cases of Hungary and Poland again, but also the Baltic states Estonia, Latvia and Lithuania.

Since the absence of conflict appears in both paths to the solution, and it has also been established that the presence of conflict was closely related to how early the EU started exerting influence, it seems clear that conflict was a strong influence on the negative outcome. This was also established in the analysis of necessity and sufficiency. However, stating that democratisation had to be peaceful to be successful or that conflict seriously derails it is trivial. For that reason I created a separate dataset with only peaceful democratisation trajectories, characteristic of ten out of the fourteen country cases. This allows for a more nuanced analysis of trajectories that happened among instances of peaceful democratisation, which should better discriminate among the remaining explanatory factors. Since the causal factor of conflict is removed from this analysis, inhibiting legacies are disaggregated back to modernisation and regime type factors, which should provide some new information. These factors are analysed together with authoritarian party dominance and the influence of EU conditionality. The resulting fuzzy set dataset with four causal conditions is displayed in the Appendix. After uploading the new dataset into the QCA software, a new configurational analysis is conducted. Table 9.11 in the Appendix shows detailed results both for the negative and the positive outcome, while the most relevant results are discussed in the following sections.

In the case of the negative outcome, weak rule of law, the parsimonious and intermediate solutions are the same:

weak rule of law = authoritarian party
dominance * inhibiting previous regime

According to this solution, the factors that most significantly contribute to problems with establishing rule of law are authoritarian party dominance combined with an inhibiting legacy of the previous regime. Comparing this solution with the one for the positive outcome reveals them as diametrically opposite. The intermediate solution for the positive outcome is:

functioning rule of law = good modernisation
preconditions * early EU influence

These kinds of findings, which treat the occurrence of an outcome separately from instances where it did not occur, are only possible with the application of set theory on which QCA is based. However, in this analysis of the positive outcome, the parsimonious solution has better consistency and coverage scores than the intermediate solution,[6] and in addition to that it further simplifies the recipe:

functioning rule of law = good modernisation preconditions

This is a striking result, which accords structural preconditions a crucial role in explaining positive democratisation trajectories. This solution covers all eight Central Eastern European cases included in this study: the Czech Republic, Estonia, Hungary, Latvia, Lithuania, Slovakia, Slovenia and Poland. After the confounding factor of conflict was removed, a very clear picture emerges whereby favourable long term structural factors play a decisive role in successful democratisation.

Separate analysis of instances of peaceful democratisation brought obvious analytical benefits in providing additional detail about the specific conditions configuring to influence more and less successful democratisation. In the analysis of the negative outcome it was able to single out regime legacy as more important than socioeconomic development among the two structural preconditions. The recipe for the positive outcome on the other hand provided a significant simplification over the initial fourteen cases analysis. This recipe makes clear that among countries that underwent peaceful democratisation, good modernisation preconditions were the key factor in their success. When these results are compared with the previous analysis of fourteen cases, several findings stand out. Table 5.5 displays all results for the purpose of easier comparison.

---

6. For the parsimonious solution the consistency is 0.96 and coverage is 0.81, while for the intermediate solution consistency is 0.97 and coverage is 0.75.

Table 5.5: Configurational analyses, summary of findings

---

14 cases analysis

weak rule of law = authoritarian party dominance *
(inhibiting legacy + conflict * brief EU influence)

functioning rule of law = absence of conflict * early EU influence
* (no authoritarian party dominance + facilitating legacy)

Peaceful democratisation analyses (10 cases)

weak rule of law = authoritarian party
dominance * inhibiting previous regime

functioning rule of law = good modernisation preconditions

First of all, in the outcome of weak rule of law, authoritarian party dominance is the central part of the causal recipe regardless of whether cases of conflict are included or not. The inhibiting legacy factor from the previous analysis is in the second analysis further specified as the influence of previous regime type. Both analyses identify Bulgaria, Slovakia and Romania as cases where authoritarian party dominance over regime change exacerbated inhibiting regime legacies to influence less successful democratisation trajectories. However, if the coverage and consistency scores of the first and second analysis are compared, the solution for weak rule of law provided in the fourteen cases analysis shows markedly higher scores – consistency score of 0.93, and coverage of 92 per cent, compared with consistency score of 0.76 and coverage of 0.79 for the ten cases dataset. Therefore it seems reasonable to establish that the analysis of fourteen cases provides more reliable recipes for less successful democratisation trajectories.

When the two analyses of positive democratisation outcomes are compared, early onset of EU democratic conditionality from the first analysis disappears in the second, which represents a significantly simplified recipe. Nevertheless, the two recipes are congruent: facilitating historical legacies from the first analysis reappear as favourable modernisation preconditions in the second analysis. However, the second analysis seems better suited to explaining the positive democratisation outcomes because it encompasses all eight CEE cases (the Czech Republic, Estonia, Hungary, Latvia, Lithuania, Poland, Slovakia and Slovenia). As a result, it also exhibits better consistency (0.97) and coverage (75 per cent) scores than the initial analysis of fourteen cases. Looking back at Chapter 4, these results could be read to confirm the argument according to which CEE states would have democratised successfully without the EU and that their European integration was a domestically driven project.

Summary of findings

In this chapter fsQCA was first used to conduct analyses of necessity and sufficiency, and then to produce configurational solutions for more and less successful democratisation trajectories in post-communist Europe. As was made evident, apart from the ability to specify necessary and sufficient conditions for an outcome, a key strength of QCA is in that it allows for asymmetric causal pathways leading to the outcome of interest. Standard statistical techniques assume that once a causal factor was established as playing a chief role in the occurrence of an outcome this must entail that it should explain the absence of an outcome as well. In contrast to that, set theoretical analysis allows for the possibility that a different condition or combination of conditions can be crucial to explaining the absence or presence of an outcome. For this reason the analysis was organised in order to reveal causal recipes for weak rule of law systems first, followed by causal recipes for successful establishment of rule of law. After that, another round of configurational analysis was conducted including cases of peaceful democratisations only in order to remove the strong condition of conflict from the analysis.

Analyses for sufficiency and necessity revealed strong relationships among each of the causal factors and the outcome, confirming findings from Chapters 3 and 4. In addition to that, fsQCA established that in European post-communist countries successful democratisation was as a rule preceded by peaceful democratisation and the magnet of EU accession. In contrast, weak rule of law was in most cases preceded by authoritarian party dominance. This relationship showed the highest scores for consistency and coverage among the examined explanatory factors. Weak rule of law systems were also almost always preceded by inhibiting structural legacies in terms of modernisation preconditions and previous regime type. Finally and not surprisingly, the occurrence of violent conflict has been established as a sufficient condition for subsequent rule of law deficiencies: no country that went through conflict has been able to establish functioning rule of law in the observed period of twenty years.

Configurational analysis revealed the asymmetric nature of set theory, whereby solutions for the negative outcome differed from those for the positive outcome. In the original dataset of fourteen countries, the analysis of the negative outcome returned more relevant results as confirmed by consistency and coverage scores. This is not surprising since the calibration process was designed with the objective to address the central research question of why countries of Southeast Europe are not catching up with levels of democratisation observed in Central Eastern European countries. It turned out that authoritarian party dominance represented a key part of the answer, as was argued throughout the study and empirically established in Chapter 4. In addition, authoritarian party dominance was combined with inhibiting legacies in some cases, and violent conflict that postponed EU integration in others. The solution for the positive outcome revealed that the strong necessary condition of absence of conflict was somewhat blurring the picture over successful democratisation trajectories.

The second configurational analysis of peaceful democratisations revealed that, while the solution for the negative outcome was very similar to that in the original analysis, for successful democratisations the solution was much more straightforward. The causal recipe for success has been the presence of facilitating modernisation preconditions. These findings reaffirm the theoretical argument according to which structural preconditions lay down the 'conditioning parameter within which choices are made and solutions are sought' (Kirchheimer 1965: 966). High enough level of economic development and the accompanying socioeconomic structure set the parameter for party systems to be competitive and democratic and they created the environment for self-driven democratic reform. The overall levels of economic, social and political development engendered democratic minded elites and societal pressure that pushed for successful establishment of the rule of law.

After establishing the main causal recipes that account for diversity in European post-communist democratisation, and confirming that party system dynamics played a uniquely important role in explaining protracted democratisation, the remaining sections of this chapter introduce the case study research presented in Chapters 6 and 7. In these chapters I employ fine-grained process tracing to establish how the explanatory factors identified by fsQCA interacted. I have argued that Croatia and Serbia made feeble progress in democratisation in the second decade after regime change, and in the case studies I focus on explaining the reasons behind this. However, in order firstly to reinstate the empirical grounds for this argument, Figures 5.2 and 5.3 show the Freedom House judiciary independence and corruption scores for the two countries in the period 2001 to 2011.

Figure 5.2: Judiciary independence in Serbia and Croatia, 2001–2011

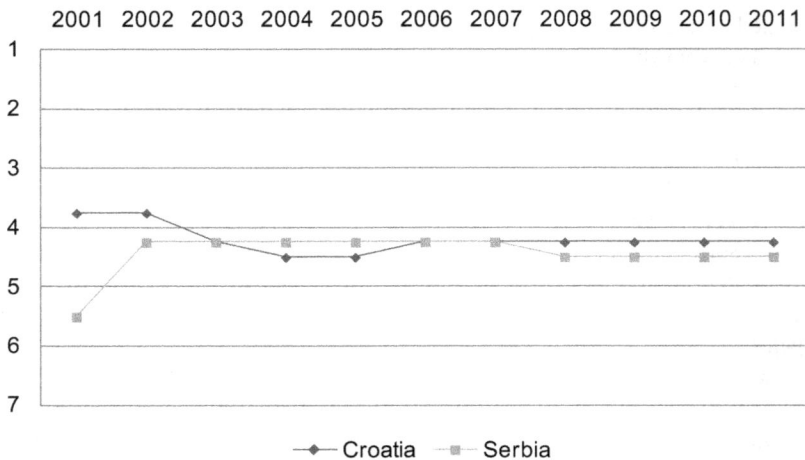

Source: Freedom House, www.freedomhouse.org

Figure 5.3: Corruption in Serbia and Croatia, 2001–2011

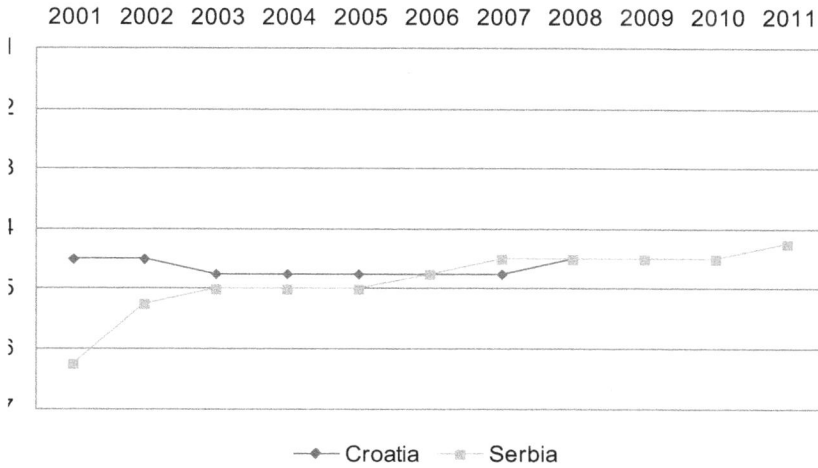

——◆—— Croatia   ——■—— Serbia

Source: Freedom House, www.freedomhouse.org

The two figures show that scores in Serbia and Croatia converged by 2003 on both dimensions of judiciary independence and corruption, and after that the dominant trend has been one of stagnation. Throughout this study I have argued that the causal mechanism which links authoritarian party dominance in the period of regime change with subsequent obstacles to democratisation are the governance practices developed by authoritarian parties that presided over regime change. These practices have been classified in Chapter 1 as falling into three groups: the concentration of executive power, the conversion of political to economic power and the politicisation of state administration. These governance practices reveal that the ruling parties treated political office as prey and the state as a resource to be harvested for private gain. They grew out of unfavourable circumstances at the moment of regime change, but once they were established, they were very difficult to undo even by more democratic subsequent governments. The case study method is uniquely positioned to delineate these governing practices and to trace how they were carried over from the moment of regime change onwards.

As argued in previous chapters, there are many similarities between the two cases, but some important differences too. Both cases were characterised by authoritarian party dominance, but in Croatia the CDU came to power by ousting the Communist Party in the first multiparty election, while in Serbia the Socialist party was a fake remodel of the Communist Party of Serbia that won the first multiparty election and stayed in power throughout the 1990s. The analysis will show that differences in party origin have influenced the differences in the resulting mode of rule. Secondly, wars and disputed statehood played out differently in the two cases. Croatia completed the state building project in 1998 and has been able to move the political agenda away from ethno-nationalism, while in Serbia the statehood project remains disputed and nationalist sentiment is still an important driving force of politics. With respect to EU influence, Croatia is scheduled to join the European Union in 2013, while Serbia only ratified the Stabilisation and Association Agreement in 2010. Finally, Croatia has more favourable historical legacies than Serbia, both in terms of overall economic development, and of a facilitating regime legacy. Tracing how these differences played into the explanation of democratisation trajectories of Croatia and Serbia is the main focus of the following chapters.

The principal method applied in the two case studies is process analysis, as is appropriate to small–n research designs. Systematic process analysis represents theory-oriented explanation which construes the task of explanation as one of elucidating and testing a theory that identifies the main determinants of a broad class of outcomes and attaches special importance to specifying the mechanisms whereby those determinants influence the outcome (Hall 2006). The objective of process analysis is to identify the most important elements in the causal chain generating an outcome; in this study this refers to obstacles to establishing a functioning rule of law system. Therefore in the following analyses the objective is to elaborate how identified explanatory factors have led to the divergent democratisation outcomes, with a special focus on establishing functioning rule of law systems. Process analysis provides the opportunity to assess the relative strength of several explanatory factors that I have identified, since social science theory is most likely to advance when it focuses on a 'three-cornered fight' among a theory, a rival theory, and a set of empirical observations (Lakatos 1970).

The case studies also scrutinise the findings of fsQCA, which suggest that democratisation trajectories of Croatia and Serbia, though similar, came about through somewhat different configurations of causes. I explore the counterfactual assumption according to which Serbia would have not avoided slow democratisation even in the absence of conflicts that erupted, while the same could not be said of Croatia. The fsQCA findings according to which authoritarian party dominance is central to explaining stagnant democratisation also justify the theoretical focus on the causal mechanism of governance practices that developed in the period of regime change. Stating that governance practices established by authoritarian parties in the 1990s transformed into a legacy that continues to burden democratisation efforts in these countries twenty years later is a path dependent argument that can only be fully explored by applying the case study method. Finally, after identifying the gap in existing literature on post-communist democratisation in the context of conflict, the following chapters aim to illuminate ways in which violent conflict interacted with other explanatory factors to negatively affect democratisation prospects.

In the following chapters basic historical knowledge of events that led to the dissolution of Yugoslavia is assumed and I move directly into the moment of regime change. The beginning of the 1990s is conceptualised as the critical juncture which holds the key to explaining why these two countries still struggle to establish functioning rule of law systems. In order to do this, I focus on the 1990s, with the aim of reconstructing the key features of the political system that continue to plague democratisation efforts. Therefore both case studies start with an examination of the historical period between 1990 and 2000, while the second part of each case study is devoted to the period after 2000. In this second period I focus on establishing continuity with governance practices that were established during the 1990s. The overall objective is to delineate ways in which governance practices that produced concentration of power, conversion of political to economic power and the politicisation of state administration help connect explanatory factors to the outcome.

chapter six | croatia

In the period 1991 to 1995, Croatia fought a war on its territory which started as an insurrection within the Serbian minority but which evolved into a full blown war against the Serbia-led Yugoslav National Army after the proclamation of Croatia's independence (Rothschild 1993, Ramet 1996). This conflict had properties of a civil war since the immediate cause was the uprising of the ethnic Serb population in Croatia, but it was in essence instigated and guided from Serbia (Kasapović and Zakošek 1997). By the end of 1991, more than 400,000 citizens of Croatia were homeless and 40 per cent of the country's industry was destroyed (Ramet 2010). Some sources estimate the total damage of this economic breakdown at US$23 billion, which caused a sharp decline in the standard of living, high unemployment rates and various other forms of social hardship (Džihić and Segert 2012). In a vehement rejection of the Yugoslav political tradition as well as in search of a new source of political legitimacy, Croatia's political elite reached back into history and revived myths and symbols of its World War Two fascist state, further 'oiling the chain reaction of competing ethnic mobilisations' (Rothschild 1993: 259).

In 1992, after the conflict spread to Bosnia and Herzegovina where ethnic Croats represent one of three constitutive nations, Croatia became involved in a conflict outside its state borders. Before its involvement in Bosnia and Herzegovina, Croatia was seen as legitimately defending its territory and was clearly identified as a victim of Serbia's attack. However, after its involvement in Bosnia and Herzegovina, Croatia's image as a victim was replaced with that of a suspicious bully (Tripalo 1993). Already feeble, the international influence that Croatia had had before the war in Bosnia and Herzegovina was further weakened (Špegelj 1993)[1]. During 1995 Croatia regained almost all of its occupied territories through military actions Flash and Storm, after which military activities and violence on its territory ceased. Nevertheless, full civilian control over the entire state territory was reinstated only in January 1998 through peaceful reintegration of Eastern Slavonia. In total, in the period between 1991 and 1995 around 14,000 people were killed and another 35,000 were wounded (Granić 2005). The broader societal impact of the conflicts was immense; between 700,000 and 800,000 people are considered to have been war victims, which is an enormous number for a country with a population of 4.5 million (Nations in Transit Report 1997).

---

1. Špegelj was Defence Minister from August 1990 to July 1991. He held a number of high ranking executive posts in the emergent Croatian Army until the end of 1992 and is considered to be the main organiser of armed defences in Croatia (Granić 2005).

Croatia's disputed claim to statehood and the subsequent conflicts that erupted were key determinants of emergent political institutions in Croatia at the beginning of 1990s. The fact that the establishment of a nation state propels nationalist rhetoric was witnessed across the post-communist world at the beginning of the 1990s. Anti-communist forces that won the first multiparty elections in Eastern Europe were frequently riding on nationalist platforms (Kasapović 1995). Nationalism and communism are compatible ideologies in that both are collectivist, paternalist and conflictual (Puhovski 1990, 1993), which may in part explain why nationalism was so successful in replacing communism across Eastern Europe. However, in countries where the state-building project was unchallenged, other platforms more compatible with democracy were also present and competing with nationalist projects. Competitive party systems across Central Eastern Europe and the Baltic states quickly evolved into democratic party constellations and the initial nationalist appeals soon gave way to other topics on the political agenda.

By contrast, in Croatia state-building was a disputed and protracted process. Croatia's claim to statehood was rejected by its 12 per cent Serbian population, and a war ensued which led to an effective occupation of a third of its territory for a number of years (Čular 2000). Such an acute threat to statehood primarily meant a prolongation of national mobilisation around the aim of establishing the state and it effectively removed all other issues from the public agenda until the problem of disputed statehood was resolved. Time of war, in essence, means that people kill each other, and this context in which you can kill another person 'creates a carte blanche for the violation of all kinds of rights'.[2] In addition to that, a long term effect of the prolonged national mobilisation was the identification of the ruling Croatian Democratic Union party (CDU) with the movement for national independence and the new state itself. A particular dynamic evolved, where the borders between the national movement, the CDU party and the state got blurred (Kasapović 1995). The consequences of this dynamic for the mode of rule in Croatia were significant and long lasting, creating a permanent tension between the formally democratic institutional framework and undemocratic practices that were undermining that framework.[3] At the same time, after ending the occupation in 1995 and fully reintegrating its territory in 1998, Croatia's state-building project was successfully completed. This enabled the development of a glorified narrative surrounding the founding of the nation. The first president of Croatia, Franjo Tuđman, described his country as 'one of the oldest European nations' and declared the establishment of an independent Croatian state as the necessary outcome of a 'millennial struggle' of the Croatian people (Zakošek 2007). The nation-building discourse that developed was based in narratives of victory, long deserved historical justice and the unity of Croatian people, which helped strengthen the legitimacy of political elites throughout the 1990s.

---

2. Author's interview with Srđan Dvornik, interview No. 15, January 2011.

3. Author's interview with Mirjana Kasapović, Interview No. 1, November 2010.

The process of state-building therefore had two primary effects: the priority of establishing the state overrode democratic reform in the period 1990–1995, while the successful completion of the state-building project created reservoirs of legitimacy for political elites after 1995. However, political and economic reforms that constituted the new regime were taking place at the same time that war was being waged, unfolding far away from the public eye and democratic scrutiny. The sections that follow delineate authoritarian governance practices that emerged from this period of regime change.

War and Tuđman as the republican monarch[4]

Chapter 4 advanced several arguments about the effects war has had on the democratisation process. First of all, war reinforces authoritarian practices because it represents a state of emergency where the head of state is often required to make executive decisions in unfavourable, unclear and risky situations. Such decision-making situations reinforce a disregard for division among branches of government and instead promote centralisation and accumulation of executive power. Centralised executive power operating under a state of emergency in turn creates ample opportunities for abuse of power. In the early 1990s in Croatia emergent political institutions were not inspired by an idea of division of government, but rather by a unity of government.[5] Though in Croatia, unlike in Serbia, the constitution was drafted and ratified after the first multiparty election, the semi-presidential system was nevertheless designed according to the preference of Tuđman and CDU for strong presidential authority (Kasapović 2008). According to the 1990 Constitution, the president had wide-reaching powers as head of state and guardian of the constitution. In addition to that, the president appoints and recalls Prime Ministers, convenes sessions of government and may dissolve Parliament (ibid.). The choice of semi-presidential system of government greatly facilitated the concentration of power in Tuđman's hands and emasculated the emergent branches of government. Between 1990 and 1999 Tuđman was in effect the undisputed chief executive with full control over the government and parliament (ibid.).

In addition to the Constitution conferring broad powers on the office of the President, the division of power between branches of government was further diminished through various presidential councils that Tuđman established, in which everyone from the governor of the Central Bank to the president of the Supreme Court took part.[6] Tuđman abused the constitutional provision that allowed the president to 'create bodies to help him discharge his constitutional duties' in

---

4.   The term republican monarch was advanced by Kasapović (2008).

5.   Author's interview with Nenad Zakošek. Interview No. 14, January 2011.

6.   Author's interviews with Žarko Puhovski (Interview No. 6, November 2010) and Nenad Zakošek, (Interview No. 14, January 2011).

order to form entities, such as the Presidential Council for National Security, that were technically legal but effectively used to bypass parliament (Kusovac 2000). Mate Granić, Vice Prime Minister in the 1991 Gregurić government, remembers that Tuđman evolved a web of para-institutional bodies and privy councils which effectively ran the state (2005). Power was informalised and personalised,[7] and important decisions were made in 'informal party coteries' (Kasapović 2008: 61).

The highest level of decision making was thus at the same time fully centralised and held outside formal institutions, without competing power centres in government. In addition to that, in the early 1990s the Prime Minister and the government were often left out of the loop, finding out about important political decisions from the press, while key decisions were made among a close circle of Tuđman and his aides (Granić 2005). In other words, political power did not reside in institutions as designed by the Constitution. Instead, Tuđman exercised full control over party and state, leading to a mode of rule in which extreme concentration of political power was in the hands of one man (Čular 2000). The powers of the presidency increased so much that the government became a mere extension of his private office (Gallagher 2003).

Such a mode of rule had lasting consequences in Croatia, since rule by discretion is by definition antithetical to the rule of law. During 1991 Tuđman issued a number of executive decrees that either replaced or supplemented existing laws, including instituting martial courts that were empowered not only in military matters but also in some instances to deal with civilians (Uzelac 2000). In a plea against one of Tuđman's executive decrees the Constitutional Court ruled that the president may use his own discretion to decide whether there is an emergency state, and without declaring it, may issue emergency decrees with statutory force; that the president may impose limitation on human rights; and that the prohibition of retroactive application does not apply to his decrees.[8] Since during 1991 the Parliament was permanently in session, this ruling was contrary to Article 17 of the Constitution which stipulated that the president could restrict constitutional rights only if the Parliament was not in session (ibid.). Presidential executive decrees and martial courts remained operational in Croatia until 1996 (Uzelac 2000).

It is important to acknowledge however that these identified features of the political regime which deviated from the democratic constitutional order were at the same time dutifully enshrined in legislation. Zakošek considers this an important distinction from the situation in Serbia, where institutions were not so much instrumentalised as simply ignored and trampled upon.[9] The 1990 Christmas Constitution unequivocally defined Croatia as a democratic state based in the principles of separation of powers and the rule of law, which is important to establish since some analysts of Croatia's democratisation claim that liberal democracy was

---

7.   Author's interview with Žarko Puhovski. Interview No. 6, November 2010.

8.   Constitutional Court Decision, June 24, 1992, *Official Gazette* 49/92

9.   Author's interview with Nenad Zakošek. Interview No. 14, January 2011.

never the intended goal of regime change in the first place and should hence not be used as a benchmark for analysis. In Article 3 of the Constitution the principle of the rule of law is upheld as one of the basic values, while Article 4 states that:

> In the Republic of Croatia government shall be organised on the principle of separation of powers into the legislative, executive and judicial branches, but also limited by the constitutionally guaranteed right to local and regional self-government. The principle of separation of powers encompasses forms of mutual cooperation and reciprocal checks and balances as stipulated by the Constitution and law[10]. (Constitution of the Republic of Croatia, Article 4)

At the same time, numerous practices from the initial period in the 1990s attest to the widespread habit among political elites of placing themselves outside the law. Both on national and municipal level legislators were 'presumed to enact laws according to explicit directives from the party leadership of the CDU' (Nations in Transit Report 1997: 110). In addition to the already described centralisation of power, the instrumentalisation of political institutions was evident in the evolution of electoral legislation in Croatia. Not a single parliamentary election between 1990 and today has taken place under the same electoral rules. In her analysis of the results of the initial three rounds of parliamentary elections between 1990 and 1995 Kasapović found comprehensive evidence of gerrymandering (1995, 2008). This kind of behaviour fortified the public perception that 'elections have little to do with democracy since they are only a powerful tool serving incumbents in keeping power' (Čular 2000). In addition to that, the war was used as an electoral strategy. The timing of the parliamentary election in 1995 was set so that the CDU would benefit from the just-completed military actions Flash and Storm (ibid.). Surveys of public support for CDU showed that the party enjoyed unprecedented levels of voter support in 1995 and 1996 (Lamza Posavec 2000).

The chief consequence of war for division of power among branches of government was the marginalisation of parliament and instrumentalisation of the judiciary. In Croatia during the early 1990s it was difficult to establish whether the seat of the legislature was the parliament – as was envisioned by the constitution – or whether the president was the lawmaker in the polity (Nations in Transit Report 1997). The judiciary system of Croatia that was being set up in 1990 did not have a tradition of independence (Uzelac 1992). On the other hand, judges in Croatia prior to 1990 were relatively well trained and independent professionals (Primorac 1994, Uzelac 2000b). This could have been due to the fact that in Yugoslavia the judiciary was not recognised as a separate branch of government, 'it was generally politically insignificant, and therefore politics mostly let it alone' (Uzelac 2000b: 2). Though potential for judiciary reform existed in Croatia at the beginning of 1990, it was not taken up; instead after regime change 60 per cent of judges were replaced at all levels of the system (Primorac 1994). Between 1990 and 1991 around 200

---

10. The full text of Croatia's Constitution in English is available on the website of its Parliament: http://www.sabor.hr/Default.aspx?art=2407. Last accessed August 18, 2012.

judges,[11] amounting to one fifth of the total number, left the judiciary (Uzelac 2001).

One crucial segment of the newly evolving judiciary was the selection of members for the High Judicial Council, the body that appoints all judges including those for the Supreme Court. The first election for members of the High Judicial Council took place in 1994. The fact that it happened so late after regime change is indicative in itself. According to acting legislation, the Lower House of Parliament nominated candidates upon collecting suggestions from the Supreme Court, the Ministry of Justice and other bodies, while the Upper House had the authority to appoint them. Notwithstanding this regulation, the thirteen initially elected members of the High Judicial Council were not those nominated by judges through secret ballot, but rather those esteemed to be loyal to the government and agreed upon in another para-institutional committee set up by Tuđman (Primorac 1994, Uzelac 2001). At the beginning of the 1990s loyalty was considered the crucial characteristic of a good judge, rather than expertise or independence (Primorac 1994, Uzelac 2001). Milan Vuković, President of the Supreme Court since 1992, was infamous for stating that Croats could not commit war crimes. Similarly, Bejaković (2002) claims that in that period mass dismissals of civil servants occurred on account of their political convictions or ethnicity, while new appointments were made on the basis of candidates' ethnicity, politics, location or status as personal friends. Such practices of cronyism and nepotism and informal influencing amounted to a thorough politicisation of the state.

Human rights groups at the time reported cases where human rights of ethnic Serbs were violated, and since this was happening outside occupied areas or conflict zones, in a sense war was fought on the entire territory of Croatia.[12] Granić (2005) recounts that during 1991 the government was receiving reports of eviction and unlawful confiscation of homes and other property from Serbs, as well as information about more serious human rights abuses. Civil society groups documented these incidents and tried to help individuals whose civil rights were being withheld (Dvornik 2009). A notorious crime happened in December 1991 when members of the Croatian police killed the Serbian family Zec in Zagreb; the mother, father and a 12-year-old daughter. Even though the killers were apprehended soon after the crime was committed, due to a procedural mistake they were released and never stood trial (Ivančić 1994).[13] It stands relatively undisputed that the so-called procedural mistake was in fact perpetrated intentionally by Croatia's legal institutions (Granić 2005). One of the killers subsequently progressed to a

---

11. This is a conservative estimate of the Croatian Legal Centre based on information provided in the Official Gazette, quoted in Uzelac 2001.

12. Author's interview with Srđan Dvornik, interview No. 15, January 2011.

13. Another dark tone is added to the story by the fact that while the crime happened in late 1991, the facts of the crime, together with the acrimonious court epilogue, only became public in April 1994 when Stjepan Mesić explicitly referred to the murder of the Zec family in an interview with satirical weekly *Feral Tribune* (Ivančić 1994).

high military rank in the Croatian Army (Butković 2004[14]). The murder of the Zec family was an early example of blatant abuse of the judiciary. A strikingly parallel sequence of events happened in the case of the Gospić massacre, when Croatian special police forces tortured, raped and killed Serbian civilians. At the behest of US Ambassador Zimmerman, Tuđman issued an order to arrest the military officer in charge. Yet in the next instance, Gojko Šušak, Tuđman's close aide and confidante, ensured that the man was arrested not by the police but by the army, and released not long after that (Granić 2005).

A parallel disciplining was going on in the muting of the political opposition. Under circumstances when national independence was fought for, what would an alternative political programme be about? The overarching societal consensus that emerged in the context of war suppressed any pluralist tendencies.[15] Many post-communist countries faced weak and non-institutionalised party systems at the onset of regime change, but this was followed by a fairly quick structuration of party space after the first multi-party election. In the case of Croatia this process was postponed (Šiber 1993). Instead, the Government of Democratic Unity was established in July 1991, effectively removing political opposition. Nearly all parliamentary parties joined this government united under CDU leadership, and that government stayed in office until the parliamentary election in August 1992. In addition, the trade unions signed the agreement with the government pledging social peace during the war, effectively silencing any societal contention (Granić 2005). While public spheres in, for instance, Poland or Hungary at the time were pluralising under the influence of intense political party competition, in Croatia there was a monolithisation of the public sphere, with only one version of the present, the past and the future of the country. In a deliberate manipulative move, the consensus across party lines that had been established due to war circumstances was broadened and reinterpreted into undisputable authority of the government, while every deviation from that position was interpreted as deliberate destabilisation of the state (Kasapović 1995).

Unfortunately the political opposition largely acquiesced to this stretched scope of consensus, contributing in that way to a weakening of political pluralism (Kasapović 1995: 23). Even though they had won a third of parliamentary seats in 1990, the Social Democratic Party (SDP) managed to make themselves virtually invisible in parliament.[16] This invalidation of the political opposition was also in part due to a complete delegitimation of the left in the initial period of the 1990s. While the left lost ground across the entire post-communist world, the disintegration of the left in Croatia was even more severe because there it was equated with Yugoslavism. When Yugoslavia became the military aggressor, in

---

14. 'Coldblooded murder', article for *Jutarnji List* daily newspaper, April 24, 2004
    http://www.jutarnji.hr/hladnokrvno-ubojstvo/7348/. Last accessed August 23, 2012.

15. Author's interview with Žarko Puhovski. Interview No. 6, November 2010.

16. Author's interview with Srđan Dvornik. Interview No. 15, January 2011.

Croatia the left became implicitly or explicitly blamed for the war, which made it vulnerable to accusation of acting against state interests (ibid.). A statement by SDP party member Marin Jurjević made in 1993 illustrates the atmosphere at the beginning of the 1990s: 'war is not a justification for postponing democracy; we have had enough of the situation where every critical word that does not suit certain individuals is branded as unpatriotic.' (1993).[17]

While the wartime context had inflicted damage on the fledgling constitutional order and rule of law, it also spurred on corruption and criminalisation in the government. Political regimes that are built on high level nationalist mobilisation are at the same time weakly accountable (Hellman *et al* 2000). Corruption is a problem in any state-building context since everyday politics is shrouded in highly symbolic rhetoric, setting aside mundane questions as to how public resources are spent. Adding to this, large scale privatisation processes have been another fertile ground for the spread of corruption (ibid.). Many studies have shown that across the board, post-communist countries experienced problems with corruption after regime change, from Bulgaria and Romania to Slovenia and the Czech Republic. In non-conflict settings the success in combating corruption depended on domestic public scrutiny, pressure from below as well as international pressure. War on the other hand amplified conditions favourable for the spread of corruption (Štulhofer 1998). Raising the stakes and increasing decision-making risk creates a context where no questions are asked, and it becomes easy to divert resources, trade in information and benefit loyalists. The mode of rule that silenced the political opposition and instrumentalised the judiciary and legislature was able to go about business in a political system with few functional checks and balances.

The privatisation process in Croatia was fully centralised in the hand of the state run Privatisation Fund, which had extensive discretionary rights to decide on a case-by-case basis (Bićanić 1993). Legislation regulating privatisation was adopted in April 1991, amid full-blown war on Croatia's territory. Hence there was almost no discussion prior to its enactment (ibid.), and large parts of the population were completely left out of it.[18] Though state-building generally postpones economic reform, in Croatia it created a context in which important economic restructuring was happening during war and extraordinary political circumstances, far away from the public eye. It was not before 1992 that opposition parties managed to put privatisation on the agenda in Parliament, and subsequently the press took up topics of corruption in privatisation (ibid.). In February 1993 the government issued a statement saying privatisation crime must stop and the rule of law should be upheld (ibid.) Analysts were warning of abuse of public office, procedural irregularities and political influence over privatisation decisions (Franičević 1997, Čučković 1997; quoted in Štulhofer 1998). In autumn 1994 Parliament adopted a resolution stating that it condemned breaking the law and

---

17. Information from AIM Press, November 3, 1993.

18. Author's interview with Žarko Puhovski. Interview No. 6, November 2010.

abuse of power in the privatisation process. However, as in the case of the 1993 government statement, no concrete actions were stipulated to stop further abuses (Grubiša 1995).

In 1995 the CDU government publicly acknowledged that serious irregularities occurred in the privatisation process and announced a revision of no less than 1,000 privatisation cases (Čengić 2000). The following year the Privatisation Fund identified the financing of bank loans with company money as the most frequent type of corrupt privatisations (ibid). Management buyouts were arranged so that banks issued them loans to buy shares in a company, which the management repaid with the company's money. At the same time, while company shares were used by banks as collateral when issuing loans, banks did not acquire ownership of any of the shares unless the loan defaulted. As Grubiša aptly summarised, state banks were issuing state guarantees for the sale of state enterprises.[19] In effect, individuals with information and connections could become large business owners without any capital and without taking on any business risk. This privatisation model encouraged management of former state companies to reduce the price of company shares or misrepresent the value of the company. Market valuations of companies prior to privatisations were not conducted (Čengić 2000). Adding insult to injury, after being bought by their former managers, companies were often stripped of assets and sold for their property value. Instead of a production class, a parasitical class was created.[20]

By 1996 there were six changes and amendments to privatisation legislation (Čučković 1997; quoted in Štulhofer 1998). In addition to that, the government interpreted criminal cases as occasional irregularities rather than features built into the privatisation model. The widespread irregularities of the privatisation process evolved into a moral bomb that influenced society's overall negative assessments of regime change (Županov 1994). In 1996, 71 per cent of respondents thought that the ruling political party reaped most benefits from the privatisation process, while 82 per cent thought that workers in privatised enterprises came out of the process the worst off (Štulhofer 1998). While only 23 per cent agreed that the privatisation process contributed to the transformation of Croatia into a modern, market-oriented and democratic society, a large majority of 77 per cent thought that several families acquired business empires under suspicious circumstances (ibid.). The privatisation process in Croatia played the role of grossly unjust initial capital accumulation, creating an illegitimate economic elite that was there to stay. Its effect was a widespread perception according to which the elites had committed a gross injustice to society (Kasapović 2009).

Apart from problems with corruption, during the war criminal groups infiltrated public and state institutions as a consequence of illegal arms trade. In October 1991 the UN Security Council introduced an embargo on weapons import, which

---

19. Author's interview with Damir Grubiša. Interview No. 3, November 2010.

20. Ibid.

meant that almost from the start Croatia started buying arms in illegal markets and smuggling them into the country (Granić 2005). The resulting collusion between the criminal milieu on the one hand and economic and political elites on the other was reduced after the war, but not dismantled (Kasapović 2009). Instead, members of the criminal milieu have in the meantime laundered money and slowly transformed themselves into legal businessmen (ibid.). Notwithstanding that, the web of criminal networks resurfaced in Croatia every once in a while, most recently in 2008 with the killing of two journalists in Zagreb.

The analysis in the previous sections aimed to establish causal chains between the context of conflict emerging from disputed statehood and the mode of rule that emerged, premised on subverting the rule of law through a concentration of executive power, the conversion of political to economic power and a politicisation of the state. If the rule of law is grounded in a limitation of government power, judiciary independence and overall compliance with the law, the state of emergency during war adversely affected all these dimensions as well as creating favourable conditions for the spread of corruption, abuse of public office and a criminalisation of the state. Taking all this on board, it is still not plausible to claim that wartime circumstances produced rule of law violations; for that, political action is required. However, before analysing emergent political elites in 1990s Croatia, let me introduce some structural features of the socioeconomic environment of the time.

In the early 1990s the entire population was infused with nationalist feelings and the mood could be best described as one of total nationalist mobilisation (Pusić 1994). To rephrase Walesa's famous remark,[21] the Croatian population resembled a fruit-shake rather than a fruit salad. By the time of the first multiparty elections, instead of focusing on a political rebirth, Croats feared impending war (Kusovac 2000). In 1990 when the Communist party of Croatia decided to hold multiparty elections, this was not publicly interpreted as a milestone, nor did it inspire Croatian citizens to demand rapid democratisation.[22] Instead democracy was introduced as a solution to a different, more pressing problem of the Yugoslav federation (ibid.). 'The decision of the SKH-SDP in December 1989 to hold multiparty elections for Croatia's communist reformers represented an exit from a nasty situation rather than a preferred democratic solution' (Čular 2000: 32). On the other hand, as shown in Chapter 3, Croatia was characterised by comparatively good modernisation preconditions and a national-accommodative communist regime, where the Communist party was forced to accommodate appeals to national autonomy and square the circle between national demands on the one hand and official communist ideology on the other. This ideological dichotomy provided for some pluralism in the political sphere.

---

21. Walesa is credited with comparing the post-communist condition with trying to make a fish tank out of a fish soup.

22. Author's interview with Tonči Kursar. Interview No. 4, November 2010.

In addition to that, the Yugoslav practice of self-management provided Croatia with historical experience that could have served to pluralise the public sphere and engender democratic pressure from below. In the late 1980s the interest structure in the economic sphere was to an extent pluralist. Yugoslav practice of self-management meant that production was organised through modalities different to that of Soviet type state-socialism, allowing for a complex system of interest representation and articulation (Zakošek 1995). At the same time, the economic sphere was not outside communist party control (Dvornik 2009), so these practices of interest articulation were not really analogous to Western-style neo-corporatism. Nonetheless, it seems safe to assume that preconditions for liberalisation of political culture in 1989 were at least as favourable as those in Visegrad countries.

However, in combination with the described context of conflict emerging from disputed statehood on the one hand and the resulting CDU dominance on the other, decisive liberalisation of the public sphere and pluralisation of interest articulation were slowed down. By the mid-1990s some pluralisation, as well as attempts at corporatist coordination of labour and capital, were present but the predominant modality of interest aggregation had become clientelism (Zakošek 1995). Under the state of emergency during war, democracy continued to be grounded in unquestioned support for the leading political option (Posavec 1993). In that sense the outgoing communist ideology and the incoming nationalism had a lot in common: both were collectivist, paternalistic and conflictual ideologies, grounded in the concept of struggle.[23] The class enemy was simply replaced with an ethnic enemy.

The key difference between nationalism of the kind that was present all over post-communist Europe in the first years of regime change, and the one that characterised Croatia, was the difference between words and action: here, people were actually being killed because of their ethnicity (ibid.). When the killing started, 'crazy paranoids became prophets', fuelling a chain reaction of nationalist mobilisation.[24] Wartime circumstances directly and indirectly suspended a wide range of civil and political liberties, further thwarting the pluralisation of the public sphere necessary for democratisation[25]. Croatia's society was thoroughly militarised, with warriors and warriors' mothers occupying centre stage in the nation's evolving mythology.[26] In that context a strong psychological bond was formed between the CDU and segments of the voter population such as war veterans and their families, refugees, displaced persons, Croats in Bosnia and

---

23. Author's interview with Žarko Puhovski. Interview No. 6, November 2010.

24. Author's interviews with Žarko Puhovski (Interview No. 6, November 2010) and Srđan Dvornik (Interview No. 15, January 2011).

25. Author's interviews with Dejan Jović (Interview No. 2, November 2010) and Goran Čular (Interview No. 5, November 2010).

26. Author's interview with Dejan Jović. Interview No. 2, November 2010.

Herzegovina, as well as populations in war-affected areas, based in the joint struggle for Croatia's independence. In a second step this highly emotional bond between party and voter was reinforced through preferential treatment, benefits and subsidies from the state budget.[27] That way an almost unbreakable bond had been created, charged with symbolic meaning as well as material benefits (Čular 2000). These key groups have become unrelenting CDU supporters across decades and together they form a client-patron axis that has helped transfer many features of wartime rule into subsequent years. The next sections shift the focus of the analysis to the late 1990s.

Authoritarian politics of the late 1990s

Over the initial three rounds of elections Croatia developed characteristics of a party system with a dominant party (Kasapović 1995). The CDU share of mandates in the 1990, 1992 and 1995 elections were 68.8 per cent, 63 per cent and 59.1 per cent respectively. Apart from a strong dominance in parliament and Tuđman's overarching persona as President, the CDU benefited from the atmosphere of state of emergency, across-the-board political consensus and a largely muted opposition. In other words, regime change in Croatia took place under the political monopoly of one party (Zakošek 1995). Rather than operating in a competitive multi-party setting, the CDU 'aspired to rule in the spirit of an all-encompassing political force that symbolises national unity' (Zakošek 1995: 29). The CDU used its dominant position in the political system to effectively monopolise political power, as well as turn it into economic and political capital (ibid.). Ruling under circumstances where no questions were asked contributed to the abuse of power and the spread of political corruption.

The third parliamentary election was held right after military operations in 1995 that ended the occupation of Croatia's territories.[28] In this election the CDU secured another majority in parliament and a safe period of rule for another four years, while Tuđman won the presidential election in 1997. The period of CDU rule from 1995 to 1999 was crucial for the long term democratisation trajectory of Croatia. In this period the CDU managed to transfer many of the features of its mode of rule that were forged during war into peacetime politics, with minor modifications. Even though the country was no longer under external threat from Yugoslavia or internal threat of another insurrection (primary causes of the state of emergency in the early 1990s), the crucial elements of wartime mode of rule were retained.

---

27. Author's interview with Mirjana Kasapović. Interview No. 1, November 2010.

28. What was not publicly known at the time was that during and after the military actions in August and September of 1995, more than 600 civilians were killed, more than 22,000 houses burned, and around 150,000 people (mostly Serbs) left Croatia. (Croatian Helsinki Committee Report quoted in *ZamirZine* web portal. Available online at http://www.zamirzine.net/spip.php?article10622. Last accessed August 18, 2012)

The 1995 election was different in that by that time it was publicly known that the political and economic transformation was mired in corruption and crime. Under peacetime circumstances this would erode the legitimacy of the political party in power and lead to their replacement with another party or coalition, as indeed happened in a number of post-communist countries. In Croatia the context of military victory replenished the source of CDU legitimacy and pushed aside concerns over widespread abuse of power and the corrupt privatisation process. This election was crucial for the CDU to carry over its mode of rule into the peacetime period when no real justification existed for continuing centralisation of power, instrumentalisation of institutions and other actions undermining the rule of law.

By the late 1990s, international assessments of the political system in Croatia had become more numerous, and overall they characterised the political system as having strong authoritarian tendencies. In the period 1995 to 1997 two events in Zagreb brought Tuđman's authoritarian mode of rule into particularly sharp light. The first one was the Zagreb Crisis. A provision in the 1990 Constitution stipulated that elected mayors in the City of Zagreb had to be confirmed by the President.[29] Tuđman abused this authority to veto the election of four opposition candidates to the seat of mayor of Zagreb, and installed his preferred candidate instead (Kusovac 2000, Granić 2005, Ramet 2010). The CDU used bribes and blackmail to destabilise the opposition and, where necessary, bought off opposition deputies. They gained control over Zagreb City Council in April 1997 by bribing two opposition deputies from the Croatian Peasant Party (Cviić 1997). Soon after, Tuđman tried to shut down Zagreb-based Radio 101, a well-known source of opposition to his government (ibid.). Over 100,000 people protested in Zagreb against Tuđman's decision not to prolong the radio's concession rights. Tuđman was in the US at the time and had ordered a police crackdown on the protesters by phone (Granić 2005). The police did not intervene however, echoing the circumstances that would also contribute to Milošević's downfall. On his return to Zagreb, Tuđman delivered a by-now infamous speech where he equated political opposition and civil society activities with threats to Croatia's sovereignty:

> We shall not allow these Yugo-communist leftovers, political dilettantes, mindless chickens,[30] who do not realise what is actually at stake in Croatia and the world, with all sorts of regionalist plans. We shall not allow those who align with the black devil against Croatia's liberty and independence; not only with black, but green and yellow devils as well! We shall not allow this to those who align with all those against Croatia's independence; not just align, they offer themselves to them! Not only offer, they sell themselves, for

---

29. The Constitution actually gave the President the prerogative to confirm elected county heads, but since Zagreb was administratively a county, this gave the president prerogative to confirm elected mayors of Zagreb. I thank Professor Kasapović for this clarification.

30. Thanks to Paul Stubbs for the difficult translation of 'smušenjaci' into 'mindless chickens'.

Judas's coins! They brag about receiving donations from all world centres. And they align with everyone from fundamentalist extremists to all sorts of false prophets, pseudo-democratic illusionists who preach grand ideas about human rights and freedom of the media. Yes, we made our country Croatia, also for human rights, and for media freedom. But for human rights primarily of the majority of Croats! Of course we will, with our Croatian freedom and democracy, secure these human rights and media freedom for the minority too. But we shall not allow outsiders to enforce solutions upon us. Croatia shall not be anybody's colony![31] (Franjo Tuđman speech 1997, author's translation)

Several features of this speech bear remarkable testimony to Tuđman's mode of rule in the late 1990s. First of all, his discourse is based in scaremongering. He is not identifying the threat and making it specific, but rather uses highly suggestive symbolic language of threat and impending danger over hard won state independence. He invokes the long struggle for statehood, the centuries of servitude under different empires, and implies that there are those among us who wish for this to happen again. Secondly, his discussion of human rights reveals an ethnic conception of the nation and the state. Contrary to the essence of the liberal conception of human rights, his understanding of rights is grounded in the distinction between ethnic Croats versus everyone else. He considers Croats as having a prior claim to these rights over other ethnicities living in Croatia. Thirdly, this speech reveals his conception of political opposition and the role of civil society more generally; any groups not aligned with official state positions are considered traitors (reference to Judas) and foreign mercenaries with agendas that jeopardise Croatia's hard won statehood. The monolithisation of the public sphere and de-legitimisation of opposition that was achieved at the beginning of the 1990s is thus re-established, and dissenting views to those of the government are again interpreted as a threat to the state.

Tuđman's authoritarian governance practices were not met with strong opposition. The political opposition was suffering internal divisions, with parties bickering among themselves and unable to capitalise on general disappointment with economic and social conditions (Cviić 1997). While the changed circumstances of the late 1990s should have allowed for a more competitive game in the electoral arena, Tuđman and the CDU continued to hold a predominant position in the political system. In the Duverger sense of the term, CDU was the dominant party that marked the 1990s 'with their mode of rule, rhetoric, worldview and methods, [...] and this proved to be very difficult to dismantle'.[32] As a result, obstacles to strengthening the rule of law and fighting corruption identified in the early 1990s remained.

---

31. Segment of a speech held at the Zagreb Airport Pleso, April 1997, accessed at the web portal Index.hr. Available online at http://www.index.hr/video/film.aspx?id=2528. Last accessed March 31, 2011.

32. Author's interview with Mirjana Kasapović. Interview No. 1, November 2010.

The US State Department Report from 1999 stated that judiciary in Croatia was under the sway of executive government and political influence, and that courts had such large backlogs that the citizens' right to a fair trial was seriously jeopardised.[33] According to some estimates, outside interventions into the judiciary were worse than those inflicted by the state of emergency during war (Uzelac 2001). Problems which emerged in the judiciary after the 1990–1991 purge and the subsequent staffing based on political loyalties were not amended in subsequent years. In 1999 the mandate of the Constitutional Court expired and a new set of eight judges was appointed by Parliament. The CDU pushed through their list of candidates which included five eminent CDU party members, two judges associated with the opposition, and one independent expert (Uzelac 2001). This was the continuation of political practice from the early 1990s, when the election of members of High Judicial Council was hijacked from the judiciary in a similar manner. In March 1999, the Minister of Justice and Vice Prime Minister Ramljak resigned, issuing a statement saying that he vehemently opposed proposed reforms in public administration which included the formation of strong para-institutional bodies around President Tudman (ibid.). He considered those reforms as leading towards the creation of non-transparent structures that marginalise the rule of law and government itself (ibid.).

According to an empirical study into corruption undertaken by the World Bank in the late 1990s, Croatia exhibited high state capture, and relatively low administrative corruption (2000). State capture in essence stands for practices of influencing the formation of laws and regulations so that they enable extracting rents from the state for a specific group in exchange for bribes, illicit equity stakes, informal control rights and so on (ibid.). In the period 1996–2000 there were 475 cases of corruption reported to relevant authorities, 207 cases reached trial stage and 171 resulted in conviction. However, in only 11.1 per cent of convictions did the Court impose imprisonment, and a number of cases were dismissed by courts due to the expiry of the statute of limitation (GRECO[34] Report 2002). Overall, in Croatia very few cases of corruption resulted in conviction and the sentencing policy was very mild (ibid.) According to the US State Department,

> The extensive constitutional powers of the presidency, the blurring of the roles and functions of the CDU party with those of the government and the presidency, CDU control of television and the continuing concentration of power within the one-party central government combined to make the country's

---

33. Report is available online, http://www.state.gov/g/drl/rls/hrrpt/1999/323.htm. Last accessed August 18, 2012.

34. The Group of States against Corruption (GRECO) was established in 1999 by the Council of Europe to monitor States' compliance with the organisation's anti-corruption standards. Information available online at http://www.coe.int/t/dghl/monitoring/greco/general/about_en.asp. Last accessed August 18, 2012.

nominally democratic system in reality authoritarian. (US State Department Human Rights Report for Croatia 1999).

At the end of 1999, Croatia was considered 'an autocratic regime, rife with nepotism, corruption, and economic incompetence, run by an egotistic ruler who was obsessed with historical injustices and worldwide conspiracies against his nation, and who was backed by an obedient party' (Kusovac 2000: 57). The regime was characterised by domestic and international scholars as either fully authoritarian or as some sort of a blended authoritarian democracy (Ćular 2000, Vachudova 2005, Schimmelfennig, Engert and Knobel 2006, Kasapović 2009). During the 1990s Croatia's international standing was further worsened due to its involvement in the war in Bosnia and its failure to fully cooperate with the ICTY tribunal in The Hague (Kasapović 2009). In addition, economically the country was in dire straits; in 1999 Croatia had a negative GDP growth of 0.4 per cent, with the unemployment rate at 19 per cent and with industrial input not reaching two thirds of the industrial output the country had in 1990 (Zakošek 2002).

The 2000 pro-democracy turn

After coming close to annihilation in 1992 when it barely made it into parliament, the Social Democratic Party (SDP) was over time slowly winning back votes. Figure 6.1 shows the per cent of votes in the legislature for SDP, and the Croatian Social Liberal Party (CSLP) across the four cycles of parliamentary elections between 1990 and 2000.

Figure 6.1: Per cent of votes for SDP and CLSP, 1990–2000 parliamentary elections

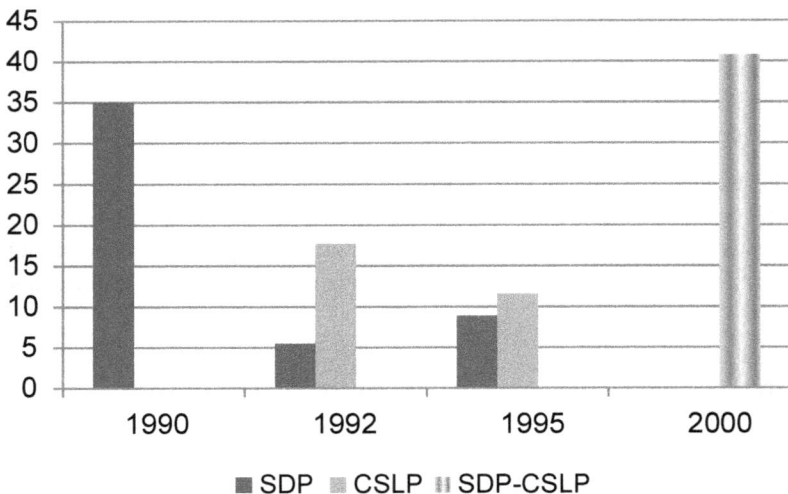

Source: Parties and Elections Database (http://www.parties-and-elections.eu/)

As can be seen from Figure 6.1, SDP fell from winning a third of parliamentary seats in the first multiparty election, to barely making it into parliament in 1992, followed by a modest recovery in 1995. The CSLP on the other hand only contested 1992 and 1995 elections on its own, with dwindling support over time. In 2000 the two parties formed a coalition and managed to win 40.8 per cent of votes,[35] inaugurating the pro-democratic government that would significantly advance democratisation in Croatia (Schimmelfennig, Engert and Knobel 2006). After the election the SDP and CSLP formed the government together with four other smaller parties: the Croatian People's Party, the Croatian Peasant Party, the Liberal party and the Istrian Democratic Forum, creating a complex government coalition of six parties. Until this election in 2000 Croatia had no experience with coalition governments, all previous governments being majority CDU governments (Kasapović 2005).

In the 2000 election, an oversized coalition of six parties came to power for the first time, producing immediate positive effects towards pluralisation in the public sphere and a democratisation of decision making in government.[36] The European Commission's Stabilisation and Association Process Report for Croatia established that 'the political environment in Croatia changed radically with the advent of the new leadership' (2002: 19). The programmatic priorities of the coalition signed in the pre-election agreement were to abolish semi-presidentialism and strengthen Parliament, depoliticise the army and police forces, strengthen civilian control over the secret service, decentralise the state, revise suspect privatisation cases, and pursue cases of corruption and abuse of power (1999).[37] The coalition's programmatic priorities serve as an apt summary of the key obstacles to democratisation in Croatia at the start of 2000.

The 2000 election proved to be a watershed event in the political development of the country. The fact that Tuđman was no longer president and that the CDU was no longer the dominant power put an end to the blurring of powers across branches of government and helped bolster independence of parliament, government and the judiciary *vis-à-vis* the president (US State Department Report 2000[38]). Crucially, the January government[39] initiated a process of constitutional reform that strengthened parliamentarism. The most important constitutional

---

35. On its own, SDP won 29 per cent, still not overtaking CDU, as the most popular party won 31 per cent of the votes (Dolenec 2009).

36. Author's interview with Mirjana Kasapović. Interview No. 1, November 2010.

37. Information from an article in Croatian daily news magazine Vjesnik, dated December 2, 1999. I accessed the article online in October 2009, but it is no longer available since the magazine has shut down.

38. Available online at http://www.state.gov/g/drl/rls/hrrpt/2000/eur/716.htm. Last accessed August 18, 2012.

39. Since the government was formed on January 3, 2011, I adopt the shorthand 'January government' to refer to the SDP-led six party coalition government that was in office until 2003.

change was the abolition of the powers of the president in the executive, while the president's power to independently bring decrees with the power of law was also radically revised (Kasapović 2008). This constitutional reform had important positive effects on the strengthening of the principle of division of powers among branches of government.

After the election in 2000 both the national program and the action plan for fighting corruption were adopted, with the main goals of strengthening the rule of law, establishing a special anti-corruption unit within the State Prosecution Office, strengthening police departments in charge of crimes of corruption, and reforming public administration, among other measures. Inaugurating a new approach to policymaking, policy measures were adopted in consultation with a broad array of stakeholders, at the initiative of nongovernmental organisations (GRECO 2002). USKOK, the Office for the Prevention of Corruption and Organised Crime, was set up as a special unit within the State Prosecution Office and became operational in December 2001. These efforts signalled commitment of the January government to tackling corruption. Since the worst breaches of justice occurred within the privatisation process, in 2001 the Parliament authorised the State Audit Office to audit the legality of the completed privatisation processes. This was a declarative measure however, since it was clear that by the time the SAO finished its work, the prosecution of most offences would have been precluded by the statutes of limitation (GRECO 2002).

Notwithstanding its initial reform resolve, by the end of the January government term the overall impression was that reform in courts and prosecutor's offices was slow and resulted in few improvements (US State Department Report 2003).[40] Similarly, the EU was not convinced about Croatia's efforts in the fight against corruption and organised crime (European Commission SAP Report 2003). With respect to the coalition government's efforts in fighting corruption, GRECO reported that 'a vast grey area of non-reported cases existed and very few cases actually resulted in conviction. In addition, the sentencing policy was deemed very mild while a predominant number of convictions on corruption charges resulted in probation sentences' (2002: 4).

As a result, while the coalition succeeded in constitutional reform that removed features of the semi-presidential system and strengthened parliamentarism, the key failure of the January government turned out to be its inability to deal with the inheritance of the corrupt privatisation process (Kasapović 2009) and to dismantle the CDU mode of rule. Already very soon after the 2000 election some domestic analysts stated that the January government was hesitating over dismantling corruption and crime within the state (Kregar 2000[41]). According to him, either the

---

40. US State Department report available online at http://www.state.gov/g/drl/rls/hrrpt/2003/27831. htm. Last accessed August 18, 2012.

41. Interview with Josip Kregar for the bi-weekly satirical magazine *Feral Tribune*, published June 24, 2000. Available online at the Digital Archive of *Feral Tribune* http://www.idoc.ba/digitalarchive/

high level crime and corruption would be *socialised*, with broader society bearing the costs, or the committed crimes would be personalised and those responsible held accountable (ibid.). In retrospect it is clear that the January government did not dismantle the 1990s mode of rule and instead *socialised* high level corruption, state politicisation and continued abuses of public office. By leaving much of the established structure of economic and political power in place they reduced their own power as well as predetermined their failure to win the following parliamentary elections. More importantly, they failed to address the major source of mistrust in political elites that was eroding the legitimacy of the political system. Hence they not only lost the subsequent election, but helped reinvigorate the 1990s mode of rule upon their removal.

Notwithstanding these weaknesses, 2001 was the first year that Croatia was scored as a free country according to Freedom House criteria. There was marked improvement in overall democratic climate and, more importantly, the dividing lines between branches of government started to exert themselves. Due to the fact that Croatia had for the first time a prime minister and a president from different political parties, and that the government was composed of a six party coalition, a plurality of political voices was represented in the public arena, and institutional autonomy was being bolstered. Relations with the media and civil society also improved significantly. These were the effects of the January government that showed up in various indices, demonstrating democratic advances in Croatia between 2000 and 2003. Apart from that, the January government made marked improvements in Croatia's foreign relations and the country's international standing more broadly. During this government Croatia became a member of the WTO, signed the Central European Free Trade Agreement (CEFTA), joined NATO's Partnership for Peace, signed the Stabilisation and Association Agreement and became a candidate country for the European Union. This new foreign policy of Croatia received a strong boost at the Zagreb Summit in November 2000, where the President of the European Commission met with heads of state of Western Balkan countries and announced that 'democracy is about to carry the day throughout this region' (Final Declaration of the Zagreb Summit 2000[42]). The Zagreb Summit and the French presidency that year in effect initiated Croatia's accession to the EU (Maki 2008).

Schimmelfennig argued that the EU starts exerting influence on political and economic reforms only after a crucial reshuffling of domestic political forces has brought democratic, EU-oriented parties to power. Once the process of EU integration is under way, a lock-in effect is created through which the political costs of trying to divert from further integration become prohibitively high. Hence

---

public/index.cfm?fuseaction=serve&ElementId=587154. Last accessed August 19, 2012.

42. The text is available online on the European Union Enlargement website http://ec.europa.eu/enlargement/enlargement_process/accession_process/how_does_a_country_join_the_eu/sap/zagreb_summit_en.htm. Last accessed August 18, 2012.

even those parties whose political practice has up to then been incompatible with a democratic framework of government develop a strong incentive to Europeanise and stay on track with European integration. The case of the reformed CDU government that came to power in 2003 supports this argument, as the following sections show.

Tuđman died in 1999, and the CDU was in disarray during the parliamentary election that took place in 2000. After Tuđman's death Ivo Sanader became party leader but internally the party was undergoing power struggles. For the first time in the role of political opposition after the January 2000 election, the CDU parliamentary strategy was initially very confrontational. The initiation of EU integration process in Croatia had meant strong pressure from the EU towards improving Croatia's cooperation with the ICTY and the prosecution of war crimes more generally, and the CDU capitalised on the public outrage these policies provoked. Probably the most serious crisis occurred at the beginning of 2001, related to the murder of the Zec family referred to earlier in this chapter. An official investigation into that case was reinstated in late 2000, and warrants for the arrest of those involved were issued in February 2001. In response, the CDU harnessed the revolt within the war veterans' population to stage a large public protest in Split, ostensibly in the honour of Mirko Norac, one of the accused who had in the meantime become a Croatian Army General. According to some analysts, at that moment the CDU hoped to topple the SDP-led coalition (Babić 2003[43]). This did not happen; instead the case went down in history as the first in which members of the Croatian armed forces were found guilty of war crimes perpetrated on Serbian civilians (ibid.).

During the first two years of the January government, the CDU was a fierce opposition party, attempting to delegitimise the government in the public eye, primarily with respect to cooperation with the ICTY. Even as an opposition party, the CDU continued to pursue successfully the tactic of delegitimising SDP as non-patriotic, treasonous communists. In addition to that, the oversized six party coalition proved difficult to handle for Prime Minister Ivica Račan. Coalition party leaders from CSLP and the Croatian Peasant Party (CPP), Dražen Budiša and Zlatko Tomčić, were not serving as ministers in the government, which meant that the Prime Minister Ivica Račan frequently had to negotiate with these two conservative parties outside the framework of regular cabinet meetings. Public communication among parties sometimes gave the impression that CSLP and CPP were opposition parties, rather than parties of government (Vlašić and Vurušić 2010[44]). The difficulty of running a coalition government had already

---

43. Article in the Croatian weekly newspaper *Nacional*, entiled 'Hrvatska napokon smogla snage da osudi svoje ratne zločince', authored by Jasna Babić, from March 26, 2003. Available online at http://www.nacional.hr/clanak/10546/hrvatska-napokon-smogla-snage-da-osudi-svoje-ratne-zlocince. Last accessed August 18, 2012.

44. Article in the Croatian daily paper Jutarnji, entitled 'Budiša i Tomčić od Račana su napravili

become evident by summer 2001. Prime Minister Račan's decision to extradite two Croatian generals, Ante Gotovina and Rahim Ademi, to The Hague Tribunal provoked resignations of CSLP ministers and a vote of confidence in Parliament. Račan's decision to go ahead with the extradition after a dramatic ten-hour government meeting was reported by major news agencies across Europe.[45] The Prime Minister faced not only hostile reactions from the CDU, which was calling his action a 'criminalisation of the Homeland War', but profound disagreement from his main coalition partner CSLP and the president of that party, Dražen Budiša. His government survived the vote of confidence in Parliament,[46] but this crisis was indicative of the difficulties his government faced from the majority of parliamentary parties as well as large segments of Croatian society. As Chapter 7 will show, a somewhat similar scenario played out in Serbia, where the democratic opposition also failed to agree on political reforms necessary for further democratisation after it came to power in 2000. In political contexts where an authoritarian party dominated over a long period after regime change, it was very difficult for the political opposition to push for decisive reforms once it came into power.

It was only after Sanader was re-elected party president in 2002 that the lock-in effect started taking hold. Sanader's victory signalled a distancing of the CDU from radical right policies and the party started decisively rebranding itself as a European Christian Conservative party. Ivo Sanader initiated this transformation of an ethno-nationalist organisation into a Christian Democratic party (Zakošek 2002, Fish and Krickovic 2002, Dolenec 2009). However, since its core voter base remained conservative nationalists, the party had to maintain a double dance, convincing Europe of their democratic credentials while at the same time appealing to the authoritarian sentiments of their voter base.

While the rebranding of the CDU was important for winning the 2003 parliamentary election, evidence of the lock-in effect appeared after it returned to power. Upon receiving the mandate to form a government in 2003, Sanader invited the Serbian Democratic Party to act as junior partner in government, and showed up at the Christmas party of the Serbian community that year. This was interpreted as a clear move towards normalising relations between Croats and Serbs in Croatia. Coalition with the Serbian party and subsequent extradition of General Gotovina to The Hague were at the time hailed as important signals of the CDU's commitment to European integration. With the benefit of hindsight, it

---

Don Quijotea 'revolucije', authors Boris Vlašić and Vlado Vurušić, from January 2, 2010. Avaiable online at http://www.jutarnji.hr/ivan-jakovcic--budisa-i-tomcic-od-racana-su-napravili-don-quijotea-nase-revolucije/445762/. Last accessed August 18, 2012.

45. Article by the Croatian News Agency Archive, from July 8, 2001, available online at http://www.hrt.hr/arhiv/2001/07/08/HRT0003.html. Last accessed August 18, 2012.

46. Article on the Croatian Radiotelevision News Archive, from July 16, 2001. Available at http://www.hrt.hr/arhiv/2001/07/16/HRT0005.html. Last accessed August 18, 2012.

now seems that these moves primarily signalled a new era of CDU politics driven by pragmatism. The CDU adjusted their rhetoric and made several concessions necessary for advancing Croatia's European integration process, but these were mainly of a tactical nature. Sanader was an autocratic ruler in the CDU and he proceeded to equally centralise his power in government.[47] Building on Tuđman's heritage, he developed a party culture where no questions were asked as long as he was winning in the polls.[48] In parallel, he strengthened clientelism as the primary integrative mechanism of his rule, buying acquiescence from political actors and wide segments of society and making sure everyone knew that their continued prosperity depended on him personally.[49] While it appeared that Croatia had finally entered the smooth waters of democratic advancement, beneath the surface, ripples of corruption were spreading across the political system.[50] However, this had not become evident before mid-2009.

Croatia applied for EU membership in February 2003 and in June 2004 the EU proposed to open accession negotiations with Croatia on the condition that it 'maintain full cooperation with the ICTY and take all necessary steps to ensure that the remaining indictee [General Ante Gotovina] is located and transferred to The Hague' (European Council Presidency Conclusions 2004). The Gotovina case proved to be the bone of contention for the Sanader government, as well as the turning point in the history of the CDU as a political party. The January government had agreed to extradite Generals Ademi and Gotovina to the ICTY back in 2002. However, while Ademi was at the disposal of the authorities, Gotovina was at large. A game of nerves was played during 2003 and 2004 between the Croatian government on the one hand and the ICTY Chief Prosecutor Carla Del Ponte on the other. As time passed, the ICTY prosecutor applied increased pressure on Croatia, claiming that the government had information on Gotovina's whereabouts and was not doing everything in its power to apprehend him and extradite him to The Hague. The Croatian authorities could not convince the ICTY prosecutor that they were doing everything possible to apprehend Gotovina. This speaks directly to the tense cost-benefit calculus that the CDU was making on whether it could extradite Gotovina and still maintain its power. War veterans and their families represented a significant part of the CDU electorate and they vehemently rejected the jurisdiction of the ICTY over the Homeland War. Initially March 2005 had been set as the date for opening negotiations, but since Gotovina remained at large, negotiations were postponed in the last minutes of the October European Council meeting (Presidency Conclusions 2005). Then, in a thriller twist, on 3 October 2005 the Chief Prosecutor for the ICTY, Carla Del Ponte, announced that Croatia

47. Author's interviews with Dejan Jović (Interview No. 2, November 2010), and Žarko Puhovski (Interview No. 6, November 2010).

48. Author's interview with Goran Čular. Interview No. 5, November 2010.

49. Author's interview with Mirjana Kasapović. Interview No. 1, November 2010.

50. Author's interview with Tonči Kursar. Interview No. 4, November 2010.

was cooperating fully (Maki 2008). On the same day Croatia's applicant status to the EU was officially recognised. General Gotovina was subsequently arrested in Spain on 7 December 2005 and brought before the ICTY to stand trial (ibid.).

The first Progress Report that the European Commission issued for Croatia in 2005 stated that 'improving the functioning of the judiciary remains a major challenge for Croatia' (2005: 15). The Report highlighted structural difficulties such as the inefficiency of courts, the excessive length of court proceedings, weaknesses in the selection and training of judges and difficulties with the enforcement of judgements. Large backlogs of cases were weakening judicial capacity (1.6 million cases in 2005), and a coherent strategy for removing systemic problems was still lacking. Nevertheless, while during the 1990s breaches to the rule of law concerned primarily violation of the independence of the judiciary, after 2000 key problems in the judiciary seemed to refer to insufficient capacity rather than violations of judiciary independence. At the same time, in 2005 the European Commission considered corruption a serious problem that continued to affect society at large. To complicate the problem, the judiciary was considered one of the most affected areas aside from the health and construction sectors (2005). Since its inception, USKOK failed to successfully prosecute a number of highly publicised cases. This was explained by shortcomings in the legislation regulating its work, and amendments to that law were introduced in 2005 (ibid.).

In summary, neither the January government nor the 2003 CDU-led government managed to reform the judiciary and public administration or satisfactorily tackle organised crime and corruption (Kasapović 2009). According to the Nations in Transit Report, at the time of the 2007 elections corruption was still one of the key challenges for Croatia (2008). Corruption was considered pervasive throughout public institutions, particularly health and judicial institutions, while at the same time a para-institutional web of connections between large national companies and state officials generated high-level corruption in public tenders through insider information and pre-established arrangements (ibid.). With respect to the judiciary, problems regarding the capacity and efficiency of the courts, as well as politicisation of war crimes cases remained. By 2007 corruption became the key issue for the electorate, and both parties incorporated anti-corruption stances into their programmes (ibid.). Transparency International in Croatia (2007) noted that anti-corruption efforts seemed primarily driven by the EU conditionality process, rather than emerging from domestically driven political agendas.

As a result of stagnation in reform, after 2005 Croatia's accession to the EU slowed down considerably. The judiciary was still not deemed sufficiently independent from political interference while informal and corrupt networks set up in the 1990s were not successfully dismantled (Kasapović 2009). The CDU was continuously balancing EU demands to strengthen the rule of law with the costs that reforms would incur for its domestic power base. The calculus repeatedly went in favour of preserving the mode of rule established in the 1990s, which rested on subverting the rule of law in favour of extracting rents from the state both for private gain and as a way of financing the party machine.

Outstanding challenges to the rule of law in Croatia

In April 2008 the CEO of the Zagreb Highways utility company, Ivan Rađenović, was brutally beaten up outside his home for attempting to stop criminal activities in the company where he worked.[51] In June 2008, Dušan Miljuš, a journalist well known for following the activities of organised crime, was subjected to a serious physical assault in Zagreb.[52] This was followed in September 2008 by another brutal attack on a company CEO, Josip Galinec, in Zagreb. In October of the same year, Ivana Hodak, daughter of the lawyer who was at the time defending an indicted Croatian Army General, was murdered in downtown Zagreb in broad daylight. Later that same month the well-known journalist and owner of weekly magazine *Nacional*, Ivo Pukanić, was assassinated. These attacks and killings of prominent public figures were interpreted in Croatia's public sphere as a result of organised crime showdowns, and the Prime Minister was under pressure to react. In October 2008 he made a public statement saying that 'the moment has finally come in which we must tackle the mafia, regardless of who is at stake'.[53] He fired the minister of the interior, the minister of justice and the head of the police (Kasapović 2009).

With respect to the rule of law, issues that were closely monitored by international organisations were trials for war crimes committed during the Homeland War in Croatia. The fact that some cases under the jurisdiction of The Hague Tribunal had been transferred to Croatia to be tried domestically was considered a test of the impartiality and professionalism of the judiciary, which was not always successfully passed. A war crime case that perhaps best exemplifies the troubling features of Croatia's political system that linger into the present concerns the trial of Branimir Glavaš. In summer 2005 a suspect in the killings of Serbian civilians in Osijek back in 1991 implicated him as responsible for these murders. Glavaš had been the so-called wartime governor in Slavonia during early 1990 and a prominent CDU member and Member of Parliament until 2005. In 2005 he founded a regional political party, the Croatian Democratic Alliance of Slavonia and Baranja (CDASB), and after his fallout with the CDU he came under investigation.[54] When he was taken to custody in October that year, Glavaš started

---

51. As reported in the online news portal *Dnevnik.hr*, on May 16, 2008. Available online at http://dnevnik.hr/vijesti/crna-kronika/pretucen-igor-radzenovic-direktor-zagrebackih-cesta.html . Last accessed August 19, 2012.

52. Both physical attacks were made using baseball bats, and both victims were attacked in front of their homes.

53. As reported in the online news portal *Index.hr*, on October 3, 2008. Available online at http://www.index.hr/vijesti/clanak/reakcije-na-ubojstvo-ivane-hodak-svatko-razuman-sada-osjeca-strah/404805.aspx. Last accessed August 19, 2012.

54. This chronology was published by the Croatian daily newspaper *Jutarnji List*, on May 8, 2009. Available online at http://www.jutarnji.hr/sudenje-glavasu-u-sjeni-politike/204755/. Last accessed

a hunger strike and both investigations were stopped due to his deteriorating health. Investigations were reinstated in 2007, and charges were brought against him. In the first case, dubbed Sellotape, he was charged with the murder of ten people as well as one attempted murder, while in the second case, dubbed Garage, he was alleged to be responsible for the torture of Serbian civilians under his military command in Osijek.

Both trials were marred by procedural problems, witnesses retracting statements, and other irregularities. In January 2008 Glavaš was released because he had been re-elected to Parliament. His immunity was again revoked for the purpose of continuation of the trial, but he was not returned to custody in spite of the fact that witnesses in the trials against him had claimed that they were being harassed. When the trial finally ended, in May 2009 he was found guilty on both charges and sentenced to ten years in prison. Glavaš' response to the sentence was to flee the country. It was clear at the time that he had anticipated the sentencing and had prepared an escape route to Bosnia and Herzegovina.[55] After his appeal, in 2010 the Supreme Court upheld the ruling, but reduced his sentence to eight years in prison, on account of mitigating circumstances. The Supreme Court ruled that Glavaš had had no previous convictions while on the other hand he was credited with a marked role in Croatia's defence during the war. According to the Court, the crime was committed within a state of war.[56] The apologetic arguments forwarded by the Court were met with public disappointment and bewilderment. After Glavaš was found guilty of the heinous crimes of torture and murder of Serbian civilians, the Supreme Court reduced his sentence by considering war circumstances mitigating in a war crimes trial, while disregarding the human rights of his victims. Adding insult to injury, though a Member of Parliament and leader of a political party, Glavaš had escaped custody in clear contempt of Croatia's judiciary and legal order. After his sentence was confirmed before the court in Bosnia and Herzegovina, he decided to serve his sentence in a Bosnian prison. In October 2010 investigations were opened concerning several of Glavaš's associates, alleging that they attempted to bribe judges of the Supreme Court into reducing Glavaš' sentence.[57]

The Glavaš case reveals persistent weaknesses in the rule of law in Croatia. It illustrates how members of the political elite are habituated to being outside the reach of law. At the same time, that the case opened only after Glavaš was no longer

---

August 19, 2012.

55. As reported in the Croatian daily newspaper *Večernji List* on July 30, 2010. Available online at http://www.vecernji.hr/vijesti/na-dan-izricanja-presude-glavas-je-bih-sredivao-nove-dokumente-clanak-173887. Last accessed August 19. 2012.

56. As reported by Nikola Jelić in Croatia's weekly newspaper *Globus*, on August 8, 2010.

57. As reported in the Croatian daily newspaper *Večernji list*, on October 18, 2010. Available online at http://www.vecernji.hr/vijesti/slucaj-glavas-uskok-istrazuje-tadica-jos-cetiri-osobe-clanak-204583. Last accessed August 19. 2010.

close to the CDU party leadership suggests that the State Prosecution Office may have been influenced by the executive branch of government. Secondly, the fact that Glavaš managed to get re-elected as an MP while standing trial for war crimes committed against civilians speaks to the fact that large segments of Croatia's voters still reject the idea that Croats could have committed crimes during the Homeland War. This helps reinforce the notion that the law does not apply equally to everyone. Thirdly, the fact that both cases were tried in Zagreb even though the primary jurisdiction was with the County Court in Osijek testifies to the realistic fear of bias in the judiciary when it comes to prosecuting war crimes. International reports on human rights abuses in Croatia, including the European Commission, have stressed this problem continuously. Fourthly, after Glavaš' re-election to Parliament in 2007, the Parliament refused to revoke his immunity from being kept in custody. Even though this was a high profile controversial trial, he was allowed out of custody with full access to the media. After his sentencing, Glavaš managed to escape imprisonment in Croatia, signalling another instance where the police and State Prosecution Office failed to act promptly and stirring doubts as to whether rules were bent to let this happen. In addition to that, his escape as well as his conduct during the trials showed contempt for Croatia's legal order and judiciary. Finally, the Supreme Court ruling was no less controversial. Through finding him guilty for serious war crimes, the Court reduced his sentence by invoking his role in the Homeland War. Instead of arguing that his high standing and responsibility as a military officer during the war made his crimes that more serious, the Court made the opposite argument according to which his contribution to the war effort partly exculpated him from the crimes he committed. In that judgement, the Court once again reinstated the widespread belief that the law should not apply equally to everyone.

The surprise resignation of Prime Minister Ivo Sanader in September 2009 announced a wider political crisis that was evolving in Croatia. Jadranka Kosor replaced Sanader as Prime Minister at the head of the CDU-led coalition government in the midst of a global financial crisis. Growing citizen dissatisfaction manifested itself through peasant demonstrations, union-organised strikes, student protests and blockades, direct citizen actions and civil disobedience. At the same time, when Sanader left the post of Prime Minister and resigned as party president, a sort of informal political embargo on anticorruption activities was removed (Kasapović and Boban 2011). During 2009, and especially in 2010, several dozen investigations and criminal proceedings were instituted against individuals belonging to the political and economic elite, mostly individuals holding high ranking positions in the CDU government – including the former defence minister and former Deputy Prime Minister.

In December 2010 criminal proceedings were instigated against former Prime Minister Ivo Sanader. After the State Attorney's Office requested that his parliamentary immunity be revoked, Sanader fled the country and was apprehended in Austria. From December 2010 until July 2011 he was in custody of the Salzburg court, and after that he was held in Zagreb prison until the first of several trials at the end of October 2011. Before criminal proceedings were instigated against him, a number of executives of state enterprises and the Customs Administration were investigated under suspicion that Sanader extended them preferential treatment in business deals with the government, in exchange for which they illegally funded the CDU as well as, it is suspected, Sanader personally (Kasapović and Boban 2011). In September 2011 the testimony of the CDU's accountant was leaked to the press, in which she directly accused top CDU members of receiving money from so-called black funds i.e. money siphoned out of public companies or through other illegal means and into the party treasury. Though the CDU leadership with Jadranka Kosor was trying to pin all criminal activities on Sanader, over time it became more and more difficult for the CDU to escape the image of a deeply corrupt organisation. The thread that kept all the trials, indictments and investigations together pointed to a para-institutional network of power relations infused with corruption and crime that penetrated diverse aspects of state and society: the government, the public administration, the judiciary, state enterprises, agencies and institutions, private corporations and agencies, the media, the health and education systems (Kasapović and Boban 2011). This unfolding of recent events is evidence that the main features of the 1990s mode of rule, though hidden from the public, remained present throughout the 2000s.

Paradoxically, the CDU was in power as its officials became indictees. It is rare in political history that a cleaning up of a political party happens while it is still in office. The CDU was handling this predicament primarily by trying to convince the public that the party had excised its own infected parts while portraying political corruption as pervasive across party lines in the hope of dissuading disenchanted voters from changing tickets. The consequence was a growing political crisis that further delegitimised the entire political elite. The indictments brought against Sanader and other high ranking officials seemed to offer ample evidence that the 1990s governance practices of power concentration, the conversion of political to economic capital as well as the politicisation of the state were alive and well twenty years later.

In late 2010, the prevailing social climate shifted from a situation where it was impossible to convict someone for corruption into a situation where it seemed impossible not to convict.[58] This was raising doubt regarding the capacity of Croatia's judiciary to ensure fair and impartial trials. However, in 2010 the European Commission's Progress Report stated that good progress was made regarding the independence of the judiciary, which was strengthened through amendments to the Constitution and the laws on the State Judicial Council (SJC), the state attorneys' offices and the courts (2010). With respect to fighting corruption the Commission highlighted positive legislative reforms but a lack of convincing implementation, concluding that 'A track record of effective investigation, prosecution and court rulings remains to be established, especially for high level corruption' (2010: 54). These concerns reflected lesson learning on the part of the EU from its experience with the accession of Bulgaria and Romania.

---

58. Author's interview with Tin Gazivoda. Interview No. 13, December 2010.

Croatia closed accession negotiations with the EU in June 2011 and signed the Accession Treaty in December of the same year. Croatia's accession to the EU is foreseen for 1 July 2013 (EC Press Release 30/6/2011[59]). Amid an unprecedented series of criminal investigations, each of which further unmasks the mode of rule in Croatia as subversive of the rule of law, the European Commission's statement upon closing negotiations revealed hope rather than conviction:

> Croatia has launched reforms in critical areas, strengthening the independence and efficiency of the judiciary, in the fight against corruption and protection of fundamental rights. These are essential to bringing results in the near future in support of the rule of law for the benefit of all citizens. (European Commission Press Release 30/6/2011)

The end of 2011 also brought to power a new coalition government, led by the Social Democratic Party, while the CDU suffered a predicted electoral failure. With the signing of the Accession Treaty and the inauguration of a new government, the political agenda has shifted decisively towards dealing with the country's dire economic performance, austerity measures, high unemployment and the looming prospect of further downgrades of Croatia's standing on the international money markets. While the trials of high ranking CDU politicians are still ongoing, political reform and corruption were no longer the focus of public attention in 2012, except as obstacles to economic recovery. Like in early 2000, the Social Democratic Party managed to enter office only when contesting a CDU that was in complete shambles during the parliamentary election, as well as again inheriting a dramatic economic situation that takes precedence over further political reforms.

While the SDP-led January government in the period 2000–2003 undoubtedly influenced Croatia's democratisation trajectory in a positive way, it did not manage to dismantle the economic-political nexus of the entrenched power structure in place since early 1990s. When the CDU came back to power in 2003, it kept the foreign policy orientation of joining the EU, but the party equilibrated between EU demands that would strengthen the rule of law on the one hand, and its habitual mode of rule on the other. The difficulties for CDU of reconciling the costs of compliance with EU demands and holding on to power were reflected in the protracted and frustrating six-year accession process. Even though twenty years after regime change SDP came into power for the second time, and the European integration process has come to a close, the rule of law in Croatia has not reached a level comparable to that in the Czech Republic or Slovenia. This analysis attempted to show that this was due to the mode of rule that developed in the early 1990s as a result of authoritarian party dominance in the context of war and disputed statehood. Once it coalesced and became entrenched through a long period of CDU dominance, it became a long term obstacle to the establishment of rule of law, as witnessed by the recent trials of top government officials in Croatia.

---

59. Available on the European Commission website, http://europa.eu/rapid/pressReleasesAction. do?reference=IP/11/824. Last accessed August 19. 2012.

In Central Eastern European countries the initial period of regime change, with its wholesale economic and political reforms, also created ample opportunities for abuse of power and politicisation of the state. But, in contrast to Croatia, there the immediate development of party competition within a democratic framework, coupled with domestic and international scrutiny, created limitations on political power. New elites that ruled over Croatia in the early 1990s did so in extreme circumstances, legitimised by mass nationalist mobilisation, and operating far away from international scrutiny. The result was a deep disregard for limitations to power including most importantly those imposed by the rule of law. By the time stronger party competition, political reform and the process of European integration were initiated, ten years had already gone by. The authoritarian mode of rule was by then deeply entrenched and difficult to dismantle, shedding light on the reasons why in 2011 Croatia still faced obstacles to a functioning rule of law system.

chapter seven | serbia

Tito had been the primary *gelling ingredient* of Yugoslavism, and his death in 1980 produced both a power vacuum and a crisis of succession (Vladisavljević 2008). After his death the republican communist organisations started increasingly diverging with respect to how the country should be organised and run. Serbia wanted more authority for the central government, while almost everyone else agreed that confederation was the way forward, with maximum autonomy for the constituent republics. In this way, 'the stage was set for an open interethnic conflict in Yugoslavia' (Kasapović and Zakošek 1997: 23). Between 1981 and 1989 Serbia was suppressing claims for rights and more autonomy of Albanians in Kosovo, transforming the Serbian Communist Party into a nationalist organisation and virtually abolishing the autonomy of two provinces of Vojvodina and Kosovo (Banac 1992).

However, as Slovenia and Croatia started moving towards secession it became clear that Milošević had in mind the creation of a Greater Serbia. His intention was to incorporate Serb populations in Croatia and Bosnia into the same political community (Banac 1992, Mazower 2002, Ramet 1996, Ramet and Wagner 2010). The Milošević-led Yugoslav Army aided the Serbian uprising in Croatia in the late 1990 and Serbian militias occupied large chunks of territory in Croatia during 1991, and Bosnia and Herzegovina during 1992. Serbia was planning to annexe the Republic Srpska from Bosnia and the majority Serb populated region of Krajina in Croatia into Greater Serbia or 'some other type of union of Serbian states' (1993)[1]. Furthermore, Serbia-cum-Yugoslavia was involved in violent conflicts in its province of Kosovo, which began in early 1998 and ended with NATO bombing in March 1999.[2]

Tragically, Serbian citizens were fighting in wars for almost a decade. The wars were attempts to gain territories within former republics of Yugoslavia as well as attempts to keep and regain control over territories that Serbia considered

---

1. As reported in the AIM news report on November 10, 1993.

2. In 2001 Human Rights Watch issued the report *Under Orders: War Crimes in Kosovo*, documenting war crimes committed by Serbian and Yugoslav government forces against Kosovar Albanians between March 24 and June 12, 1999, the period of NATO's air campaign against Yugoslavia. It reveals a systematic campaign to terrorise, kill, and expel the ethnic Albanians of Kosovo that was organised by the highest levels of the Serbian and Yugoslav governments in power at that time. This report is available online at http://www.hrw.org/reports/2001/10/26/under-orders-war-crimes-kosovo. Last accessed August 19, 2012. http://www.hrw.org/campaigns/kosovo98/timeline.shtml

constitutive to its historical state borders. However, by 1999 the borders of Serbia were almost back to where they were at the end of the nineteenth century (Mazower 2002). In addition to an almost decade-long experience of violence, sanctions and international isolation, Serbia went through a complex process of state identity shifting. After Slovenia, Croatia, Bosnia and Herzegovina and Macedonia seceded in 1991, the only remaining former republics of the Yugoslav federation were Serbia and Montenegro. The two republics established the Federal Republic of Yugoslavia (FRY) in 1992, aspiring to be the legal successor state to the former Socialist Federal Republic of Yugoslavia (SFRY). This was disputed by the international community, and eventually Serbia and Montenegro accepted the opinion of the Badinter Arbitration Committee about shared succession and applied for UN membership as the State Union of Serbia and Montenegro. This union was a loose confederation, which ended in 2006 when Montenegrins voted in favour of independence. In the same year Serbia declared independence as a sovereign state, signalling hope that the country was finally able to clearly delineate its territory and establish its state sovereignty.

However, the dissolution of confederation with Montenegro did not end Serbia's stateness problem because the issue of Kosovo remains unresolved since Kosovo proclaimed independence in 2008. Serbia did not accept this unilateral claim for independence and filed a complaint before the UN disputing Kosovo's right to secede, and the case was put before the UN's International Court of Justice. During this time Belgrade placed an embargo on Kosovo goods following the 2008 declaration of independence, breaching the terms of the Central European Free Trade Agreement, CEFTA.[3] In 2010 the ICJ ruled that Kosovo's unilateral declaration of independence from Serbia did not violate international law. Serbia's reaction to the ICJ ruling was that it would 'never recognise the unilaterally proclaimed independence of Kosovo'.[4] The dispute over Kosovo's independence remains a chief obstacle to Serbia's statehood issue, stalling not only its European integration process but its democratisation more broadly. Neighbouring Bosnia and Herzegovina, like several other EU member states with large minorities,[5] have not recognised Kosovo for fear that this case might serve as a precedent. Kosovo and Republika Srpska in Bosnia and Herzegovina[6] remain chief sources

---

3. As reported by the *Balkan Insight* news portal, in an article on July 26, 2011. Available online at http://www.balkaninsight.com/en/article/kosovo-police-seize-northern-border-points. Last accessed August 19, 2012.

4. AS reported by BBC web portal in an article 'Kosovo independence move not illegal, says UN court', July 22, 2010. Available online at http://www.bbc.co.uk/news/world-europe-10730573. Last accessed August 19, 2012.

5. For instance Cyprus, Greece, Slovakia, Spain and Romania.

6. Early in 2011 Republika Srpska was threatening to hold a referendum on independence. The situation was diffused through EU intervention, but it illustrates the precariousness of the situation. More information is available in the International Crisis Group report available online at

of instability in Southeast Europe and the future of both these entities depends to a large extent on Serbia. In the summer of 2011 new clashes erupted at the border crossings in Serb-controlled North Kosovo. The fact that some Serbian officials were suggesting the partition of Kosovo as a solution to the problem[7] sent a warning signal of continuing sources of instability.

This introductory analysis serves to show that Serbia's state borders and territorial integrity have not been fully established to this day – keeping its stateness problem centre stage in the domestic political arena. In 2011 Serbia was still not a political community with a clearly defined population and internal sovereignty on a clearly demarked territory[8] (also Pavićević 2010). The following sections trace how the stateness problem influenced the evolution of the mode of rule under Slobodan Milošević throughout the 1990s, and how it continues to hamper democratisation in Serbia.

Milošević as the people's tyrant[9]

Until April 1987 Slobodan Milošević was a 'little-known Serbian Communist apparatchik' (Bideleux and Jeffries 2007: 241). On April 24 he delivered the infamous speech in Kosovo, inflaming the already widespread sentiments of victimisation among Serbs by saying 'No one dare beat you!' This speech was broadcast on national television, propelling Milošević to the forefront of the Serbian nationalist revival (ibid.). In the period 1987 to 1989 together with allies in the state apparatus, the Yugoslav Army and Yugoslav League of Communists he organised mass rallies and media events. He skilfully exploited the position of Serbs in Kosovo and he used nationalist ideology as his selling point. The wholesale mobilisation of Serbian nationalism and the accompanying anti-bureaucratic revolution helped Milošević win the presidency of Serbia in December 1987 (ibid.).

Milošević was brought to power on the wave of a deeply undemocratic mobilisation movement. While democratic revolutions were taking place in countries of Central Eastern Europe, during the late 1980s Serbia's intellectual elite was developing a political platform deeply imbedded in traditionalism, nationalism and an authoritarian rejection of democracy. Perović (1996) analysed

---

http://www.crisisgroup.org/en/regions/europe/balkans/bosnia-herzegovina/214-bosnia-what-does-republika-srpska-want.aspx. Last accessed on August 19, 2012.

7. As reported by the *Balkan Insight* news portal, on May 18, 2011. Available online at http://www.balkaninsight.com/en/article/idea-of-kosovo-partition-back-in-the-air. Last accessed on August 19, 2012.

8. Author's interviews with Hedvig Morvaj Horvat (Interview No. 8, November 2010) and Slaviša Orlović (Interview No. 16, February 2011).

9. I draw this term from the title of a book by the Serbian writer Vidoslav Stevanović , *Milošević: the people's tyrant* (2004)

columns published in Serbia's most widely read daily newspaper *Politika* since the late 1980s, tracing the development of an elaborate scholarly argument against multi-party democracy, for the unification of Serbs and for the re-establishment of Serbian statehood rooted in traditional ideas of national sovereignty. The antibureaucratic revolution further homogenised Serbian citizens, evoking collectivism and essentialist concepts of the nation as ethnic community. The ruling party exploited the citizens' fear of losing social rights and the fear of capitalism, which were encouraged during the state socialist regime, and transformed it into the fear of losing national identity and Serbia's statehood (Obradović 1996). In a nutshell, Serbia was rejecting the wave of democratic and market reforms that had swept across post-communist Europe.

Events in 1989 and 1990 set Serbia's trajectory clearly apart from the rest of post-communist Europe, ushering communist revival supplanted with ethnic nationalism (Vejvoda 2000). In July 1990 the ruling Serbian League of Communists merged with the Socialist Alliance of the Working People of Serbia to form the Socialist Party of Serbia (SPS), led by Milošević (Bideleux and Jeffries 2007). SPS inherited the connections, patronage, financial and infrastructural assets of its predecessors and grew into a political organisation that dominated Serbia's politics throughout the 1990s. While Bulgaria and Romania were also characterised by a continuation in power of former Communist parties under a new guise, the case of Serbia is unique in that the SPS never rejected socialist ideology or bothered to put on a reformed modern Social Democratic face. This was in full contrast to the Croatian Communist Party, which reformed into the Social Democratic Party and tried to shed any continuity with their previous incarnation (Goati 2004).

In its 1990 programme, the SPS declared itself to be a party maintaining continuity with the League of Communists of Yugoslavia, aiming to reinvigorate socialism by purging it of bureaucratic deformations (Obradović 1996). Another key component that set the SPS platform apart from the Socialist parties in Bulgaria and Romania was hostility towards the West, which was equated with imperialism (Obradović 1996, Perović 1996). At the same time, for all the inflammatory rhetoric Milošević is best understood as a pragmatic that deployed nationalism, warfare and media control in order to neutralise rivals and remain in power (Gordy 1999, Gagnon 2004; quoted in Bideleux and Jeffries 2007). His objective was to use the trappings of power to the fullest, and he relied on the family as the strongest social institution in the Balkans to achieve that (Gallagher 2003).

Multipartyism was legalised in the summer of 1990, and the first multiparty elections were held in December 1990. Though the election was announced as late as possible in order to disable opponents from preparing, it was contested by several parties that subsequently became a permanent part of the political landscape in Serbia. The Serbian Renewal Movement (SRM) was a nationalist party under the leadership of Vuk Drašković. The Democratic Party (DP) attracted Serbian intelligentsia of various stripes such as Vojislav Koštunica on the one hand and former Praxis critics of Tito's Yugoslavia such as Ljuba Tadić[10] on the other. From the very outset the DP was characterised by internal strife that would become characteristic of Serbia's political opposition. The DP had already split into nationalist and anti-nationalist factions before the first election (Miller 1997; quoted in Bideleux and Jeffries 2007). The lack of a coherent oppositional political vision to that of Milošević became a lasting feature of party politics during the 1990s, removing a crucial check on Milošević's mode of rule.

In 1990 the new constitution for Serbia was drafted and ratified by the SPS and Milošević before the first parliamentary election took place. This timing was carefully planned in order to pre-empt any power sharing in deciding on the constitutional setup of Serbia. The undemocratically ratified Constitution conferred extensive powers on a directly elected president and established a British style first-past-the-post electoral system that gave SPS successive majorities in Parliament (Bideleux and Jeffries 2007). In the first election in December 1990 the SPS had 46.1 per cent share of the vote, winning 194 out of 250 seats in Parliament. SMR came second with 15.8 per cent vote share and DP third with 7.4 per cent vote share. The 1990 constitution effectively legalised Milošević's almost unlimited personal power (Vejvoda 2000), while the overwhelming SPS parliamentary majority further cemented it. The regimes that emerged in Croatia and Serbia revolved around two men with unchecked power in their hands, leading the two biggest and most important Yugoslav republics (Vejvoda 2000).

At that point in time virtually all parties in Serbia offered the same agenda to the electorate (Stojanović 1996), primarily in advocating the policy of all Serbs in one state. Divisions surfaced primarily with respect to the future of the Yugoslav federation and the preservation of the socialist economy (ibid.). Similarly to Croatia, the moment of regime change was characterised by a homogenisation of the elites as well as citizens, effectively removing the sources of pluralist party competition. However, though national homogenisation was probably of comparable strength in the two cases, the deeply reactionary and isolationist nature of national mobilisation in Serbia was more strongly adverse to democratisation.

Though Serbia did not wage wars on its own territory in the early 1990s, it was strongly affected by them through loss of human lives, compulsory conscription, economic and social devastation as well as a large influx of refugees (Vejvoda 2000, Clark 2008, also Interview No. 8 with Morvaj Horvat 2010). By mid-1993, around 590,000 refugees were registered in Serbia, with actual figures probably 20–30 per cent higher (Clark 2008). Large population shifts were happening amidst a disastrous economic situation. By 1993 the average daily food consumption required 17.5 German marks, while the minimal monthly salary was 14 German marks (1993).[11] In August 1993 coupons were introduced for rationed supplies of

---

10. Ljuba Tadić was the father of Boris Tadić, the President of the Democratic Party (2004–current) and the President of Serbia between 2004 and 2012.

11. As reported in the Serbian magazine *Borba*, November 4, 1993.

basic foodstuffs such as flour, oil, sugar and detergent (Obradović 1996). Added to that, the Serbian monetary system was collapsing; in November 1993 the exchange rate between the German mark and the Serbian dinar went from 1:500,000 to 1:1,500,000.[12] As a journalist succinctly summarised, money in Serbia had value for about as long as it took an ice cream to melt.

At the same time, wars legitimised the rhetoric and practice of the SPS regime (Obradović 1996). Wars inflamed and strengthened nationalist mobilisation, proving a strong source of legitimacy for the regime (Obradović 1996, Lazić 2008). When this situation is compared to Croatia, it seems that wartime circumstances played similar roles in the two countries. Furthering the general atmosphere of crisis, the political ideology of SPS deliberately instigated social tension and crisis in order to erode institutions as instruments for resolving social conflicts (Obradović 1996). Instead, political power was informalised and personalised. By mid-1992 the so-called rump Yugoslavia was an international pariah (Pridham 2001). In May 1992 the UN imposed a trade embargo on Yugoslavia, which fuelled smuggling and illegal trade, over time strengthening the growth of Balkan mafias. The unintended result of UN sanctions was that in large part the Serbian economy was outside of international law, resulting in heavy criminalisation (Clark 2008). In such a context, the destruction of the legal system was a deliberate state strategy to circumvent blockades and enable the provision of goods (Lazić and Sekelj 1997). The criminalisation of the state and the legitimisation of criminal practice grew into a new system of social organisation (ibid.).

Subsequently indicted war criminals such as Radovan Karadžić and Ratko Mladić were warlords during the early 1990s, operating across former Yugoslavia (Clark 2008). As in Croatia, in Serbia wartime circumstances enabled people from marginal backgrounds to push their way to the forefront. International sanctions in both cases contributed to the subversion of the rule of law in pursuit of provision of goods. Also, using war as a policy instrument required employing 'people not lacking in recklessness, cruelty or rank opportunism' (Gallagher 2003). In both countries petty criminals, heads of sports clubs, released prisoners and returning diaspora became wealthy on the proceeds of goods seized in ethnic warmongering (ibid.). Wealth was accumulated through wholesale seizure of private property, often at the point of a gun. In both cases dubious privatisation schemes enabled the transference of state assets to the ruling elite.

Notwithstanding these similarities however, Serbia's regime was considerably more repressive, not afraid to use violence against its citizens or against any form of dissent that was deemed threatening. Milošević built up a police force to near-parity with the Yugoslav army. By 1996, the police were supplied with artillery rockets, tanks and armoured personnel carriers, with officers even being trained to fly helicopter gunships (ibid.). The Serbian police have been dubbed Milošević's Praetorian Guard, which he repeatedly used to suppress protests and demonstrations during the 1990s (Orlović 2008). The heavily armed police force,

---

12. As reported by the AIM news portal, November 1993.

estimated at 100,000 strong, was guilty of extensive and systematic human rights abuses (US State Department Report 1995).[13]

Economic hardship and growing international isolation fuelled social opposition to the Milošević regime. The Yugoslav National Army had difficulties in recruiting soldiers for its military campaigns into Croatia because thousands of young men were avoiding conscription. In a closed session of the Serbian parliament in September, it was announced that the response of reservists in Serbia was 50 per cent, but in Belgrade only 15 per cent (Gallagher 2003). In 1992 the opposition parties captured the growing anti-war sentiment in Serbia, organising a mass rally in Belgrade in March 1992 attended by 50,000 people. The success of the rally encouraged the opposition to launch the Democratic Movement of Serbia in May 1992, known under the acronym DEPOS. The main members were SRM, Koštunica wing of DP, New Democracy as well as the Peasant and Liberal parties. While they were campaigning on a peace platform, the parties did not risk 'national betrayal' by offering a substantially different political programme with respect to Serbia's claim on territories in Bosnia and Croatia (Stojanović 1996). In 1992 all major parties in Serbia still supported the ethno-nationalist programme of all Serbs in one state, which means that Serbia's political party constellation at the time could be classified as undemocratic across the board.

Both Serbian parliamentary elections and Yugoslav federal elections were held in December 1992. However, the election for the new federal parliament in rump Yugoslavia was boycotted by opposition parties in Serbia and Montenegro, apparently to no other effect apart from marginalising themselves yet further. As a result, SPS won 73 of the 138 seats, while the ultra-nationalist Serbian Radical Party (SRS) under the leadership of Vojislav Šešelj came second. The 1992 elections for Serbia's Parliament were seriously flawed due to media manipulation, manipulation of voter registers, lack of voting secrecy and other irregularities. Repeating their success in the federal election, the Serbian Radical Party dramatically increased its representation, gaining a 22.6 per cent share of the vote, while SPS won with 28.8 per cent (Gordy 1999; in Bideleux and Jeffries 2007). DEPOS came third with 16.9 per cent vote share, working in a Parliament where SPS and SRS held 174 out of 250 seats. The key characteristic of the 1992 election was that Milošević's ethno-nationalist platform was outflanked by an even more radically authoritarian political actor. Between 1992 and 2008, Šešelj's Radicals were the single most popular political party in Serbia.

Šešelj's SRS alternated in the roles of loyal partner to the Socialists and their rival, but it was never a truly oppositional party to the Milošević regime. In 1993 Šešelj accused Milošević of being the top mafia boss in Serbia, stealing and transferring vast amounts of state money to private offshore accounts. After Milošević counter-accused Šešelj of war crimes, Šešelj replied that his

---

13. The US Department of State Country Report on Human Rights Practices in Yugoslavia, published in 2005, is available online at http://www.unhcr.org/refworld/category,COI,,,SRB,3ae6aa1a0,0. html. Last accessed August 19, 2012.

paramilitary forces deployed in Croatia and Bosnia were armed by Serbian police, publicly exposing Milošević's regime as waging wars in Croatia and Bosnia and Herzegovina. In September 1993 Šešelj and the SRS proposed a vote of no confidence in the Serbian government. Milošević responded by dissolving the parliament, throwing opposition parties into disarray (Thomas 1999).

In the early 1990s Milošević had little to fear from the opposition, which was fragmented and hesitant about advancing a different vision of Serbia's political future. In the period 1990–1994 the main opposition parties in the ostensibly democratic bloc – the DPS, the SPO and the DP – supported Serbia's expansionist aspirations and everyone toed the ethno-nationalist line. The Democratic Party, which was supposed to be the axis of the Milošević opposition, supported the secession of Republic Srpska from Bosnia and Herzegovina during 1993 and 1994 (Goati 2004). Adding to the lack of alternative political programmes, Milošević effectively controlled the media (Cviić 1997, Gallagher 2003). Research has shown that SPS and its smaller sister party JUL had 1.5-10 times more air time than other political parties (Pavlović and Antonić 2007). Though political opposition was allowed to exist, when it was perceived as a threat to the regime its actions were extinguished (Thomas 1999). At the same time, due care was taken that such actions were 'clothed in the language of legality' whereby the judiciary was instrumentalised in legalising the actions of the regime. Serbia under Milošević was 'a country where the laws had fallen silent' (Thomas 1999: 424).

Overall, though formally democratic institutions of multiparty elections and the division of branches of power did exist, they were seriously trampled upon. Power was used arbitrarily and it was personalised in Milošević.[14] Elections were manipulated, while appointments to executive and legislative posts both at the federal level and in Serbia were directed by Milošević. He dominated the judiciary, filling it with pliant supporters (Thomas 1999, Gallagher 2003, Orlović 2008) and he controlled and manipulated state media (Goati 2001). In Serbia 'often no distinction existed between having a state career and personally serving the ruler' (Gallagher 2003: 176). As a result, no real separation of powers among branches of government existed and the state was merged with the Socialist Party of Serbia (Thomas 1999). The regime made the rule of law practically meaningless, replacing the constitution and legal system with an informal network based on loyalty.[15] An observer at the time described the regime as follows: 'We have one ruler, his wife and two kids. The whole system is based on him personally. Milošević symbolises the final attempt of Serbia to escape from modernisation' (Grubatić, quoted in Gallagher 2003).

---

14. Author's interview with Slaviša Orlović. Interview No. 16, February 2011.

15. Author's interview with Nebojša Vladisavljević. Interview No. 12, November 2010.

The incident involving SRM party leader Vuk Drašković offers a vivid example of suppression of the political opposition. In June 1993 he was arrested, seriously beaten by the police and jailed for allegedly obstructing the police and enticing riot (Bideleux and Jeffries 2007). This was a warning to the opposition not to step beyond the narrow limits in which the regime allowed it to operate (Gallagher 2003). Similarly to the situation in Croatia, in Serbia the opposition was viewed by the regime as an enemy and traitor to the nation, and often accused of promoting foreign interests (Vejvoda 2000), not unlike the tactics undertaken by Putin in Russia in more recent times. However, while in Croatia the political opposition never suffered physical abuse and direct repression, in Serbia this was common practice. In the next few sections I reflect more specifically on Serbia's historical legacies of patrimonialism and traditionalist political culture, which provided poor reservoirs for political pressure for democratisation from below.

Serbia entered the twentieth century as an economically backward, poor and agrarian country with a patrimonial political regime characterised by personalised relations in the state apparatus on the one hand and corruption on the other (Lazić 2004). The communist period brought elements of modernisation in terms of industrialisation, urbanisation and education, but this material development came about without the corresponding change in individual value orientations characteristic of Western democracies (Perović 2006). Parallel to industrialisation, urbanisation and the spread of education the regime nurtured many features of traditional collectivist values. In these societies 'only collectivities [we]re candidates for the role of political subjects' (Puhovski 1993: 87). By the end of the twentieth century collectivism and individualism, egalitarianism and market relations coexisted, creating a kind of normative value dissonance for the average Serbian citizen. The character of social relations was contradictory, and deep ambivalences were embedded into individual value orientations (Lazić 2004). As a result, the main cleavage structuring voter-party linkages in Serbia since the early 1990s was between civic versus nationalist value orientations.[16] This cleavage corresponds to the traditionalist versus modernist value clusters identified in Inglehart's work. Milošević's regime reinforced traditionalist and conservative norms, with nationalism becoming the dominant value orientation that structured other values for most of society (Lazić 2004). The minority core of civicness in the vastly impoverished but resilient Serbian middle class helped topple Milošević in 2000[17] (also Lazić 2004). However, the limited reach of reform after 2000 suggests that civic democratic forces in society were not strong enough to articulate a political alternative for Serbia's citizens (Vujadinović 2006). Empirical research into value orientations of Serbia's citizens throughout the 1990s repeatedly found a dominance of authoritarian values, concentrated primarily in supporters of the

16. Author's interview with Slaviša Orlović. Interview No. 16, February 2011.

17. Author's interviews with Sonja Licht (Interview No. 9, November 2010) and Slaviša Orlović (Interview No. 16, February 2011).

Socialist Party of Serbia and the Serbian Radical Party which constituted the majority of Serbia's voters (ibid.). In opposition to this dominant authoritarian political culture, 'another Serbia',[18] which stands for civic values continues to coexist, but within a highly polarised society (Ramet 2011, Dulić 2011).

Serbia's structural preconditions in terms of its level of socioeconomic development and the legacy of the previous regime support the fsQCA finding from Chapter 5 according to which Serbia would not have escaped slow democratisation even had it escaped the wars in Yugoslavia. This is reinforced by the fact that prior to the dissolution of Yugoslavia, during the late 1980s, Serbia was undergoing an intellectual revival of anti-modernist and reactionary values. The Serbian Academy of Arts and Sciences published a Memorandum in 1986 which chartered the intellectual underpinnings of Serbian politics in decades to come. It formulated the narrative of a general threat faced by Serbs in Yugoslavia and postulated the supremacy of ethnicity in that it made the very possibility of the realisation of civic rights conditional on the realisation of ethnic rights (Milosavljević 1996). When analysing solutions to Serbia's problems, the Memorandum advocated a return to authentic socialist values and did not mention any type of democratic reform (Madžar 1996). In other words, at the end of the 1980s Serbia was rejecting democratisation. Even if the dissolution of Yugoslavia had been peaceful, it is plausible to assume that democratic reforms in Serbia would have been protracted.

Milošević's regime systematically postponed and subverted political and economic reform so that state patronage and dependency became dominant features of political culture. Serbia was the only European post-communist country where the initiated process of privatisation was annulled to return economic assets back to the state portfolio. Initially the privatisation unfolded much like everywhere else, through dubious privatisation schemes that enabled the transference of state assets to the ruling elite (Gallagher 2003). Only a few years into Milošević's rule, the process of privatisation in Serbia was generally perceived as a giant robbery. In addition, outrageous rates of inflation, which in the period February 1993 to February 1994 exploded to 116 trillion per cent, enormously reduced the cost of shares in company buyouts. As a result of international sanctions and failed domestic economic policies, Serbia experienced an economic disaster. Between 1990 and 1997, Serbia's economic performance decreased by 60 per cent and unemployment rose from 19.7 per cent in 1990 to 30 per cent in 1997 (Džihić and Segert 2012). After the war in Kosovo and NATO intervention, the country's Gross National Product was at only 50 per cent of its 1989 level, while employment climbed to 50 per cent (ibid.). These extremely adverse economic conditions in turn endangered the survival of interest based organisations, civil society groups and even basic societal institutions (Goati 2004). Serbia experienced rising numbers of 'factories without workers, banks without money, schools without pupils, institutes without research projects, courts without judgements and civil

---

18. This expression comes from the title of Ivan Čolović's book *Another Serbia*, published in 1992, which originally referred to the anti-war intellectual and civic circles in Serbia.

servants without civil service' (Bolčić 1994; quoted in Goati 2004). Far from having established interest groups that would articulate social demands and help structure party competition, Serbia was an atomised society. As a result of the deeply unjust and corrupt privatisation process, the idea of political office as an opportunity to amass a private fortune developed into a widespread cultural trait.[19]

In the summer of 1994 the Democratic Party proposed a law on the revaluation of property rights, intended to correct injustices in the privatisation during hyperinflation, when managers bought company shares for next to nothing. The SPS however realised a different potential, and allowed this law to pass through Parliament.[20] A property revaluation ensued, through which private ownership was 're-socialised' (Lazić and Sekelj 1997). Under the *Property Transformation Revaluation Act* privatisation was annulled in 87 per cent of transformed enterprises, in effect returning the bulk of the economy to state control (ibid.). The SPS judged that direct control over big enterprises enabled full merging of economic and political power and virtually unchecked abuse of public resources. As a result, high ranking SPS and JUL officials were at the same time directors of large state enterprises. Two-thirds of Serbia's economic elite were directly or indirectly part of the former socialist nomenclature (Lazić 2008). These circumstances fuelled widespread corruption and criminalisation, which became constitutive to the regime. The shadow economy was estimated at around 40 per cent in 1995 (ibid.). In 1997 several close associates of the Milošević family were gunned down on the streets of Belgrade with no one held responsible (ibid.). Zoran Todorović, secretary general of JUL and director of a Belgrade oil company, was also assassinated in 1997, illustrating the close ties between the Milošević family, large business and organised crime (Nations in Transit Yugoslavia Report 1998).

By the mid 1990s Serbia had a non-restructured, inefficient economy that was drained of resources to fuel personal fortunes, political battles and service voters through clientelist networks. Add to this general impoverishment and international isolation, and the picture became even grimmer. The vast majority of the population throughout the 1990s was poor and dependent on the state for survival. Such economic and social conditions could not foster the development of the self-expression values needed to generate a bottom-up demand for democratisation (Inglehart and Welzel 2005). The inhibiting regime legacy that Serbia inherited in the form of patrimonialism and a traditional agrarian society were not overcome during Milošević's rule but rather reinforced with new forms of clientelism and politicisation of the state. The merging of political and economic power enabled the transfer of power to an illegitimate economic elite that represents the chief source of continuity from Milošević's era until today.[21]

---

19. Author's interview with Slaviša Orlović. Interview No. 16, February 2011.

20. It was the first and last proposal of an opposition party ever accepted by the Serbian Parliament under the rule of the Socialist party (Lazić and Sekelj 1997).

21. Author's interview with Sonja Licht. Interview No. 9, November 2010.

fsQCA results from Chapter 5 suggested that Serbia would have had a hard time following the trajectory of fast democratisation in the early nineties due to inhibiting historical legacies. This analysis supports that finding in two ways. Earlier sections have shown both how the dominant intellectual climate in Serbia in the late 1980s was nationalist, undemocratic and parochial, and portrayed political culture in Serbia as authoritarian. Taken together, these structural preconditions drew the conditioning parameter in which political choice was severely constrained: at the beginning of 1990s, as I have shown, there was no alternative political programme to ethno-nationalism in Serbia. Democratic political opposition was fragmented and weak, while the two political allies of the Socialists were the extremist parties – the SRS and the SRM. The continuous threat to state sovereignty combined with wars and international isolation further exacerbated these circumstances, enabling the development of an authoritarian rule that was deeply inimical to establishing the rule of law. All in all, in the 1990s several foundational preconditions for democratisation of Serbia were missing.

If Schumpeter (1947) is right in saying that attitudes are like coins because they do not easily melt, then it is plausible to expect that the political culture in Serbia should also change very slowly. Comparing the World Values Survey data for 1995 used in Chapter 3 to the European Values Survey data for 2008 might shed some light on this question. Figure 7.1 shows data on Inglehart and Welzel's value dimension of post-materialism from the two datasets in 1995 and 2008 for Serbia and Croatia, which are also compared to the averaged value for the fourteen countries in the study.

Figure 7.1: Post-materialist values in Serbia and Croatia, 1995 and 2008

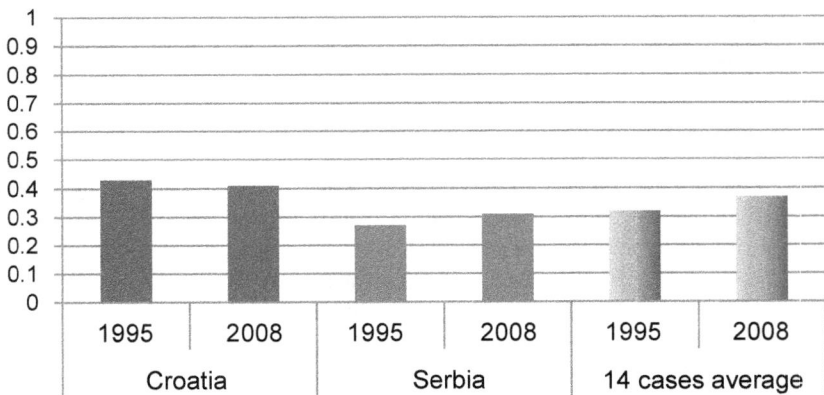

Sources: WVS1995, EVS 2008; author's calculations

Figure 7.1 primarily confirms that very little has changed over time, supporting the well-established claim according to which dominant societal values are very durable. The proportion of Croatia's citizens supporting democratisation was higher than the fourteen cases average both in 1995 and 2008, while conversely the proportion of such citizens in Serbia remained below the average for all fourteen countries studied both in 1995 and 2008. These findings support the contention according to which political culture in Serbia has been a comparatively weak source of democratic pressure from below.

Growing authoritarianism of the regime

In the face of many difficulties, oppositional parties managed to form a coalition under the name Together in the autumn of 1996. After peace agreements were signed in Dayton and Erdut for Bosnia and Croatia respectively, during 1995 the Democratic Party softened its nationalist rhetoric and focused on demands for further democratisation. In 1996 it decided to abandon its isolationist politics and focus on building an oppositional political coalition (Goati 2004). As a result, the coalition Together was composed of the Serbian Renewal Movement, the Democratic Party, the Civic Alliance of Serbia and the Democratic Party of Serbia.

Initially the opposition had a good chance of winning the federal presidential election but after its presidential candidate stepped down two weeks before the election, that potential was wasted (Vejvoda 2000). Nevertheless, in the 1996 municipal elections Milošević suffered his first electoral defeat. The opposition coalition Together won a number of urban centres such as Belgrade,[22] Niš, Novi Sad, Kragujevac, Čačak and others (Vejvoda 2000). Milošević initially refused to accept electoral defeat, provoking massive civic protests by the social movement called the Other Serbia (ibid.). Apart from that, he abused the judiciary to overturn oppositional victories in cities (Nations in Transit Yugoslavia Report 1998). Eventually conceding defeat in the face of domestic and international pressure, he emptied the municipality treasuries before handing them over to opposition parties so as to thwart their plans (Cviić 1997). Regrettably, the coalition Together fell apart six months after it was crafted, reaffirming the inability of the opposition to formulate an alternative political option (Goati 2004). Throughout the 1990s, the opposition was programmatically and politically divided and unable to seriously challenge SPS's grip on power (Goati 2001).

Milošević suffered another blow at the 1997 parliamentary election, despite the fact that he temporarily shut down 77 private radio and TV stations before the election (Nations in Transit Yugoslavia Report 1998). Since the SPS lost a number of seats, Milošević was forced to enter a coalition in order to form a government. After six months of negotiations, a coalition was formed, consisting of the ultra-right Serbian Radical Party, the SPS and JUL (Vejvoda 2000). JUL was the party of Milošević's wife and close confidante, Mira Marković. Ostensibly Marxist, this

---

22. The first elected oppositional mayor of Belgrade was Zoran Đinđić from the Democratic Party.

was actually a party of regime profiteers who acquired wealth and status in the 'lawless conditions that had emerged when the productive economy had largely collapsed in the early 1990s' (Gallagher 2003: 178). After the electoral defeat of the oppositional coalition, Vuk Drašković of the SRM left the coalition and aligned with the ruling SPS, confirming the argument according to which they were not an oppositional party to Milošević's regime.

After changing allegiances, the SRM party ousted Đinđić from his post as Mayor of Belgrade and took control of the only independent TV station in Belgrade, Studio B (Vejvoda 2000). When Serbia's presidential election came up in 1997, Milošević could no longer run, having exhausted his two terms in office as the President of Serbia. However, in order to thwart this constitutional stipulation, in 1997 he simply changed offices, the federal parliament electing him President of Federal Yugoslavia (Gallagher 2003). The key feature of the 1997 Serbian presidential election was the rise and near victory of Vojislav Šešelj (Vejvoda 2000). As was shown, the Serbian Radical Party had strong and steady support in the Serbian electorate throughout the 1990s, outflanking Milošević's authoritarianism with an even more radical political platform. At the time, the situation in Kosovo was worsening, adding fuel to ethno-nationalist radicalisation in Serbia. The local leadership in Kosovo kept pushing for independence and Milošević kept up the repression. During state breakdown and violence in neighbouring Albania in 1997, a lot of weapons made their way into Kosovo. By late 1997, the Kosovo Liberation Army (KLA) began attacks on Serbian security forces in Kosovo (Nations in Transit Yugoslavia Report 1998).

This brief account of events during 1996 and 1997 reveals several important features of Serbia's political party system. First of all, Milošević's SPS was flanked by two other ethno-nationalist parties: Šešelj's SRS and Drašković's SRM. These two parties were often make-pretend opposition to Milošević, principally aimed at securing votes so as to strike a deal with Milošević once in power (Pavlović 2001).The SRS was a militant proto-fascist party, heavily involved in paramilitary activities in the wars in Croatia and Bosnia, and notwithstanding that it managed to sustain high popularity in Serbia (Vejvoda 2000). Not all votes cast for this party were extremist votes however, but represented disgruntled voters of SPS and SRM as well (ibid.). Taken together, these three parties commanded the vast majority of Serbia's electorate in the 1990s.

The moderate democratic bloc consisting of DP, DPS and the Civic Alliance of Serbia (CAS) actually had fairly weak democratic credentials. Apart from the CAS, led by Vesna Pešić on a convincingly liberal democratic platform, Đinđić's DP was middle-of-the-road, while Koštunica's DPS was a nationalist conservative party. Initially civic oriented and democratic, over time both DP and DPS moved towards rightwing national orientation (Stojanović 1996). Overall, party competition in Serbia does not map onto the general left-right axes, either by looking at the cultural or the economic dimensions. Instead political parties in 1990s Serbia are best aligned along an authoritarian-democratic continuum, where the large majority was in the authoritarian part of the spectrum (SPS, SRS; SRM), DPS and DP somewhere in the middle, and no one except small urban political elites in the fully democratic part. In addition to the absence of a strong democratic alternative, the key problem of the political opposition in Serbia was the fact that these parties could not cooperate effectively, but competed over which would have the strongest standing in order to make deals with Milošević (Pavlović 2001).

Between 1990 and 1998, the SPS won four parliamentary elections (in 1990, 1992, 1993 and 1997), it won the federal elections in May and December 1992 as well as those held in 1997 (Goati 2004). None of these elections was considered free and fair since opposition parties were routinely denied access to the state media, and the regime manipulated the electoral process in various ways (Nations in Transit Yugoslavia Report 1998). Beginning with 1998 the key features of Milošević's regime intensified. The initial marginalisation of the opposition turned into ruthless prosecution, while rules of the political game were not only manipulated but openly trampled upon (Goati 2004). After the SPS-JUL-SRS coalition was formed in April 1998, the regime evolved into authoritarianism 'stripped bare' (ibid.). In the autumn of 1998 Milošević dismissed the army and secret service chiefs, purged universities of dissenters and continued the crackdown on independent media in his ongoing construction of a private regime composed of loyalists completely dependent on the patronage of the state (Vejvoda 2000).

The revised law on public broadcasting in 1998 significantly restricted media freedom in Serbia (Goati 2001, 2004). Between 1998 and 2000 no less than 1,700 members of the oppositional civic movement Otpor were arrested or brought to court, while in 2000 police broke into Otpor headquarters and confiscated its equipment (ibid.). Slander trials were used against opposition leaders, journalists and lawyers defending media, protesters and opposition politicians (ibid.). Vuk Drašković, who had suffered police abuse in 1993, subsequently survived two attempted assassinations, while the former President of Serbia, Ivan Stambolić, was kidnapped and assassinated by the Special Operations Unit that was part of Serbia's secret service. Criminal investigations were used to intimidate and harass political opponents including Vuk Drašković, Zoran Đinđić and Vojislav Šešelj (Nations in Transit Yugoslavia Report 1998). In addition to full control over police and secret services, Milošević financed non-institutional paramilitary groups which were used to deal with activists at anti-government demonstrations (Antonić 2002; quoted in Goati 2004). By the end of the 1990s in Serbia the police, paramilitary groups and organised crime networks were closely intertwined (Goati 2004). Discretionary use of power held the central place that in democracies belongs to constitutionalism (Dimitrijević 2004; quoted in Goati 2004). This political repression was happening in parallel with the campaign to expel ethnic Albanians from Kosovo, which provoked the 1999 NATO bombardment of Serbia. As a result, Milošević's regime has been characterised as competitive authoritarianism (Pavlović and Antonić 2007, Vladisavljević 2010). The term was coined by Levitsky and Way (2002: 52) to define regimes in which formal democratic rules are in place, but they are violated by incumbents to such an extent 'that the regime fails to meet conventional minimum standards for democracy'. Schedler (2009) employs a similar term of electoral authoritarianism, stressing the electoral process as the key characteristic that makes these regimes hybrid.

Levitsky and Way (2002) listed Croatia under Tuđman and Serbia under Milošević as examples of competitive authoritarianism. However, while both regimes were arguably hybrid, case evidence presented here suggests there were important differences among them. Though Tuđman and the CDU centralised executive power, marginalised political opposition and emasculated the judiciary and parliament, elections in Croatia were free of large scale manipulation and fraud, the political opposition did not face repression and political parties were able to articulate alternative political programmes. In Serbia, by contrast, all these features were part and parcel of SPS mode of rule. While Tuđman manipulated electoral rules and constitutional provisions to his advantage, he confined his fight against the political opposition to institutional means, and political protests were not met with state repression. In contrast, Milošević used the full scale of intimidation, prosecution and repression against his political opponents. In addition to that, the criminal underground and the state in Serbia merged (Antonić 2002; in Goati 2004), while in Croatia the criminal milieu had more marginal access to the state. These are differences primarily of degree rather than kind of phenomenon, but when taken together the case evidence suggests that Croatia was a democratic regime diminished by authoritarian governance practices, while Serbia was a repressive authoritarian regime where formal democratic institutions served as little more than decor.

In addition to that, by the late 1990s Tuđman's mode of rule was weakening while Milošević's grew more repressive. While in the late 1990s Tuđman held on to the grand narrative of Croatia's hard won independence and the ethnic conception of the nation, the changed circumstances of full sovereignty and peacetime were weakening the legitimacy of his authoritarian rule. In Serbia in contrast, the renewed escalation of the conflict in Kosovo, together with the failure of warmongering in Croatia and Bosnia had meant that the legitimacy of Milošević's authoritarian rule was amply replenished with the fear and frustration of Serbia's citizens. While in Croatia Tuđman's death led to reform in the CDU and a peaceful alternation in power in 2000, Milošević was neither expecting electoral defeat nor was he willing to concede it.

The 2000 election and beyond

The victory of DOS coalition (DP, DPS and 13 other parties) at the September 2000 federal election removed SPS and Slobodan Milošević from power, representing a pro-democratic turn in Serbia's politics (Schimmelfennig 2005). Losing both the federal parliamentary and presidential elections shocked Milošević and the SPS, and they desperately attempted to undo this defeat. Their refusal to concede defeat led the opposition coalition DOS to the streets, sparking protests which led to a mass popular uprising. On October 5, despite police repression, more than 700,000 people took to the streets of Belgrade, besieging the Parliament building and the national TV broadcaster RTS (Bideleux and Jeffries 2007). Though Milošević had sent special police forces known as the Red Berets[23] to break the protest, instead of intervening they joined the protesters, effectively precipitating the fall of the Milošević regime. As later became clear, the co-opting of security services enabled a peaceful transfer of power, but it subsequently compromised decisive democratic reforms (Subotić 2010, Ejdus 2010). These circumstances evoke a parallel with Romania, where regime change was also made possible through the consent of Ceauşescu's army and secret police, whose 'agreement to a change of regime was intended as a sort of life insurance', i.e. a guarantee of survival in the new regime (Mungiu-Pippidi 2006: 314). On October 6 Vojislav Koštunica was confirmed as President of Yugoslavia, while DOS formed the federal government. In December 2000 DOS won another victory at Serbia's republican parliamentary election and formed the government in January 2001. This sequence of events was met with the approval of the international community. In a quick response, the EU lifted the remaining sanctions against Serbia, though maintaining a freeze on state assets and visa restrictions in an attempt to prevent Milošević and his loyalists from escaping abroad (Bideleux and Jeffries 2007). The Federal Republic of Yugoslavia was readmitted to the UN in November, which was followed by a restoration of diplomatic relations with the USA, UK, France and Germany. FR Yugoslavia was invited to the Zagreb Summit in November 2000, where Macedonia signed the SAA and Croatia opened negotiations for signing the SAA (ibid.).

Immediately after the 2000 election it became clear that the DOS coalition was deeply divided among the two leading parties, DP and DPS. There was strong animosity between DP's Zoran Đinđić and DPS' Vojislav Koštunica (Goati 2004). While Đinđić denied legitimacy to the previous regime and worked intensively on undoing it, Koštunica insisted on following legal procedures, legitimising the previous regime by treating the 2000 election as a routine alternation in government (Goati 2004, Pešić 2007, Popović 2010, Orlović 2008). According to Popović,[24] Koštunica was a compromise choice agreed between the democratic opposition and the old regime. After becoming President, Koštunica was protecting elements of the old regime in the police, army and security services, while at the same time he was obstructing Đinđić's reform efforts (Popović 2010).

The DOS government found itself in the situation described by O'Donnell (2004), when acting formally according to the law entails the application of discriminatory or undemocratic rules. The state apparatus was criminalised across

---

23. This group, officially called the Special Operations Unit, was formed as a paramilitary unit in 1990 to stir up Serbian rebellion in Croatia and its members have been accused of committing some of the most heinous atrocities in the Yugoslav wars. After the end of the war, Milošević officially merged the Red Berets with regular security forces, and they remained part of official police forces after Milošević was ousted from power, making them much more difficult to disband and prosecute (Subotić 2010).

24. Author's interview with Srđa Popović. Interview No. 10, November 2010.

the board, from the judiciary and the army, security and intelligence services.[25] It was impossible to govern a state apparatus that was working against the newly elected government in fear of lustration and the ICTY, so many shortcuts were applied including improvisation, deceit and shrewdness (ibid.). Due to the nature of Milošević's regime, change had to be implemented through a combination of institutional and para-institutional means (Lazić 2008). Notwithstanding their democratic reformist intentions however, the DOS government's continued disregard for rule of law constituted a prolongation of the mode of rule inimical to democratisation.

The main problem for the DOS government from 2000–2003 was the fact that a hybrid regime remained that was not exercising effective control.[26] Describing his time in office Zoran Điđić said: 'When you asked yourself where the power resides after we go home, you realised there was no power. It existed while we were all together, but as soon as we dispersed it was gone. And when you asked yourself whether the Socialists had mechanisms which operated when they were away, the answer was yes' (quoted in Popović 2010: 227, my translation).

The missed opportunity to fully dismantle levers of the old regime led to a consolidation of the network merging state security services and organised crime (Orlović 2006). According to some analysts, organised crime remained the principal economic sector, and much of the functional mechanisms of the old regime were left in place (Sekelj 2001). While the armed insurrection of the Red Berets in November 2001 exposed the seriousness of this challenge, the full implications of not dismantling elements of the old regime were revealed in the assassination of Zoran Đinđić in 2003 (Orlović 2006).

The period 2000-2003 is perhaps best characterised as a state of emergency, an unstable period of non-regime.[27] The first report of the European Commission on Serbia within the SAP framework (2002: 5) emphasised the 'problem of dualism, the continued presence of elements of the old regime even within the new structures', which created a climate of constitutional uncertainty. Corrupt elements of the old regime remained present either in, or parallel to, the new structures, opposing reforms. As a legacy of the previous regime, public confidence in the judicial and prosecutorial system, as well as general legal awareness and perception of law, were negative (EC, ibid.). Furthermore, open conflicts within the ruling coalition undermined the authority and transparency of institutions, complicating the situation further. Commenting on the judiciary, the European Commission report stressed that the climate of legal insecurity was helped by the constitutional court which was inefficient with little sense of independence. Implementation of laws was often lacking and influence was sometimes exerted by extra-judicial means.

---

25. Author's interview with Srđa Popović. Interview No. 10, November 2010

26. Author's interviews with Srđa Popović (Interview No. 10, November 2010) and Nebojša Vladisavljević (Interview No. 12, November 2010).

27. Author's interview with Nebojša Vladisavljević. Interview No. 12, November 2010.

After the October 2000 overthrow state structures were experiencing a purge. There was a wholesale replacement of cadres in the state administration, the public sector and state enterprises, guided by the same spoils system that characterised the 1990s mode of rule (Sekelj 2001, Orlović 2002, Golubović 2004). DOS tried to take control over all major state institutions, while the state media that used to be Milošević's weapon now turned against him with the same bias and one-sidedness[28] (also in Pavlović and Antonić 2007). Opposition activists took control of the national bank, Serbian police and customs office, and there were forcible takeovers of major banks, key companies and factories (Bideleux and Jeffries 2007). Students and staff expelled the rector and senior administration from the University of Belgrade (ibid.). Other characteristics of the 1990s mode of rule that survived into the DOS government were centralisation of power and decision making in the DOS coalition cabinet, absence of control mechanisms over executive power and a continued marginalisation of parliament (Golubović 2002). In addition to that, the criterion of party loyalty was used in the nomination of judges and, overall, the judiciary remained dependent on the executive branch (Radojević 2002).

Apart from differing in their fundamental stance *vis-à-vis* Milošević's regime, DP and DPS disagreed on the direction that reform in Serbia should take[29] (also in Golubović 2002). DP was advocating speedy reintegration of Serbia into mainstream European politics, which included accepting the jurisdiction of The Hague Tribunal. DPS in contrast was vigorously against cooperation with The Hague. The two parties continue to disagree on the fundamental direction of Serbia's politics.[30] The cohabitation of DP and DPS was marred by rivalries and disputes that hindered Serbia's reform process (International Crisis Group 2001).[31] In a revealing instance of how the DOS government was functioning, Koštunica only found out about the extradition of Milošević to The Hague after the fact and reacted by withdrawing his party from Serbia's parliament and the federal parliament in June 2001 (Bideleux and Jeffries 2007). By mid-2002 it was evident that though the two parties were in government together, Koštunica's DPS constituted the chief opposition to Đinđić's government.

After 2000 there was no shortage of elections in Serbia. Between 2000 and 2008, four parliamentary elections were held (in December 2000, December 2003, January 2007 and May 2008) as well as five presidential elections (in September 2002, December 2002, November 2003, June 2004 and January 2008). Unlike in the 1990s, the elections after 2000 were generally considered free and fair –

28. Author's interview with Nebojša Vladisavljević. Interview No. 12, November 2010.

29. Author's interview with Srđa Popović. Interview No. 10, November 2010.

30. Author's interview with Slaviša Orlović. Interview No. 16, February 2011.

31. International Crisis Group, Europe Report No. 117, published on September 21, 2001. The Report is available at: http://www.crisisgroup.org/en/regions/europe/balkans/serbia/117-serbias-transition-reforms-under-siege.aspx. Last accessed on August 20, 2012.

marking a key dimension along which Serbia made democratisation advances.[32] However, while confirming that in Serbia politicians were indeed competing for office, competitive elections did not produce the radical shift in the mode of rule that Serbia required in order to establish a functioning rule of law. According to Bideleux and Jeffries (2007), Serbia's 2002 presidential election had to be repeated because Šešelj, the SRS and SPS urged their supporters to boycott the second round in order to make the election invalid. Pavlović and Antonić (2007) on the other hand quote Čedomir Jovanović, head of the Liberal Democratic Party and Đinđić's close associate, as saying that after realising Koštunica might win the election, Đinđić decided to make the election void by lowering turnout. Two days before the presidential election, Prime Minister Đinđić spoke on national TV saying that no harm would come out of a failed election, and state run media were used to manipulate voters (ibid.).

Similar tactics were used in the repeated election in December 2002. It again confirmed Koštunica as the most popular candidate, but the turnout was too low (45 per cent) so the election was declared invalid. Koštunica was publicly accusing Đinđić's government of rigging the voter register (Bideleux and Jeffries 2007). Since two rounds of presidential elections were deliberately made unsuccessful, the Speaker of the Parliament took the office of President following stipulations in the Constitution of Serbia. The office of President of Serbia was filled by Nataša Mičić, Đinđić's associate (Pavlović and Antonić 2007). These events testify to a continued manipulation of state institutions and public office. Though Đinđić's government was undoubtedly pursuing European integration and democratic reforms for Serbia, it continued to abuse the prerogatives of executive power to steer the legislative and judiciary branch, as well as to control the media and other state institutions. The sometimes desperate means used to steer events in the difficult aftermath of the overthrow of Milošević were hardly conducive to Serbia's transformation into a democratic regime.

The governance crisis in Serbia escalated further in 2003. In February that year Đinđić narrowly survived an assassination attempt (Bideleux and Jeffries 2007). However, very soon after that, on March 12 the Prime Minister Zoran Đinđić was assassinated by sniper outside the main government building in Belgrade. The blame was immediately pinned on Milorad Luković Legija, head of the Zemun criminal underground clan, who had previously been accused of the murder of former Serbian president Ivan Stambolić and the attempted assassination of Vuk Drašković. Legija was the personification of Milošević's regime; he was the chief drug mafia boss and at the same time the former commander of the infamous Red Berets. After the assassination it was alleged that Legija had struck a deal with Đinđić back in 2000 to support the DOS government in return for immunity from extradition to The Hague. Legija's suspicion that he might still end up in The Hague was speculated to have led to the assassination of the Prime Minister.

---

32. Author's interviews with Dušan Pavlović (Interview No. 7, November 2010), Srđa Popović (Interview No. 10, November 2010) and Sonja Licht (Interview No. 9, November 2010).

Those inside the plot to assassinate the Prime Minister used the code name Stop The Hague for this operation, indicating that Đinđić was murdered to stop further ICTY investigations and extraditions (Subotić 2010).

After the assassination of the Prime Minister, a state of emergency was declared that lasted until April 22 (Pavlović and Antonić 2007). By the end of March over 3,000 people had been arrested. The president of Serbia's Supreme Court and the republic's Chief Prosecutor were dismissed, while the Deputy State Prosecutor Milan Sarajlić was arrested for alleged links to the Zemun clan. Sarajlić subsequently confessed to taking money from the Zemun clan and passing on secret information about the investigation of Đinđić's assassination (Bideleux and Jeffries 2007). In addition to that, he admitted to obstructing investigations into a number of other actual or attempted assassinations including the killing of journalist Slavko Ćuruvija, general manager of Yugoslav Airlines Žika Petrović and deputy interior minister Radovan Stojičić, as well as the attempted assassination of SMR's Vuk Drašković. This demonstrates the extent to which elements of the old regime were subverting the direction of reform set by the Đinđić government, and how the criminal underground and the state were merged in Serbia. Though those responsible for Đinđić's assassination were tried and sentenced to maximum penalties in 2007, the trial did not incorporate political circumstances surrounding the assassination, which bore elements of an attempted coup d'état (ibid.). The main intended effect of Đinđić's assassination was accomplished, in that reforms in Serbia slowed down (Orlović 2008). According to Popović, after the assassination most of Đinđić's reforms were dismantled apart from the objective of joining the EU.[33] The long term negative legacy of Đinđić's assassination was the breaking of resolve in Serbia for fast and far reaching reform (ibid.). It also removed ambiguities regarding party alignments and their democratic credentials. After the assassination it became clear that Koštunica and DPS were cut from the same cloth as SPS, SRS and SRM, while DP was also aligned both with colluders with the old regime parties and those advocating decisive reforms (Popović 2010).

The December 2003 election was free and fair, and the Democratic Party went peacefully into opposition, signalling an important step in the democratisation of Serbia. At the same time, this election featured indicted war criminals, Slobodan Milošević and Vojislav Šešelj, heading electoral party tickets for the SPS and SRS (Subotić 2010). SRS won 28 per cent of votes, while SPS won 8 per cent of votes. Considering that the conservative and nationalist DPS and Koštunica won 18 per cent of the votes, the results of this election suggested that a large part of Serbia's voters was still supporting authoritarian nationalist politics. Serbia seemed unready for a radical break with the politics that had led to several wars, international isolation and economic impoverishment of the country. Vojislav Koštunica became Serbia's new Prime Minister after this election, presiding over a minority coalition government composed of DPS, G17+, SNR and the New Serbia party. In contrast to Đinđić's programmatic priorities, Koštunica stressed the problem of Kosovo

---

33. Author's interview with Srđa Popović. Interview No. 10, November 2010.

and Serbia's territorial integrity as his primary concern, which was followed by the objective of strengthening the state union with Montenegro (Orlović 2008). The new government announced that it would no longer recognise indictments based on command responsibility, that no further indictees would be transferred to The Hague, and that domestic courts would take over ICTY trials (Subotić 2010).

Serbia's European integration slowed down (Pešić 2007). Though some economic reforms were implemented, in 2003 the grey economy still amounted to 29.1 per cent of GDP (Pavlović 2006). Koštunica's minority government had tacit support from the Socialists, offering another signal that the division between old and new regime parties was only skin deep (Pešić 2007). Also, in the 2003 election the Serbian Radical Party emerged as the most popular, signalling that the 2000 turnover did not represent a permanent reorientation among Serbia's voters towards democratic demands and principles (Vasović 2003). The majority of Serbia's citizens hold traditional values and they generally side with nationalist parties (Orlović 2006). Authoritarian political legacy was strengthened through a decade of ethno-nationalist and authoritarian rule, giving it time to grow deep roots in contemporary Serbian society (Vujadinović 2006). Even long after all conflicts ended, the ethnic conception of the nation and nurtured intolerance represent a long term obstacle to democratisation (ibid.).

At the presidential election in June 2004, the new leader of DP, Boris Tadić, beat the Serbian Radical Party candidate Tomislav Nikolić to the office of President of Serbia. The DP and DPS switched roles.[34] Koštunica's government strengthened the politicisation of the state administration, using mechanisms of power diffusion as elaborated in Chapter 1. Once ministry portfolios were agreed among the coalition parties, the given sector was fully under control of that party, almost as if it was private property (Pešić 2007). Ruling parties presided over nominations across the entire civil service and the public sector, including enterprises, agencies, funds, schools, hospitals and so on. The same system of *feudal* appointments at the central level was repeated at local level. Pešić (2007) uses the example of the city of Novi Sad, where a change of party in office meant a full scale staff replacement based on party stripes. Over time political parties in Serbia developed solidarity over their common interest in remaining in power, allowing competition to go only as far as not endangering the system of spoils.[35] Since the state has been thoroughly politicised, real political struggle has been undermined (ibid.). Furthermore, political and economic powers remain intertwined. Data for 2004 showed that 45.8 per cent of total capital and 43.5 per cent of total economic resources were concentrated in 17 state enterprises (Pešić 2007). Pavlović (2006) characterises Serbia since 2004 as a captured state, where economic elites pressure the government towards discretionary and privileged treatment of regime insiders.

---

34. The difference being that DPS's Vojislav Koštunica was President of Federal Republic Yugoslavia, while DP's Boris Tadić became President of Serbia.

35. Author's interview with Srđa Popović. Interview No. 10, November 2010.

The EU had reacted to Milošević's ousting with 'great enthusiasm and instant rewards', quickly removing economic sanctions against Serbia and pledging $2 billion in reconstruction aid (Subotić 2010: 599). An additional $300 million a year was set to follow over the following seven years and a trade agreement was signed allowing tax free access to European markets for most Serbian exports (ibid.). The key priority of Đinđić's government was European integration. In announcing his programme, he set the goal of Serbia's membership in the EU within ten years (Orlović 2008). However, Đinđić and Koštunica disagreed on this policy that was vital for further European integration of Serbia (Orlović 2008). In addition to that, due to many in Serbia's elite fearing ICTY prosecution, the new government faced serious internal hurdles to complying with EU demands (Subotić 2010). In April 2001 Milošević was arrested in Belgrade and taken to prison, where he was indicted for embezzlement of state funds. A few days later the ICTY presented a warrant for his arrest and after some internal wrangling Serbia passed a decree allowing for extradition of indictees to The Hague. Milošević was extradited to The Hague on June 28, 2001, in breach of the Constitutional Court ruling to freeze the extradition. The extradition took place one day before the international donors' conference for Serbia in Brussels, leaving analysts in no doubt as to the government's motives, and confirming the influence of the lock-in effect.

However, when Koštunica became Prime Minister in 2004, government cooperation with The Hague soured, creating a stumbling block for Serbia on the road to Brussels (Subotić 2010). Over time this stagnation in European integration became politically unpopular, so Koštunica's government tried to square the circle by declaratively complying with the European Commission's requests. In October 2004 Serbia's Parliament adopted the Resolution on the Accession to the EU, stating that Serbia was prepared to fulfil all necessary preconditions for a speedy accession to the EU and that it was determined to apprehend all individuals on its territory who were suspected of war crimes (Pavićević 2010). This was followed by the opening of negotiations for the signing of the Stabilisation and Association Agreement between Serbia and the EU in 2005.

Though commending Serbia for positive democratisation steps, the initial Feasibility Report of the European Commission assessing the country's readiness to enter into the Stabilisation and Association framework established that 'in Serbia the rule of law remained weakened by the legacy of the Milošević regime, i.e. the persistent links between organised crime, war crimes and political extremism, and their continued obstructive presence within parts of the current political, institutional, military and state security systems.' (2005a: 6). This report played a crucial role in Koštunica's changed stance towards the ICTY (Subotić 2010). In 2005 the Koštunica government adopted a strategy of so-called 'voluntary surrenders' whereby a dozen indictees were arrested and transferred to the ICTY in a period of a few months. This model was borrowed from Croatia, where the state made a deal with indictees that those who voluntarily surrendered were released on bail to await charges, and their families given financial assistance (ibid.).

This lock-in effect was therefore present in Croatia and Serbia, whereby the government decided to compromise its domestic power base in order to stop the discontinuation of the European integration process. The EU's reaction to these actions was positive and after another feasibility study was conducted, Serbia was given the go-ahead to start negotiations for the SAA in April 2005. The first Progress Report of the European Commission (2005b) confirmed that constitutional and legal certainty in Serbia remained precarious. The functioning of the judiciary exhibited serious weaknesses, especially with respect to judicial independence, which continued 'to be severely undermined by political pressure on the appointment of judges and prosecutors and their activities, and the system remain[ed] heavily burdened with the legacy of the previous regime' (2005b: 15).

Despite declaratory support for cooperation with the ICTY and some tactical concessions, Serbia's cooperation with respect to the capture and extradition of several key indictees for war crimes remained weak. The ICTY was demanding extradition of the two most wanted indictees, Radovan Karadžić and Ratko Mladić, and Serbia's inability to convince the ICTY of its full commitment eventually led to the suspension of negotiations for the signing of SAA (Subotić 2010, Pavićević 2010). This played out negatively for the government internationally and domestically, putting it under considerable strain. Luckily for Serbia, the EU favourably assessed its new 2006 Constitution, even though the International Crisis Group characterised the constitution and the process by which it was passed as illustrating that 'Koštunica continue[d] to transform Serbia into something closer to authoritarian authoritarianism than liberal democracy' (International Crisis Group 2006).[36] In addition to that, in 2006 Montenegrins voted to leave the State Union of Serbia and Montenegro. This turned out to be the least challenge for Serbia in 2006 since this was the year in which negotiations over the status of Kosovo were initiated (Pavićević 2010). SAA negotiations resumed in June 2007 after the ICTY established that Serbia was committed to full cooperation, even though at that point neither Karadžić nor Mladić had been apprehended.

The SAA was eventually signed in June 2008, seven years after it had been signed with Croatia, and in spite of no major steps forward being taken in cooperation with the ICTY. Subotić (2010) interprets the EU's move as aimed at strengthening pro-European forces within Serbia on the eve of parliamentary elections scheduled for May 2008. The move was successful, though with an ironic twist since the reformist Democratic Party formed a government with the Socialist Party. The new government acted decisively, arresting Radovan Karadžić in Belgrade in July 2008. This move was praised by the international community and welcomed by the EU. Serbia's candidacy status remained tied to the arrest of Ratko Mladić, but in 2008 renewed tension over Kosovo put the issue of war crimes

36. International Crisis Group Report 'Serbia's New Constitution: Democracy Going Backwards', published November 8, 2006. The report is available at http://www.crisisgroup.org/en/regions/europe/balkans/serbia/b044-serbias-new-constitution-democracy-going-backwards.aspx, last accessed August 20, 2012.

on the backburner (Subotić 2010). At the EU-Serbia Forum held in Belgrade in September 2011, Tadić reaffirmed Serbia's resolve over the issue of Kosovo. In a subtly threatening tone he emphasised that asking Serbia to remove its institutions from the north of Kosovo was unrealistic and may have catastrophic consequences. Furthermore, he stressed that should 'a new attempt to change the reality in the field through violence occur, with the support or silent approval of certain international factors, the consequences may be dire'.[37] In his speech at the same event, the President of the European Council, Herman Van Rompuy, called on Serbia to tackle corruption, organised crime and judicial reform, thus identifying the main obstacles to securing the rule of law in Serbia. In October 2011 the European Commission issued an Opinion on Serbia's application for membership of the European Union (COM(2011) 668)[38] where it re-emphasised these key obstacles, but it also commended Serbia for stepping up necessary reforms since the 2008 government came into office. In the end however, it recommended that Serbia be granted candidacy status and the opening of negotiations for membership, under the condition that it improves relations with Kosovo. As analysts have observed, the story of contemporary Serbia begins and ends with Kosovo.

Outstanding challenges to the rule of law in Serbia

Bearing in mind that almost a decade has passed during which the electoral process has been a functional democratic mechanism but without bringing significant democratisation advances, worrying questions emerge about the entrenched mode of rule in Serbia.[39] A World Bank Anticorruption Report in 2006 found signs of improvement in Bulgaria, Romania and Croatia but a worsening situation in Serbia. The highest levels of state capture in Southeast Europe were recorded in Bosnia and Herzegovina, Albania, Macedonia, and Serbia and Montenegro (ibid.). In 2006 Serbia ratified the new Constitution without any public debate (Pešić 2007, Pavićević 2010), echoing the circumstances surrounding the ratification of the 1990 Constitution. Even the Members of Parliament that voted on it were not given the draft version, and there was no debate in Parliament (Pešić 2007). Instead, Serbia's new constitution was the product of inter-party barter (Pavićević 2010) and it also signalled Tadić's flirtation with the nationalists (Bochsler 2009). The official explanation for the hurried adoption of a new Constitution was the provision on Kosovo, which was officially declared part of Serbia. In another troubling sign over governance practices, while under international pressure in

---

37. I accessed Tadić's speech on the Serbian government's website http://www.srbija-eu.rs/en/forum_speeches_boris-tadic. The page was no longer available on August 20, 2012.

38. The text of the Opinion on Serbia's application for membership of the European Union (COM(2011) 668 is available on the European Commission website http://ec.europa.eu/enlargement/pdf/key_documents/2011/package/sr_rapport_2011_en.pdf. Last accessed August 20, 2012.

39. Author's interview with Dušan Pavlović. Interview No. 7, November 2010.

2002 Serbia introduced the first draft act on establishing an anti-corruption agency (Pešić 2007); however, the Agency was only established in 2010.

After the new Constitution was ratified, the parliamentary election was held in January 2007. The Serbian Radical Party was again most popular, followed by the Democratic Party. The government coalition was composed of DP, DPS and G17+, and its programmatic priorities were keeping Kosovo in Serbia, speeding up the European integration of Kosovo, cooperation with The Hague Tribunal and economic recovery (Orlović 2008). Like in previous instances, forming of the coalition was fraught with bickering over portfolios and patronage (ibid.). In order to increase leverage in coalition negotiations with Boris Tadić, Koštunica's DPS supported the nomination of Tomislav Nikolić from the Radicals for the office of the Speaker of Parliament. After a lot of haggling, Nikolić was withdrawn and the DP-DPS government was sworn in at the last minute. Following earlier established procedures, the *feudal* allocation of posts, offices and spheres of influence within the state apparatus and the public sector ensued (ibid.).

After Boris Tadić won the presidential election in 2008, the DP became stronger than the DPS both in the executive and legislative branches. Though the two parties were in coalition, DPS had not supported Tadić's presidential candidacy. After the presidential election the DPS left the coalition, prompting a new parliamentary election in 2008. The 2008 presidential and parliamentary elections strengthened the position of the DP and Boris Tadić as the strongest political party in Serbia. The 2008 election brought about a development in the party system that was compromising for the DP at the time since it was seen as an unprincipled coalition, but which has since been hailed a sign of democratisation – the Socialist Party of Serbia entered the government as junior partner. As was elaborated in Chapter 4, the rebranded and moderated policies of the Socialists were followed by a split in the Radical party soon after, another sign that parties were abandoning extremist platforms.[40] The emergent Serbian Progressive Party would go on to win the parliamentary and presidential elections in 2012.

Even though the 2006 constitution strengthened the role of the government as the centre of executive power, the office of president in Serbia remained overbearing in the executive branch.[41] The President directly supervises ministers in the government, controls and directs both domestic and foreign policy and holds the reins of executive power (Pavićević 2010). In his term as President in the period 2008-2012, Tadić continued to usurp the division of power.[42] In Serbia the executive branch is equated with the state, while the other two branches service it. Even more importantly, Serbian society is wedded to the notion that the state, like a king, cannot break the law since its will is the law (ibid.).

---

40. Author's interview with Mladen Lazić. Interview No. 18, February 2011.

41. Author's interviews with Hedvig Morvaj Horvat (Interview No. 8, November 2010), Srđa Popović (Interview No. 10, November 2010) and Sonja Licht (Interview No. 9, November 2010).

42. Author's interview with Srđa Popović. Interview No. 10, November 2010.

Civilian control over security services remains one of the weakest-functioning segments of the executive branch. Since the adoption of the 2006 Constitution there has been considerable improvement in the normative framework surrounding security and intelligence services, yet in 2009 the Minister of Defence said there was no instrument available through which a government minister could find out what was really going on in security and intelligence (Ejdus 2010). The most recent Global Competitiveness report from the World Economic Forum (2011) rated Serbia's judiciary independence and corruption the worst in Southeast Europe. The belated judiciary reform that took place in 2009 was judged very important (Pavlović 2010, Belgrade Centre for Human Rights 2010, also interview No. 9 with Sonja Licht 2010). However, the election of judges after the necessary legislation was adopted was controversial. The institution of High Judiciary Council was introduced to guide the nomination of judges, but the process itself was disputed since through a single decision taken on 16 December 2009, 1,531 judges were confirmed to a full-time post and another 876 elected for the first time. Several hundred judges were dismissed without any explanation.[43] The Serbian Society of Judges unsuccessfully appealed to the Constitutional court claiming that such a general election of judges was unconstitutional. According to Pavlović,[44] something designed as judiciary reform ended up as another partisan purge.

Many institutional reforms have been introduced within the requirements postulated by the European integration process.[45] While numerous new agencies have been established and charged with supervisory and control functions, once they expose irregularities or violations of the law, no consequences ensue. Regulatory and control institutions still lack the teeth needed to implement sanctions against wrongdoers.[46] Corruption stems from political parties, which abuse the state and public sector through cronyism, clientelism and plain theft, both for party and personal gain.[47] Since 2000 political parties have implemented a thorough politicisation of the state and at the same time they control wide segments of the economic sphere[48] (also in Popović 2010).

The 2000 election which ousted Milošević and inaugurated the DOS government marked a watershed in contemporary politics in Serbia when the country decided to join all other post-communist countries on the path to democratic reform and European integration. Twelve years later there has been marked progress from the Milošević era which was characterised by authoritarian politics and a blatant

---

43. Author's interview with Dušan Pavlović. Interview No. 7, November 2010.

44. Ibid.

45. Author's interview with Hedvig Morvaj Horvat. Interview No. 8, November 2010.

46. Author's interviews with Dušan Pavlović (Interview No. 7, November 2010), Hedvig Morvaj Horvat (Interview No. 8, November 2010) and Sonja Licht (Interview No. 9, November 2010).

47. Author's interview with Hedvig Morvaj Horvat. Interview No. 8, November 2010.

48. Author's interview with Sonja Licht. Interview No. 9, November 2010.

disregard for democratic principles and institutions. As the October 2011 opinion of the European Commission states, Serbia now has a constitutional and legislative framework which is 'largely in line with European principles and standards' (COM(2011) 668 final). Overall there has been marked improvement in the rule of law through reforms to the judiciary, establishing the Anti-Corruption Agency and enhancing international cooperation in preventing organised crime (ibid.). At the same time, challenges remain in the areas of judiciary independence and efficiency, the fight against corruption and organised crime.

This case study has focused on delineating features of the mode of rule that survived Milošević. It has shown that, albeit with reformist intentions, pro-democratic governments after 2000 continued to centralise power, breach the division among branches of government and undermine the rule of law by exercising power through informal party networks. In addition to that, the DP and DPS governments continued to politicise the state along party lines and extract resources from the state, both for the financing of party machines and for private gain. High level corruption and crime continue to undermine the rule of law in Serbia while further democratic advances represent formidable challenges for domestic sources of change.

As a result, since the mid-2000s Serbia has been described as an authoritarian democracy. While elections have established the system of vertical accountability, the system of horizontal accountability remains a permanent weakness.[49] In addition, Serbia only completed Huntington's test of the second turnover in the most recent election in May 2012, so it remains to be seen whether political parties of the Milošević regime have become confirmed democrats that will not jeopardise the security of Southeast Europe. At the presidential election in 2012, Boris Tadić lost against Tomislav Nikolić from the Serbian Progressive Party. In another subtle indication of the contempt that Serbia's elites have for the rule of law, Boris Tadić had contested the election a third time even though only two terms as president are allowed by the Constitution. The formal loophole he used was the fact that during his first term in office he was presiding over a different state entity (the State Union of Serbia and Montenegro). And this is behaviour from the democratic spectrum of Serbia's political space, which does leave everyone worried about the country's future prospects. With no political group determined to change the mode of rule in Serbia,[50] the Kosovo question still open, as well as occasional troubling signals from the Republika Srpska in Bosnia and Herzegovina,[51] in 2012 Serbia's democratisation process remains burdened with serious obstacles.

---

49. Author's interviews with Nebojša Vladisavljević (Interview No. 12, November 2010) and Hedvig Morvaj Horvat (Interview No. 8, November 2010).

50. Author's interview with Nebojša Vladisavljević. Interview No. 12, November 2010.

51. Several high ranking officials from Republic of Srpska publicly stated during 2012 that Republic of Srpska is a state, even though under the Dayton Accords it has the status of an entity within the state of Bosnia and Herzegovina.

chapter eight | conclusion

Throughout this study, an argument has been put forward according to which the rule of law was the weakest link in Southeast European democratisation. The failure of these states to establish a functioning rule of law system has been suggested as representing the chief obstacle to closing the gap between authoritarian and democratic systems. While it is not difficult to understand why communist governments failed to engender a rule of law culture, the question was posed as to why and how authoritarian mode of rule continued to reproduce itself after the introduction of formal democratic institutions at the beginning of the 1990s. I will summarise the empirical findings of this study by starting with the case studies of Croatia and Serbia in Chapters 6 and 7.

The two case studies reconstructed ways in which the mode of rule that evolved in the early 1990s subsequently reproduced itself well into the 2000s despite constitutional frameworks that postulated division of power between branches of government, multipartyism, regular and competitive elections and other formal institutions of democracy. Both case studies empirically traced the three processes of power mutation which represent the causal mechanism that contributed to stalled democratisation processes in Southeast Europe. It was shown how the process of power concentration occurred through the personalisation of power in the hands of Tuđman and Milošević. Both leaders abused the institutions through arbitrary rule, they concentrated power in the executive branch and violated the division of power by emasculating the judiciary and legislature. In both cases political power was merged with economic power through the conversion of common societal resources and infrastructure into private fortunes. Privatisation processes were used to create economic tycoons, while economic reform went only so far as to ensure that insider advantages were secured. Finally, a process of state politicisation took place whereby the state apparatus and the public sector were abused for patronage and clientelist relationships. Instead of professional hiring and advancement, informal networks of loyalty became the structuring principle of governing. This produced feudalised bureaucracies which were weak and unaccountable, as well as revitalising the family as the 'strongest social institution in the Balkans' (cf. Gallagher 2003).

When these findings are compared with democratisation processes in Bulgaria and Romania (drawing from Gallagher 1996, Karasimeonov 1996, Vachudova 2005, Ganev 2007 and others), the analysis showed that these countries share principal features of the identified mode of rule. Similarly, case evidence from Chapter 4 suggests that the initial transformation processes in Albania and Macedonia closely mirrored those of the rest of the Southeast European countries, coupled with comparatively greater challenges in terms of structural preconditions of economic and social development. Albania and Macedonia were classified as indeterminate cases when it comes to the one characteristic that distinguishes democratisation in Serbia and Croatia from that in Bulgaria and Romania – the outbreak of violent conflicts. Case studies of Serbia and Croatia showed how the evolution of new regimes under extreme circumstances of war exacerbated several features of power mutation. Circumstances of war added further legitimacy to authoritarian politics and to the processes of power concentration, conversion and dispersion that were already in motion across countries of Southeast Europe. Nationalist mobilisation further aided the personalisation of power and the exercise of arbitrary rule. In addition to that, the UN and EC's 1991 arms embargo that applied to all of the territory of the former Yugoslavia had the perverse effect of subverting the rule of law since, in both cases, states undermined the rule of law by engaging in illegal trade.

With respect to key differences among the two cases, the case study analysis delineated ways in which the state-building project in Croatia eventually had a positive impact on democratisation due to the fact that it was successfully completed, while the open-endedness of Serbia's state crisis continues to negatively influence the country's politics. Next, while the populations of both countries underwent nationalist mobilisation at the onset of regime change, the character of the anti-bureaucratic revolution in Serbia was more regressive and less compatible with democratisation. Though both countries underwent the destructive ethnification of politics, the mobilisation recipe in Serbia in the late 1980s included rejecting the wave of democratic regime change that swept across Eastern Europe. Another important characteristic that distinguishes the two cases is the fact that Milošević's regime was more repressive and criminalised while political opposition to Milošević's rule was weaker and more fragmented than was the case in Croatia. Throughout the 1990s the election process in Croatia was considered free and fair, while this was not the case in Serbia. Tuđman and the CDU resorted to gerrymandering, while Milošević and the SPS employed ballot rigging, intimidation, media control and outright ballot theft.

As a result, the 2000 pro-democratic turn and the democratic reforms that ensued in the following decade were faced with greater challenges in Serbia. The case studies paid close attention to analysing obstacles to democratisation that the DOS government faced in the period 2000-2003. While the January government in Croatia also faced internal strife, disagreement over cooperation with the ICTY and finally a vote of confidence in parliament, in the end it survived. In contrast, the DOS government was blocked both by the old regime as well as members of its own coalition in carrying out democratic reforms. The horrible extent to which old regime forces were threatened by democratisation of Serbia became clear with the assassination of Prime Minister Zoran Đinđić in 2003. In both countries democratic reforms slowed down after the elections in 2003. In Croatia the CDU came to power as an ostensibly reformed democratic party, but was later exposed as having held on to its well-established practices of state politicisation, patronage and corruption. In Serbia the balance of forces after 2003 tipped in favour of Koštunica's DPS, a party that unsuccessfully equilibrated between the demands of democratisation and European integration on the one hand, and preserving the described mode of rule from the 1990s. In this period between 2003 and 2007 the two countries exhibited similar strategies with respect to compliance with the ICTY, which was postulated as the chief political criterion for advancement in their respective European integration processes. In declaratively accepting ICTY jurisdiction but not delivering key indictees, both governments were attempting to 'talk the talk without walking the walk' (Jacoby 2002). In the end however, EU conditionality proved effective in that both Serbia and Croatia delivered all indictees from the most wanted list. Sixteen years after he had been indicted, Ratko Mladić was extradited to The Hague in May 2011.

At the same time, the case studies built on various assessments, both domestic and international, according to which the rule of law and corruption remain permanent weaknesses in both Serbia and Croatia. Since aberrations from democratic principles were more pronounced in Serbia, as case evidence made clear, the reach of subsequent democratic reforms there was also more limited than in Croatia. While in Croatia the former Prime Minister and a whole swathe of top government officials are currently undergoing trials that should uncover the depth and breadth of ways in which the state was used as political party resource, Serbia only made the first steps in this direction in 2010 when it instituted the Agency against corruption. Such differences are present in the extent to which the judiciary has been reformed, in the professionalisation of the bureaucracy and the extent to which other aspects of formal democratic institutions have been strengthened. As a result, qualitative case study analyses overall support quantitative measurements of democratisation such as the Freedom House which, in Figure 8.1, show that the two countries have followed a similarly shaped trajectory, but with Serbia continuously exhibiting lower scores than Croatia:

Figure 8.1: Democratisation trajectories of Croatia, Serbia and Slovenia 1991–2010

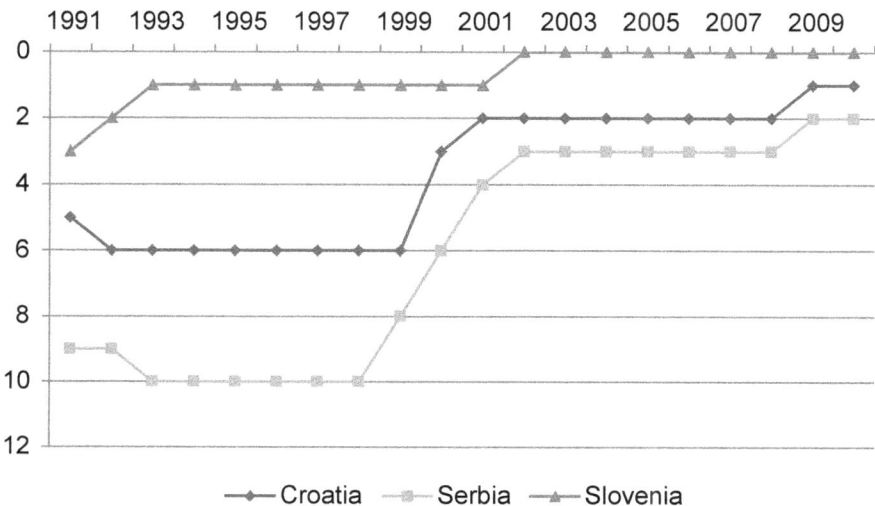

Source: Freedom House

Figure 8.1 compares democratisation trajectories of Croatia and Serbia to that of Slovenia in order to return to the originally postulated divergence among countries of Southeast and Central Eastern Europe. Since the three countries used to belong to the same state, the marked difference in the three trajectories is instructive. Notwithstanding that these countries were different already while in Yugoslavia, it seems evident from Figure 8.1 that the period of the 1990s was an important source of divergence when it comes to subsequent success in democratic reforms. Slovenia capitalised on favourable economic and social preconditions, avoided the war and made decisive steps forward at the very onset of regime change. Already in 1992 Slovenia had a high democracy score of two, a score which Serbia reached only in 2009. While the violence and state-building surely account for the very low scores of Croatia and Serbia in the 1990s, the fact that after 2000 they still did not reach Slovenia's 1990s scores suggests negative path dependency. The case studies offer strong evidence for the argument according to which the mode of rule from the 1990s survived well after the 2000 pro-democratic turn, slowing down further democratisation. The slight curve upwards in the last period suggests that this influence might be waning, but it remains to be seen whether this translates into permanent democratic advances in the two countries.

Going back to the overall design of this study, I aimed to discover why democratisation in countries of Southeast Europe failed to reach levels comparable with countries of Central Eastern Europe in the second decade since regime change. The argument that I proposed placed the crucial focus on authoritarian party dominance, which produced a mode of rule inimical to functioning rule of law systems. This mode of rule continued to obstruct the establishment of rule of law system even after the initial authoritarian party dominance was broken because their governance practices coalesced into fundamental features of these regimes that have proven difficult to dismantle. In addition to this central proposition, an argument was developed about how structural preconditions conditioned political events surrounding regime change. While initial structural preconditions are understood to condition the supply of political party alternatives as the strongest predictor of success in democratisation, in cases where violent conflicts occurred this exacerbated unfavourable trajectories or derailed originally positive ones. Similarly, according to the proposed argument the role of EU as external democracy promoter either accentuated favourable combinations of facilitating legacies and democratic elites, or helped reorient originally less decisively positive democratisation trajectories.

These propositions were analysed by applying various methods across Chapters 3–7. The first level of empirical analysis in Chapters 3 and 4 focused on exploring the diversity of the fourteen country cases behind the two regional labels. Numerous indicators were compared to enable an empirical assessment of theoretical propositions, starting from indicators of social and economic development and previous regime types all the way to election and party data, and the character of the process of European integration in post-communist Europe. Initial verification of the theoretical framework was provided through analysis of bivariate relationships which established association between key explanatory factors and divergent democratisation trajectories. Regression analysis on data from post-communist Europe confirmed the well-established relationship between economic development and democracy. Descriptive analysis of economic and social indicators in the period after 1990 revealed that the fourteen analysed countries do not group according to the political regions of Central Eastern and Southeast Europe, which may be understood more as the result of contemporary geopolitical concerns than long term historical divisions. Looking at post-communist Europe from the perspective of global development, differences in socioeconomic development or predominant values in the population are not large, which in part reaffirms the homogenising impact of the historic period of communist rule. Those important differences that do emerge can in part be attributed to cultural legacies of Orthodoxy and Catholicism, as well as to the fact that the communist regimes across Europe differed in the scope of their modernisation projects; here the difference between Yugoslavia on the one hand and Albania on the other comes immediately to mind.

Inglehart and Welzel's (2005) work on the World Values Survey data was replicated to create composite variables that capture dimensions of the survival – self-expression cluster. Using 1995 survey data, the analysis re-established the association between citizens' preferences and democratisation. The more the self-expression cluster of values is present in the population of a given country, the better its democratisation trajectory. Though the established correlation was not very high, this analysis served the purpose of triangulating the already established relationship between modernisation preconditions and democratisation on a different set of data. Overall, empirical analyses confirmed theoretical predictions according to which levels of socioeconomic development, communist regime type and citizens' value orientations are important factors of subsequent democratisation.

The analysis of party system dynamics drew from scholarship that emphasised competitiveness and constellation as two major features of party systems important for democratisation. Schimmelfennig's concept of party constellation was extended to define an authoritarian party as a party that concentrates power in the executive, converts political to economic power through rigged privatisations and politicises the state apparatus and the public sector for party and private gain. Analysing the relationship between political party competitiveness and constellation, an argument was developed according to which the constellation of political parties conditions the influence that competitiveness has on democratisation. The first part of the analysis focused on two features of party system dynamics: communist exit and the two-turnover test. It showed that, among the six countries of Southeast Europe, only in Croatia did the communist party lose the first multiparty election, while everywhere else the communist parties undertook slow or declaratory reforms while remaining in power. In four cases the former communist party dominated the regime change period: Bulgaria, Macedonia, Romania and Serbia. Though in Albania two large parties alternated in office during regime change, and in Croatia an anti-communist party was in office, the essential characteristic that all six cases share was that authoritarian parties were entrusted with the development of democratic institutions in the initial period of regime change.

The two-turnover test further emphasised differences among the countries of Central Eastern and Southeast Europe. While the five countries from Central Eastern Europe passed the two-turnover test by 1998, Serbia only reached this threshold of democratic consolidation in mid-2012. The two-turnover test also focused attention on the fact that in seven cases the party which won the initial elections stayed in power for six to ten years. This was the case in Romania, Bulgaria, Macedonia, the Czech Republic, Slovakia, Croatia and Serbia. Two countries that emerged from the same federation, Slovakia and the Czech Republic, were both characterised by a long period of one-party dominance, the HZDS and the ODS respectively. The resulting divergence in their initial democratisation trajectories serves as a good illustration of the relationship between political party constellation and competitiveness. While in the Czech case of democratic party constellation the absence of alternation of power did not negatively affect democratisation, in the Slovak case of authoritarian party dominance over regime change, the absence of alternation of power exacerbated negative effects on democratisation.

After key authoritarian parties were identified in the six cases from Southeast Europe, party system competitiveness and constellation were analysed for their association with democratisation. Though both dimensions showed the expected negative association with democratisation, the party constellation dimension showed markedly stronger association with the outcome, strengthening the argument according to which party system constellation conditions the strength of the effect that party system competitiveness has on subsequent democratisation. Nevertheless, since both dimensions were found to contribute to the outcome, the composite authoritarian party dominance was created, and its association with democratisation analysed. The results of bivariate correlation pointed to a very strong association between authoritarian party dominance and the difficulties in establishing rule of law in the post-communist context, empirically verifying the argument according to which authoritarian party dominance plays a key role in explaining lasting rule of law deficiencies.

Chapter 4 also provided operationalisations and analysis of the relationship between the process of European integration and democratisation. The fact that emergent regimes had time to consolidate authoritarian practices and various forms of authoritarian politics before the EU's political conditionality came into force was argued to explain in part why the influence of the European Union was less effective in Southeast Europe. In addition to that, the involvement of the EU in this region was more confounded, not least due to conflicts and security challenges. A brief comparative overview of EU relations with the Western Balkans in Chapter 4 traced the evolution of the EU's involvement in the region, paying special attention to security challenges in Macedonia and in Kosovo. The character of these emergent regimes was less compatible with the mechanism of EU conditionality than was the case with countries of Central Eastern Europe, which underwent a largely self-driven process of reform that was required for entering the EU. The results of bivariate correlations suggested that the EU represented an important part of the explanation for divergent democratisation trajectories in post-communist Europe, confirming the argument according to which the early onset of EU influence was positively related to successful democratisation trajectories.

Fuzzy set QCA analysis in Chapter 5 explored relationships of necessity and sufficiency, tested the theoretical framework and produced configurational recipes. The analyses for sufficiency and necessity revealed strong relationships among each of the explanatory factors and the outcome, strengthening findings from earlier analyses. It established that weak rule of law was in most cases preceded by authoritarian party dominance. This relationship showed the highest scores for consistency and coverage among the examined explanatory factors. Weak rule of law systems were also almost always preceded by inhibiting structural legacies in terms of modernisation preconditions and previous regime type. Finally and not surprisingly, the occurrence of violent conflict has been established as a sufficient condition for rule of law deficiencies; no country that went through conflict has been able to establish functioning rule of law in the observed twenty year period.

Configurational analysis revealed the asymmetric nature of applying set theory, since solutions for the negative outcome differed from those for the positive outcome. Authoritarian party dominance was shown to be the key ingredient in the recipe for stalled democratisation. It was combined with inhibiting legacies in some cases, and violent conflict that postponed EU integration in others. However, since the factor of conflict was somewhat confounding the picture regarding successful democratisation trajectories, a separate analysis of peaceful democratisations was conducted to learn about recipes for successful democratisation. The causal recipe for success turned out to be very simple, requiring good modernisation preconditions, confirming the hypothesis according to which structural preconditions lay down the 'conditioning parameter within which choices are made and solutions are sought' (Kirchheimer 1965: 966). High enough level of economic development and the accompanying social structure engendered democratic and competitive party systems, propelling domestically driven democratic reform.

While this study has focused on explaining the recent historical occurrence of democratic stagnation in countries of Southeast Europe in the second decade after regime change, it does allow for some tentative predictions regarding further democratisation of these countries in the future. Some countries face more formidable obstacles to further democratisation than others. Unresolved statehood disputes burden Macedonia and Serbia, representing sources of instability that make it more difficult for these states to abandon authoritarian politics. While it does not have open statehood problems, Albania's democratisation is the most precarious of the group since it possesses the weakest structural preconditions. Bulgaria, Croatia and Romania on the other hand have stable democratic regimes, the future quality of which depends on how successfully these political systems draw on domestic sources of political and social change.

The main implication of this study however is that democracy cannot be engineered through smart design of formal institutions. Instead, the level of socioeconomic development and previous regime legacy influence whether democratic contenders compete for power, or whether authoritarian parties preside over regime change. In circumstances when authoritarian parties dominated regime change, the introduction of formally democratic institutions was undermined by authoritarian politics. In other words, no sudden jumps forward can be expected in the democratisation trajectories of countries of Southeast Europe. This study shows that political change happens gradually, through the strengthening of independent social spheres, citizens and groups which demand fair treatment by the state and grow into endogenous sources of opposition and control of the political system. Political abuse of power represents the root cause of the lack of legitimacy across the region of post-communist Europe. Before political elites are forced into accepting limitations on their power there will be no democratic deliberation on how to improve the political systems of these countries towards political emancipation, equality and social justice.

| appendices

Datasets

Table 9.1: Post-communist Europe regime type and democracy scores in 2010

Country	Communist regime type	Democracy scores 2010
Albania	1	8
Bulgaria	1	10
Croatia	2	11
Czech Republic	3	12
Estonia	1.5	12
Hungary	2	12
Latvia	1.5	10
Lithuania	1.5	12
Macedonia	1	8
Poland	2.5	12
Romania	1	10
Serbia	1.5	10
Slovakia	1.5	12
Slovenia	2	12

Sources: Kitschelt *et al* (1999) typology, authors operationalisations, Freedom House democracy scores

Table 9.2: Post-communist Europe citizens' democratic values and democracy

Country	Democratic values	Democracy scores
Albania	0.31	8
Bulgaria	0.31	10
Croatia	0.41	11
Czech Republic	0.44	12
Estonia	0.32	12
Hungary	0.33	12
Latvia	0.34	10
Lithuania	0.29	12
Macedonia	0.29	8
Poland	0.32	12
Romania	0.29	10
Serbia	0.33	10
Slovakia	0.38	12
Slovenia	0.40	12

Sources: World Values Survey 1995, Freedom House democracy scores

Table 9.3: Party system competition and constellation variables

Country	Length of one-party dominance, in months	Political party constellation	Freedom House summed democracy scores 2010	Freedom House judicial framework 2010
Albania	10	3	8	2.75
Bulgaria	81	2	10	4
Croatia	115	2	11	2.75
Czech Republic	95	1	12	5
Estonia	17	1	12	5.5
Hungary	48	1	12	5
Latvia	13	1	10	5.25
Lithuania	20	1	12	5.25
Macedonia	93	2	8	3
Poland	38	1	12	4.25
Romania	77	2	10	3
Serbia	117	2	10	2.5
Slovakia	99	2	12	4
Slovenia	31	1	12	5.25

Sources: author's calculations, Freedom House

Table 9.4: Values for the composite variable authoritarian party dominance

Country	Political party constellation	Length of rule	Authoritarian party dominance (composite)
Albania	3	1	3
Bulgaria	2	2	4
Croatia	2	2	4
Czech Republic	1	2	2
Estonia	1	1	1
Hungary	1	1	1
Latvia	1	1	1
Lithuania	1	1	1
Macedonia	2	2	4
Poland	1	1	1
Romania	2	2	4
Serbia	2	2	4
Slovakia	2	2	4
Slovenia	1	1	1

Source: author's calculations

Table 9.5: Length of EU influence and democratisation

Country	Length of EU influence (yrs)	Freedom House judicial framework	Freedom House summed democracy 2010
Albania	8	2.75	8
Bulgaria	19	4	10
Croatia	11	2.75	11
Czech Republic	21	5	12
Estonia	17	5.5	12
Hungary	21	5	12
Latvia	17	5.25	10
Lithuania	17	5.25	12
Macedonia	11	3	8
Poland	21	4.25	12
Romania	19	3	10
Serbia	6	2.5	10
Slovakia	21	4	12
Slovenia	16	5.25	12

Source: author's calculations, Freedom House

Table 9.6: Rule of law and control of corruption in 1996, 2002 and 2008

Country	rol96	corr96	rol02	corr02	rol08	corr08
Albania	-0.1	0.03	-0.9	-0.9	-0.6	-0.45
Bulgaria	-0.1	-0.8	-0.017	-0.027	-0.1	-0.17
Croatia	-0.6	-0.6	0.02	0.27	0.08	0.12
Czech Republic	0.83	0.63	0.77	0.36	0.85	0.37
Estonia	0.51	-0.02	0.73	0.73	1.05	0.94
Hungary	0.87	0.66	0.89	0.64	0.82	0.55
Latvia	0.15	-0.6	0.35	0.11	0.73	0.29
Lithuania	0.3	-0.1	0.4	0.31	0.58	0.18
Macedonia	-0.2	-1.1	-0.6	-0.7	-0.3	-0.11
Poland	0.7	0.44	0.61	0.36	0.49	0.38
Romania	-0.2	-0.2	-0.3	-0.4	-0.05	-0.06
Serbia	-1	-1	-0.9	-0.7	-0.5	-0.16
Slovakia	0.2	0.39	0.29	0.13	0.52	0.43
Slovenia	0.83	1.1	0.99	0.87	0.91	0.95

Source: World Bank Governance Indicators

Table 9.7: Dataset for macro condition 'inhibiting legacy'

Country	Low modernisation	Inhibiting regime legacy	Inhibiting legacy
Albania	0,985	0,95	0,9675
Bulgaria	0,695	0,95	0,8225
Croatia	0,32	0,5	0,41
Czech Republic	0,175	0,05	0,1125
Estonia	0,35	0,82	0,585
Hungary	0,325	0,5	0,4125
Latvia	0,375	0,82	0,5975
Lithuania	0,335	0,82	0,5775
Macedonia	0,86	0,95	0,905
Poland	0,48	0,18	0,33
Romania	0,92	0,95	0,935
Serbia	0,565	0,82	0,6925
Slovakia	0,395	0,82	0,6075
Slovenia	0,0	0,5	0,25

Source: author's calculations

Table 9.8: Peaceful democratisations fuzzy dataset

Country	Low modernisation	Inhibiting regime type	Authoritarian party dominance	Brief EU influence	Weak rule of law
Bulgaria	0,695	0,95	1	0,14	0,55
Czech Republic	0,175	0,05	0,82	0,05	0,13
Estonia	0,35	0,82	0,05	0,35	0,05
Hungary	0,325	0,5	0,05	0,05	0,13
Latvia	0,375	0,82	0,05	0,35	0,08
Lithuania	0,335	0,82	0,05	0,35	0,08
Poland	0,48	0,18	0,05	0,05	0,42
Romania	0,92	0,95	1	0,14	0,89
Slovakia	0,395	0,82	1	0,05	0,55
Slovenia	0,0	0,5	0,05	0,5	0,08

Source: author's calculations

Results of fsQCA configurational analysis

Table 9.9: Configurational analysis for weak rule of law outcome, fourteen cases

	Complex solution	Parsimonious solution	Intermediate solution
Weak rule of law	inhibiting legacy * ~conflict * authoritarian p.d. Conflict * authoritarian p.d. * brief EU	inhibiting legacy*authoritarian p. d. Conflict Brief EU	authoritarian p.d. * inhibiting legacy authoritarian p.d. * brief EU * conflict
Coverage	0.84	0.93	0.92
Consistency	0.93	0.77	0.93
Cases	First solution: Romania, Bulgaria, Albania, Slovakia Second solution: Croatia, Serbia, Macedonia	First solution: Albania, Romania, Macedonia, Bulgaria, Serbia, Slovakia Second solution: Croatia, Serbia, Macedonia Third solution: Serbia, Albania, Croatia, Macedonia	First solution: Albania, Romania, Macedonia, Bulgaria, Serbia, Slovakia Second solution: Croatia, Serbia, Macedonia

Table 9.10: Configurational analysis for functioning rule of law outcome, fourteen cases

	Complex solution	Parsimonious solution	Intermediate solution
~weak rule of law	~conflict * ~authoritarian p d.* ~brief EU ~inhibiting legacy * ~conflict *~brief EU*	~authoritarian p. d. ~inhibiting legacy * ~brief EU ~inhibiting legacy * ~conflict	~brief EU *~conflict *~inhibiting legacy ~brief EU *~authoritarian p. d. * ~conflict *
Coverage	0.75	0.93	0.75
Consistency	0.92	0.93	0.92
Cases	First solution: Hungary, Poland, Estonia, Latvia, Lithuania Second solution: the Czech Republic, Poland, Hungary	First solution: Estonia, Hungary, Latvia, Lithuania, Poland, Slovenia Second solution: the Czech Republic, Poland, Hungary Third solution: the Czech Republic, Slovenia, Poland, Hungary	First solution: the Czech Republic, Poland, Hungary Second solution: Hungary, Poland, Estonia, Latvia, Lithuania

Table 9.11: Configurational analyses for peaceful democratisations

	Complex solution	Parsimonious solution	Intermediate solution
Weak rule of law	~brief EU * inhibiting regime * authoritarian party dominance	inhibiting regime * authoritarian p.d.	authoritarian p.d. * inhibiting regime
Coverage	0.78	0.79	0.79
Consistency	0.79	0.76	0.76
Cases	Bulgaria, Romania, Slovakia	Bulgaria, Romania, Slovakia	Bulgaria, Romania, Slovakia
~weak rule of law	~low modern * ~ brief EU	~ low modernisation	~low modern * ~ brief EU
Coverage	0.75	0.81	0.75
Consistency	0.97	0.96	0.97
Cases	the Czech Republic, Hungary, Estonia, Latvia, Lithuania, Slovakia, Poland	Slovenia, the Czech Republic, Hungary, Estonia, Latvia, Lithuania, Slovakia, Poland	the Czech Republic, Hungary, Estonia, Latvia, Lithuania, Slovakia, Poland

List of interviews in chronological order

November 2010

1.   Mirjana Kasapović, Faculty of Political Science of the University of Zagreb, university professor and leading expert in Croatia on electoral systems and author of *Key Terms on Elections* (2003) .

2.   Dejan Jović, Faculty of Political Science of the University of Zagreb, university professor and political advisor to the President of Croatia, author of *Yugoslavia: A State that Withered Away* (2009).

3.   Damir Grubiša, Faculty of Political Science of the University of Zagreb, expert on the politics of corruption.

4.   Tonči Kursar, Faculty of Political Science of the University of Zagreb, university professor and specialist on theories of democracy.

5.   Goran Čular, Faculty of Political Science of the University of Zagreb, author of edited volume *Elections and the Consolidation of Democracy in Croatia* (2005).

6.   Žarko Puhovski, Faculty of Philosophy of the University of Zagreb, public intellectual in Croatia.

7.   Dušan Pavlović, Faculty of Political Science of the University of Belgrade, author of *Consolidation of Democratic Institutions in Serbia after 2000* (2007, with Slobodan Antonić).

8.   Hedvig Morvai Horvat, Executive Director of the European Fund for the Balkans.

9.   Sonja Licht, President of the Belgrade Fund for Political Excellence and leading civil society figure in Serbia.

10.   Srđa Popović, attorney at law, represents Đinđić's family in a trial aimed at uncovering the political background to the PM's assassination, public intellectual in Serbia.

11.   Daniel Bochsler, researcher at the Centre for Comparative and International Studies at ETH-Zürich, author of *Territory and Electoral Rules in Post-Communist Democracies* (2010).

12.   Nebojša Vladisavljević, Faculty of Political Science of the University of Belgrade, author of *Serbia's Antibureaucratic Revolution: Milošević, the Fall of Communism and Nationalist Mobilisation* (2008).

December 2010

13.   Tin Gazivoda, Advisor to the Open Society Foundation in Croatia, civil society actor in Croatia.

January 2011

14.   Nenad Zakošek, Faculty of Political Science of the University of Zagreb, university professor and author of *Croatia's Political System* (2002).

15.   Srđan Dvornik, independent analyst and civil society actor in Croatia, author of *Actors without Society* (2009).

February 2011

16.   Slaviša Orlović, Faculty of Political Science of the University of Belgrade, author of *Political Life of Serbia: Between Partitocracy and Democracy* (2008).

17.   Dragana Nikolić Solomon, Head of Media Department, OSCE Mission to Serbia.

18.   Mladen Lazić, Sociology Department, Faculty of Philosophy of the University of Belgrade, author of *Change and Resistance* (2005) and *Waiting for Capitalism* (2011).

| bibliography

Acemoglu, D. and Robinson, J. A. (2006) *Economic Origins of Dictatorship and Democracy*, Cambridge: Cambridge University Press.

Adamson, K. and Jović, D. (2003) 'The Macedonian–Albanian political frontier: the re-articulation of post-Yugoslav political identities', *Nations and Nationalism*, 10(3): 293–311.

Almond, G. A. and Verba, S. (1963) *The Civic Culture: Political attitudes and democracy in five nations*, Princeton: Princeton University Press.

Antić, M. and Dodić, M. (2008) 'The parliamentary election in Croatia November 2007' *Electoral Studies*, 27: 740–773.

Arat, Z. F. (1988) 'Democracy and economic development: modernization theory revisited', *Comparative Politics*, 21(1): 21–36.

Arendt, H. (1968) *The Origins of Totalitarianism*, New York: Harvest Books.

Aslund, A. (2007) *How Capitalism Was Built: The transformation of Central and Eastern Europe, Russia and Central Asia*, Cambridge: Cambridge University Press.

Ayers, A. J. (2008) '"We all know a democracy when we see one": (neo)liberal orthodoxy in the 'democratisation' and 'good governance' project', *Policy and Society*, 27: 1–13.

Banac, I. (1992) 'Post-Communism as Post-Yugoslavism: The Yugoslav Non-Revolutions of 1989–1990', in I. Banac, *Eastern Europe in Revolution*, Ithaca: Cornell University Press.

Bates, R., Grief, A., Levi, M., Rosenthal, J. L. and Weingast, B. (1998) *Analytical Narratives*, Princeton: Princeton University Press.

Batt, J. (2007) 'The Western Balkans', in S. White *et al.* (eds) *Developments in Central and East European Politics*, London: Palgrave Macmillan.

Bechev, D. (2006) 'Carrots, sticks and norms: the EU and regional cooperation in Southeast Europe', *Journal of Southern Europe and the Balkans*, 8(1): 27–43.

Bejaković, P. (2002) 'Corruption in Croatia – institutional settings and practical experiences', *Politička misao*, 39(5): 128–155.

Belgrade Center for Human Rights (2010) Human Rights in Serbia– A Comprehensive Report for 2009, available at http://english.bgcentar.org. rs/index.php?option=com_content&view=article&id=452&Itemid=129 (accessed 20 August 2012).

Bellamy, R. (2007) *Political Constitutionalism: A republican defence of the constitutionality of democracy*, Cambridge: Cambridge University Press.

Berend, I. T. (1996) *Central and Eastern Europe 1944–1993: Detour from the periphery to the periphery*, Cambridge: Cambridge University Press.

— (1997) 'Transformation and Structural Change: Central and Eastern Europe's Post-communist Adjustment in Historical Perspective', in T.

Hayashi (ed.) *The Emerging New Regional Order in Central and Eastern Europe*, Sapporo: SRC Hokkaido University.

— (2001) Decades of Crisis: Central and Eastern Europe before World War II, Berkeley: University of California Press.

Berglund, S., Ekman, J. and Aarebrot, F. H. (2004) *The Handbook of Political Change in Eastern Europe*, Northampton: Edward Elgar.

Bermeo, N. (2003) 'What the democratization literature says – or doesn't say – about postwar democratization', *Global Governance, 9*: 159–177.

— (2010) 'Interests, inequality and illusion in the choice for fair elections', *Comparative Political Studies*, 43(8–9): 1119–1147.

Bićanić, I. (1993) 'Privatization in Croatia', *East European Politics and Societies, 7*: 422–439.

Bicchi, F. (2006) '"Our size fits all": normative power, Europe and the Mediterranean', *Journal of European Public Policy,* 13(2): 286–303.

Bideleux, R. and Jeffries, I. (2007) *The Balkans: A post-communist history*, London: Routledge.

Birch, S. (2005) 'Lessons from Eastern Europe: Electoral Reform Following the Collapse of Communism', paper prepared for the conference on 'Electoral Reform in Canada: Getting Past Debates about Electoral Systems', Mount Allison University, Sackville, New Brunswick, Canada, 10–12 May, 2005.

Blondel, J. (1999) 'The Role of Parties and Party Systems in the Democratization Process' in I. Marsh, J. Blondel and T. Inoguchi (eds) *Democracy, Governance and Economic Performance: East and Southeast Asia*, Tokyo, New York, Paris: United Nations University Press.

Blondel, J. and Müller-Rommel, F. (2001) *Cabinets in Eastern Europe*, New York: Palgrave.

Bochsler, D. (2008a) 'Parliamentary election in Serbia 21 January 2007', *Electoral Studies, 27*: 151–190.

— (2008b) 'Hawk in dove's clothing: political trajectories of political parties in Serbia 2003–2008', *Central European Political Studies Review*, 10(4): 292–319.

— (2009) 'Political Parties in Serbia', in V. Stojarova and P. Emerson (eds) *Party Politics in the Western Balkans*, London: Routledge.

Boix, C. (2003) *Democracy and Redistribution*, Cambridge: Cambridge University Press.

Boix, C. and Stokes, S. C. (2003) 'Endogenous Democratization', *World Politics, 55*(4): 517–549.

Börzel, T. A. and Risse, T. (2004) 'One Size Fits All! EU Policies for the Promotion of Human Rights, Democracy and the Rule of Law', paper presented at Workshop on Democracy Promotion, Oct. 4–5, Stanford University.

Brady, H. E. and Collier, D. (2004) *Rethinking Social Inquiry: Diverse tools, shared standards*, Lanham: Rowman & Littlefield Publishers.

Brown, W. (2011) 'We are all democrats now…', in G. Agamben (ed.) *Democracy in What State?*, New York: Columbia University Press, pp. 44-60.

Bruszt, L. and Stark, D. (1998) *Postsocialist Pathways: Transforming politics and property in East Central Europe*, Cambridge: Cambridge University Press.

Bunce, V. (1999a) *Subversive Institutions: The design and destruction of socialism and the state*, Cambridge: Cambridge University Press.

— (1999b) 'The political economy of post-socialism', *Slavic Review,* 58(4): 756–793.

Capoccia, G. and Ziblatt, D. (2010) 'The historical turn in democratization studies: a new research agenda for Europe and beyond', *Comparative Political Studies,* 43(8/9): 931–968.

Caratan, B. (2009) 'The European Union, South-Eastern Europe and the Europeanization of Croatia', *Politička misao*, 46(5): 171–180.

Carothers, T. (1998) 'The rule of law revival', *Foreign Affairs*, 77(2): 95–106.

— (2002) 'The end of the transition paradigm', *Journal of Democracy,* 12(1): 5–21.

Čengić, D. (2000) 'Vladajuća elita i proces delegitimacije privatizacijskog projekta: ima li pouka za budućnost?' *Društvena istraživanja*, 9 (4–5): 497–525.

Centre for the Study of Democracy (2010) *Organised Crime and Corruption: National characteristics and policies of the EU member states*, Sofia: CSD.

— (2009) *Crime Without Punishment: Countering corruption and organized crime in Bulgaria*, Sofia: CSD.

Clark, J. N. (2008) *Serbia in the Shadow of Milošević: The legacy of conflict in the Balkans*, London: Tauris Academic Studies.

Collier, D. and Collier, R. B. (1991) *Shaping the Political Arena: Critical junctures, the Labour movement, and regime dynamics in Latin America,* Princeton: Princeton University Press.

Collier, D. and Levitsky, S. (1996) 'Democracies with Adjectives: Conceptual Innovation in Comparative Research' , Working Paper 230, available at http://www.nd.edu/~kellogg/publications/workingpapers/WPS/230.pdf, (accessed 20 August 2012).

Consolidation of Democracy in Central and Eastern Europe 1990–2001, dataset available from Gesis.

Čular, G. (2000) 'Political development in Croatia 1990–2000: fast transition postponed consolidation', *Croatian Political Science Review*, 5: 30–46.

— (2005) 'Politčke stranke i potpora demokraciji' in G. Čular (ed.) *Izbori i konsolidacija demokracije u Hrvatskoj*, Zagreb: Fakultet političkih znanosti.

Cviić, K. (1997) 'Plus ça change in former Yugoslavia?', *The World Today,* 53(10): 247–249.

Cviić, K. and Sanfey, P. (2008) *Jugoistočna Europa od konflikta do suradnje*, EPHLiber, Zagreb.

Dahl, R. A. (1971) *Polyarchy: Participation and opposition*, New Haven: Yale University Press.

—   (1998) *On Democracy*, New Haven: Yale University Press.
Dahrendorf, R. (1990 [2004]) *Reflections on the Revolutions in Europe*, Piscataway, N. J.: Transaction Publishers (originally published in German in 1990).
Dalton, R. J. and van Sickle, A. (2005) 'The Resource, Structural, and Cultural Bases of Protest', Center for the Study of Democracy, UC Irvine, available at http://escholarship.org/uc/item/3jx2b911.
Darden, K. and Grzymala Busse, A. (2006) 'The great divide: literacy, nationalism, and the communist collapse', *World Politics,* 59(1): 83–115.
Daskalovski, Z. (2004) 'Democratic consolidation and the 'stateness' problem: the case of Macedonia', *The Global Review of Ethnopolitics,* 3(2): 52–66.
Dawisha, K. and Deets, S. (2006) 'Political learning in post-communist elections', *East European Politics and Societies*, 20: 691–728.
De Ridder, E. and Kochenov, D. (2011) 'Democratic conditionality in Eastern enlargement: ambitious window dressing', electronic copy of the article available at: http://ssrn.com/abstract=1930911. Last August 20, 2012.
Di Palma, G. (1990) *To Craft Democracies: An Essay on Democratic Transitions*, Berkeley: University of California Press.
Diamandouros, P. N. and Larrabee, F. S. (2000) 'Democratization in South-Eastern Europe: theoretical considerations and evolving trends', in G. Pridham and T. Gallagher (eds) *Experimenting With Democracy: Regime Change in the Balkans*, London and New York: Routledge.
Diamond, L. (2000) 'Is Pakistan the (reverse) wave of the future?', *Journal of Democracy*, 11(4): 81–107.
—   (2002) 'Thinking about hybrid regimes', *Journal of Democracy*, 13(2): 21–35.
Diamond, L. and Morlino, L. (2004) 'Quality of democracy', *Journal of Democracy*, 15(4): 20–31.
Dolenec, D (2008) 'Europeanization as a democratising force in postcommunist Europe: Croatia in comparative perspective', *Croatian Political Science Review*, 5: 23–46.
—   (2009) 'Demokratizacija stranačkog sustava u Hrvatskoj: ponuda i potražnja javnih politika', in Z. Petak (ed.) *Stranke i javne politike. Izbori u Hrvatskoj 2007*, Zagreb: Biblioteka Politička Misao.
Downs, W. M. and Miller, R. V. (2006) 'The 2004 presidential and parliamentary elections in Romania', *Electoral Studies*, 25: 393–415.
Dulić, D. (2011) 'Serbia After Milošević: The Rebirth of a Nation', in O. Listhaug, O., Ramet and D. Dulić (eds) *Civic and Uncivic Values: Serbia in the post-Milošević Era*, Budapest: CEU Press.
Dvornik, S. (2009) *Akteri bez društva: uloga civilnih aktera u postkomunističkim promjenama*, Zagreb: Fraktura and Heinrich Boll Stiftung.
Džihić, V. and Segert, D. (2012) 'Lessons from "Post-Yugoslav" Democratization functional problems of stateness and the limits of Democracy', *East European Politics and Societies*, 26(2): 239–253.
Eagleton, T. (2011) *Why Marx Was Right*, New Haven: Yale University Press.

EBRD (1999) Life in Transition Report, available at http://www.ebrd.com/ downloads/research/transition/TR99.pdf. Last August 20, 2012.

Economist Intelligence Unit (2005) Quality of Life Report, available at http://www.economist.com/media/pdf/QUALITY_OF_LIFE.pdf. Last accessed August 20, 2012.

Eisenstadt, S. N. (2000) 'Multiple modernities', *Daedalus*, 129: 1–29.

Ejdus, F. (2010) 'Demokratsko upravljanje sektorom bezbednosti u Srbiji' in Pavlović, D. (ed.) *Razvoj demokratskih ustanova u Srbiji – deset godina posle*, Beograd: Heinrich Boll Stiftung.

Ekiert, G. (1991) 'Democratization processes in East Central Europe: a theoretical reconsideration', *British Journal of Political Science*, 21(3): 285–313.

— (2003) 'Patterns of postcommunist transformation', in G. Ekiert and S. E. Hanson (eds) *Capitalism and Democracy in Central and Eastern Europe: Assessing the legacy of communist rule*, Cambridge: Cambridge University Press.

Ekiert, G. and Hanson, S. E. (2003) 'Time, Space, and Institutional Change in Central and Eastern Europe', in G. Ekiert and S. E. Hanson (eds) *Capitalism and Democracy in Central and Eastern Europe: Assessing the legacy of communist rule*, Cambridge: Cambridge University Press.

Ekiert, G. and Kubik, J. (1999) *Rebellious Civil Society: Popular protest and democratic consolidation in Poland, 1989–1993*, Ann Arbor: University of Michigan Press.

Ekiert, G., Kubik, J. and Vachudova, M. A. (2007) 'Democracy in postcommunist world: an unending quest', *East European Politics and Societies*, 21(1): 1–24.

Elbasani, A. (2004) 'Albania in transition: manipulation or appropriation of international norms?' *Southeast European Politics*, June issue: 24–44.

Elster, J., Offe, C. and Preuss, U. K. (1998) *Institutional Design in Post-Communist Societies: Rebuilding the ship at sea*, Cambridge: Cambridge University Press.

Engström, J. (2009) *Democratisation and the Prevention of Violent Conflict: Lessons learned from Bulgaria and Macedonia*, London: Ashgate.

European Commission Reports (available at http://ec.europa.eu/enlargement/ candidate-countries/index_en.htm).

— (2012) CVM Report for Bulgaria.

— (2012) CVM Report for Romania.

— (2010) CVM Report for Romania.

— (2010) Progress Report on Croatia.

— (2009) Progress Report for Croatia.

— (2009) Progress Report for Serbia.

— (2005) Progress Report on Croatia.

— (2005a) Feasibility Report for Serbia's entry into SAP.

— (2005b) Progress Report for Serbia.

— (2003) SAP Report on Croatia.

— (2002) SAP Report on Croatia.

— (2002) SAP Report on Serbia.

European Values Survey (2008) Dataset available at http://www. europeanvaluesstudy.eu/. Last accessed August 20, 2012.

Fink-Hafner (2000) 'The case of Slovenia', in H. Riegler (ed.) *Transformation Processes in the Yugoslav Successor States between Marginalization and European Integration*, Baden und Baden: Nomos.

Fish, S. (1998) 'The determinants of economic reform in the post-communist World' *East European Politics and Societies* 12(1): 31–78.

— (2001) 'The Dynamics of Democratic Erosion' in R. D. Anderson *et al* (eds) *Postcommunism and the Theory of Democracy*, Princeton: Princeton University Press.

— (2005) *Democracy Derailed in Russia*, Cambridge: Cambridge University Press.

— (2006) 'Stronger Legislatures, Stronger Democracies', *Journal of Democracy*, 17(1): 5–20.

Fish, M. S. and Krickovic, A. (2002) 'Out of the brown and into the blue: the tentative "Christian-Democratization" of the Croatian Democratic Union', *East European Constitutional Review*, (12)2: 104–112.

Fisher, S. (2006) *Political Change in Post-Communist Slovakia and Croatia: From Nationalist to Europeanist*, London: Palgrave.

Fishman, R. M. (1990) 'Review: rethinking state and regime: Southern Europe's transition to democracy', *World Politics*, 42(3): 422–440.

Forgeard, M. J. C., Jayawickreme, E., Kern, M. and Seligman, M. E. P. (2011) 'Doing the right thing: measuring wellbeing for public policy', *International Journal of Wellbeing*, 1(1): 79–106.

Freedom House website, Freedom in the World Comparative and Historical Data, http://www.freedomhouse.org/template.cfm?page=439. Last June 1, 2010.

Fukuyama, F. (1992) *The End of History and the Last Man*, Avon Books, New York.

Gallagher, T. (1995) 'Democratization in the Balkans: Challenges and prospects', *Democratization*, 2(3): 337–361.

Gallagher, T. (1996) 'The emergence of new party systems and transitions to democracy: Romania and Portugal compared', in G. Pridham and P. G. Lewis (eds) *Stabilizing Fragile Democracies: Comparing party systems in Southern and Eastern Europe*, London and New York: Routledge.

Gallagher, T. (2003) *The Balkans after the Cold War: From tyranny to tragedy*, London and New York: Routledge.

Gallup Balkan Monitor (2010) 'Insights and Perceptions: Voices of the Balkans', available at http://www.balkan-monitor.eu/files/BalkanMonitor-2010_ Summary_of_Findings.pdf. Last August 22, 2012.

Ganev, V. I. (2001) 'The Dorian Gray effect: winners as state breakers in postcommunism', *Communist and Post-Communist Studies*, 34: 1–25.

Ganev, V. I. (2007) *Preying on the State: The transformation of Bulgaria after 1989*, Ithaca: Cornell University Press.

Geddes, B. (2009) 'Changes in the Causes of Democratization through Time', in T. Landman and N. Robinson (eds) *Sage Handbook of Comparative Politics*, London: Sage.

George, A. L. and Bennett, A. (2005) *Case Studies and Theory Development in the Social Sciences*, Cambridge: The MIT Press.

Glenny, M. (1995) 'Heading off war in the Southern Balkans', *Foreign Affairs*, May-June issue.

Goati, V. (2001) 'Priroda poretka i oktobarski prevrat u Srbiji', in I. Spasić and M. Subotić (eds) *R/evolucija i poredak: o dinamici promena u Srbiji*, Beograd: Institut za filozofiju i društvenu teoriju.

— (2004) *Partije i partijski sistem u Srbiji*, Beograd: Odbor za građansku inicijativu i Ogi Centar.

Golubović, Z. (2002) 'Karakter društvenih promena u Srbiji 2001', in V. Vasović and V. Pavlović (eds) *Postkomunizam i demokratske promene*, Beograd: Jugoslavensko udruženje za političke nauke, Fakultet političkih nauka.

— (2004) 'Socijalna i politička dinamika postoktobarske Srbije' in V. Vasović and V. Pavlović (eds) *Uslovi i strategije demokratizacije*, Beograd: Jugoslavensko udruženje za političke nauke, Fakultet političkih nauka.

Gould, J. A. (2003) 'Out of the blue? Democracy and privatization in post-communist Europe', *Comparative European Politics,* 1(3): 277–312.

Grabbe, H. (2006) *The EU's Transformative Power*, London: Palgrave MacMillan.

Granić, M. (2005) *Vanjski poslovi: iza kulisa politike*, Zagreb: Naša stvar.

GRECO Reports (available at http://www.coe.int/t/dghl/monitoring/greco/general/3.%20what%20is%20greco_EN.asp).

— Evaluation Report on Croatia 2000.

— Evaluation Report on Croatia 2002.

Green, J. C., Kreider H. and Mayer E. (2005) 'Combining Qualitative and Quantitative Methods in Social Inquiry' in B. Somekh and C. Lewin (eds) *Research Methods in the Social Sciences*, London: Sage.

Greskovits, B. (1998) *The Political Economy of Protest and Patience: East European and Latin American transformations compared*, Budapest: Central European University Press.

Grubiša, D. (1995) 'Politička korupcija u društvima u tranziciji', *Erasmus Journal for Culture of Democracy*, 14: 32–41.

Grugel, J. (2002) *Democratization: A critical introduction*, Basingstoke and New York: Palgrave.

Grzymala Busse, A. (2002) *Redeeming the Communist Past*, Cambridge: Cambridge University Press.

— (2007) *Rebuilding Leviathan: Party competition and state exploitation in post-communist democracies*, Cambridge: Cambridge University Press.

Haggard, S. and Kaufman, R. R. (1997) 'The political economy of democratic transitions' *Comparative Politics*, 29(3): 263–283.

Hall, P. A. (2003) 'Aligning Ontology and Methodology in Comparative Research', in J. Mahoney and D. Rueschemeyer (eds) *Comparative Historical Analysis in the Social Sciences*, Cambridge: Cambridge University Press.

—   (2006) 'Systematic process analysis: when and how to use it' *European Management Review*, 3: 24–31.

Hall, P. A. and Taylor, R. C. R. (1996) 'Political Science and the three new institutionalisms', *Political Studies*, 44(5): 936–957.

Hall, P. A. and Soskice, D. (2001) *Varieties of Capitalism: The industrial foundations of comparative advantage*, Oxford: Oxford University Press.

Hansen, O. and Tot, R. S. J. (2003) 'A refined Inglehart index of materialism and post-materialism', Working Paper FNU-35, Hamburg University.

Hashimoto, T. (2009) 'Victory for European Albania: democratic election as a step towards "strong states"', *European Perspectives – Journal on European Perspectives of the Western Balkans*, 1(1): 75–92.

Hawkins, D. (2009) 'Case Studies' in T. Landman and N. Robinson (eds) *Sage Handbook of Comparative Politics*, London: Sage.

Hellman, J. S. (1998) 'Winners take all: the politics of partial reform in postcommunist transitions', *World Politics*, 50(2): 203–234.

Hellman, J. S., Jones, G. and Kaufmann, D. (2000) 'Seize the State, Seize the Day: An Empirical Analysis of State Capture and Corruption in Transition Economies', World Bank Paper prepared for the ABCDE 2000 Conference.

Heywood, P. (2009) 'Corruption' in T. Landman and N. Robinson (eds) *Sage Handbook of Comparative Politics*, London: Sage.

Hislope, R. (2003) 'Between a bad peace and a good war: insights and lessons from the almost-war in Macedonia', *Ethnic and Racial Studies*, 26(1): 129–151.

Hobson, J. M. (2009) 'Comparative Politics and International Relations' in T. Landman and N. Robinson (eds) *Sage Handbook of Comparative Politics*, London: Sage.

Holmes, L. (2006) *Rotten States? Corruption, post-communism, and neoliberalism*, Durham and London: Duke University Press.

Horowitz, D. L. (1985) *Ethnic Groups in Conflict*, Berkeley and Los Angeles: University of California Press.

—   (1993) 'Democracy in divided societies', *Journal of Democracy*, 4(4): 18–38.

Horowitz, S. (2003) 'War after communism: effects on political and economic reform in the former Soviet Union and Yugoslavia', *Journal of Peace Research*, 40(1): 25–48.

Horowitz, S. and Browne, E. C. (2005) 'Sources of post-communist party system consolidation: ideology versus institutions' *Party Politics*, 11(6); 689–70.

Howard, M. M. (2003) *The Weakness of Civil Society in Post-Communist Europe*, Cambridge: Cambridge University Press.

Huntington, S. (1991) *The Third Wave: Democratization in the late Twentieth Century*, Norman: University of Oklahoma Press.

Inglehart, R. (2006) 'East European Value Systems in Global Perspective', in H.-D. Klingemann, D. Fuchs and J. Zielonika (eds) *Democracy and Political Culture in Eastern Europe*, London: Routledge.

Inglehart, R. and Norris, P. (2003) 'The true clash of civilizations', *Foreign Policy*, 135: 62–70.

Inglehart, R. and Welzel, C. (2005) *Modernization, Cultural Change and Democracy*, Cambridge: Cambridge University Press.

International Crisis Group Reports, available at http://www.crisisgroup.org.

— (2006) Serbia's New Constitution: Democracy Going Backwards, No. 44.

— (2001) Serbia's Transition: Reforms Under Siege, No. 117.

— (2000) Albania: State of the Nation, Europe Report No. 87.

Ishiyama, J. T. (1997) 'The van Sickle or the rose?: Previous regime types and the evolution of the ex-communist parties in post-communist politics', *Comparative Political Studies*, 30(3): 299–330.

Ivanov, K. (2010) 'The 2007 accession of Bulgaria and Romania: ritual and reality', *Global Crime*, 11(2): 210–219.

Jacoby, W. (2002) 'Talking the Talk and Walking the Walk: The Cultural and Institutional Effects of Western Models', in F. Bönker, K. Müller and A. Pickel (eds) *Postcommunist Transformation and the Social Sciences: Cross-disciplinary approaches*, Boulder, Col.: Rowman & Littlefield, pp.129–152.

Jowitt, K. (1992) 'The Leninist Legacy', in I. Banac (ed). *Eastern Europe in Revolution*, Ithaca: Cornell University Press.

Karasimeonov, G. (1996) 'Bulgaria's New Party System', in G. Pridham and P. G. Lewis (eds) *Stabilizing Fragile Democracies: Comparing party systems in Southern and Eastern Europe*, London and New York: Routledge.

Karatnycky, A. (1999) 'The decline of illiberal democracy', *Journal of Democracy*, 10(1): 112–23.

Karklins, R. (2002) 'Typology of post-communist corruption', *Problems of Post-Communism*, July-August issue: 22–32.

Karl, T. L. (1995) 'The Hybrid Regimes of Central America', *Journal of Democracy*, 3(4): 72–86.

Karl, T. L. and Schmitter, P. C. (1991) 'Modes of transition in Latin America, Southern and Eastern Europe', *International Social Science Journal*, 43 (2): 269–284.

Kasapović, M. (1993) 'Transition and Neoinstitutionalism: the Example of Croatia', *Croatian Political Science Review*, 2: 71–79.

— (1995) 'Izborni rezultati – analiza', *Erasmus Journal for Culture of Democracy*, 3(14): 3–23.

— (1996) 'Demokratska tranzicija i političke institucije u Hrvatskoj', *Politička misao*, 33(2/3): 84–99.

— (2000) 'Ten Years of Democratic Transition in Croatia 1989–1999', in H. Riegler (ed.) *Transformation Processes in Yugoslav Successor States Between Marginalization and European Integration*, OiiP.

— (2001) 'Demokratska konsolidacija i izborna politika u Hrvatskoj 1990–2000', in M. Kasapović (ed.) *Hrvatska politika* 1990–2000, Zagreb: Fakultet političkih znanosti.

—   (2003) 'Coalition governments in Croatia: first experience 2000–2003', *Croatian Political Science Review* 40(5): 52–67.

—   (2005) 'Koalicijske vlade u Hrvatskoj: prva iskustva u komparativnoj perspektivi', in G. Čular (ed.) *Izbori i konsolidacija demokracije u Hrvatskoj*, Zagreb : Fakultet političkih znanosti.

—   (2008) 'Semi-presidentialism in Croatia', in R. Elgie and S. Moestrup (eds) *Semi-Presidentialism in Central and Eastern Europe*, Manchester: Manchester University Press.

—   (2009) 'Croatia: strengthening the rule of law and economic competitiveness', *Südosteuropa*, 57(2/3): 217–234.

Kasapović, M. and Boban, D. (2011) 'Croatia Report' for the Bertelsmann Transformation Index Study, unpublished paper.

Kasapović, M. and Zakošek, Z. (1997) 'Democratic Transition in Croatia: Between Democracy, Sovereignty and War', in I. Šiber (ed.) *The 1990 and 1992/3 Sabor Elections in Croatia*, Berlin: Ed. Sigma.

Katz, R. S. (2007 [1980]) *Theory of Parties and Electoral Systems*, Baltimore: Johns Hopkins University Press.

King, C. (2000) 'Post-postcommunism: transition, comparison, and the end of "Eastern Europe"', *World Politics*, 53:1, 143–172.

—   (2001) 'Potemkin Democracy', *The National Interest*, 64: 93–104.

Kingdon, J. W. (1995) *Agendas, Alternatives and Public Policies*, London: Longman Publishing Group.

Kirchheimer, O. (1965) 'Confining conditions and revolutionary breakthroughs', *American Political Science Review*, 59(4): 964–974.

Kitschelt, H. (2003) 'Accounting for Post-communist Regime Diversity: What Counts as a Good Cause?' in G. Ekiert and S. E. Hanson (eds) *Capitalism and Democracy in Central and Eastern Europe: Assessing the legacy of communist rule*, Cambridge: Cambridge University Press.

Kitschelt, H., Mansfeldova, Z., Markowski, R. and Toka, G. (1999) *Post-Communist Party Systems*, Cambridge: Cambridge University Press.

Kochenov, D. (2004) 'Behind the Copenhagen facade: the meaning and structure of the Copenhagen political criterion of democracy and the rule of law', *European Integration Online Papers*, 8(10). Available at http://eiop.or.at/eiop/pdf/2004-010.pdf. Last accessed April 23, 2013.

Konitzer, A. (2008) 'The parliamentary election in Serbia May 2008' *Electoral Studies*, 28: 141–173.

Kopstein, J. S. and Reilly, D. A. (2000) 'Geographic diffusion and the transformation of the postcommunist world', *World Politics*, 53(1): 1–37.

Krastev, I. (2004) *Shifting Obsessions: Three essays on the politics of anticorruption*, Budapest: CEU Press.

Kurki, M. (2012) 'How the EU can adopt a new type of democracy support', FRIDE Working Paper, No. 112, p. 1–21.

Kusovac, Z. (2000) 'The prospects for change in post-Tudjman Croatia', *East European Constitutional Review*, summer issue: 57–62.

Kuzio, T. (2008) 'Comparative perspectives on communist successor parties in

Central-Eastern Europe and Eurasia', *Communist and Post-Communist Studies*, 41: 397–419.

Laakso, M. and Taagepera, R. (1979) '"Effective" number of parties: a measure with application to West Europe', *Comparative Political Studies*, 12(3): 3–27.

Lakatos, I. (1970) 'Falsification and the Methodology of Scientific Research Programmes' in I. Lakatos and A. Musgrave (eds) *Criticism and the Growth of Knowledge*, Cambridge: Cambridge University Press.

Lamza Posavec, V. (2000) 'Što je prethodilo neuspjehu HDZ-a na izborima 2000: Rezultati istraživanja javnoga mnijenja u razdoblju od 1991. do 1999. godine' *Društvena istraživanja*, 9(4–5): 433–471.

Lazić, M. (2004) 'Serbia: a part of both the East and the West?', *Sociologija*, XLV(3).

—   (2005) *Promene i otpori*, Beograd: Filip Višnjić.

—   (2008) 'Nacrt za istraživanja savremenih društvenih promena u Srbiji' *u Konsolidacija demokratskih ustanova u Srbiji: godinu dana posle*, Pavlović, D. (ed.), Službeni glasnik, Beograd.

Lazić, M. and Sekelj, L. (1997) 'Privatisation in Yugoslavia', *Europe-Asia Studies*, 49(6): 1057-70.

Landa, D. and Kapstein, E. B. (2001) 'Inequality, growth, and democracy', *World Politics*, 53(2): 264–296.

Lerner, D. (1958) *The Passing of Traditional Society: Modernizing the Middle East*, Glencoe ILL: The Free Press.

Levitsky, S. and Way, L. (2002) 'The rise of competitive authoritarianism', *Journal of Democracy*, 13(2): 51–65.

Levitz, P. and Pop-Eleches, G. (2010) 'Why no backsliding? The European Union's impact on democracy and governance before and after accession', *Comparative Political Studies*, 43(4): 457–485.

Lewis, P. G. (2001) *Political Parties in Post-Communist Eastern Europe*, London and New York: Routledge.

Lijphart, A. (1986) *Electoral Laws and their Political Consequences*, New York: Agathon Press.

—   (1991) 'Constitutional choices for new democracies' *Journal of Democracy*, 2(1): 72–84.

—   (1999) *Patterns of Democracy: Government forms and performance in thirty-six countries*, New Haven: Yale University Press.

Lindblom, C. E. (1977) *Politics and Markets: The world's political economic systems*, New York: Basic Books.

Linz, J. J. and Stepan, A. (1996) *Problems of Democratic Transition and Consolidation*, Baltimore: Johns Hopkins University Press.

Lipset, S. M. (1959) 'Some social requisites of democracy: economic development and political legitimacy' *American Political Science* Review, 53(1): 69–105.

—   (1994) 'The social requisites of democracy revisited: 1993 Presidential Address', *American Sociological Review*, 59(1): 1–22.

Lukic, R. (2010) 'The Emergence of the Nation-State in East Central Europe and the Balkans in Historical Perspective', in S. P. Ramet (ed.) *Central and Southeast European Politics since 1989*, Cambridge: Cambridge University Press.

Madžar, L. (1996) 'Who Exploited Whom?', in N. Popov (ed.) *The Road to War in Serbia*, Budapest: CEU Press.

Mair, P. (1997) *Party System Change: Approaches and interpretations*, Oxford: Oxford University Press.

Maki, J. M. (2008) 'EU enlargement politics: explaining the development of political conditionality of "Full Cooperation with the ICTY" towards Western Balkans', *Croatian Political Science Review*, XLV(5): 47–80.

Mazower, M. (2002) *The Balkans: A short history*, New York: Random House.

McFaul, M. (2002) 'The fourth wave of democracy and dictatorship: non-cooperative transitions in the postcommunist world', *World Politics*, 54(2): 212–244.

McFaul, M. (2005) 'Transitions from communism', *Journal of Democracy*, 16(3): 5–19.

McGregor, J. P. (1996) Constitutional factors in politics in post-communist Central and Eastern Europe', *Communist and Post-Communist Studies*, 29(2): 147–166.

Merkel, W. (1999) 'Defekte Demokratien', in W. Merkel and A. Busch (eds) *Demokratie in Ost und West*, Frankfurt am Main: Suhrkamp.

— (2004) *Transformacija političkih sustava*, Zagreb: Biblioteka Politička misao.

Migdal, J. S. (1988) *Strong Societies and Weak States: State society relations and state capabilities in the Third World*, Princeton: Princeton University Press.

Millard, F. (1994) 'The shaping of the Polish party system, 1989–93', *East European Politics & Societies*, 8(3): 467–494.

Milosavljević, O. (1996) 'The abuse of the authority of science' in N. Popov (ed.) *The Road to War in Serbia*, Budapest: CEU Press.

Moore, B. (1966) *The Social Origins of Dictatorship and Democracy: Lord and Peasant in the Making of the Modern World*, Boston: Beacon Press.

Mungiu-Pippidi, A. (2006) 'Romania: Fatalistic political cultures revisited', in H.-D. Klingemann, D. Fuchs and J. Zielonika (eds) *Democracy and Political Culture in Eastern Europe*, London: Routledge.

Nations in Transit, Freedom House Reports available at http://www.freedomhouse.org/template.cfm?page=17. Last accessed August 20, 2013.

— (2010) Macedonia Report.

— (2008) Croatia Report.

— (1998) Yugoslavia Report.

— (1997) Croatia Report.

North, C. D. (1999) 'In Anticipation of the Marriage of Political and Economic Theory', in J. E. Alt, M. Levi and E. Ostrom (eds) *Competition and Cooperation: Conversation with Nobelists about economics and political science*, New York: Russell Sage Foundation.

Noutcheva, G. and Bechev, D. (2008) 'The successful laggards: Bulgaria and Romania's accession to the EU', *East European Politics and Societies*, 22(1): 114–144.

Obradović, M. (1996) 'The Ruling Party' in N. Popov (ed.) *The Road to War in Serbia*, Budapest: CEU Press.

O'Donnell, G. A. (1994) 'Delegative democracy', *Journal of Democracy*, 5(1): 55–69.

— (2004) 'Why the Rule of Law Matters', *Journal of Democracy*, 15(4): 32–46.

O'Donnell, G. A., Schmitter, P. C. and Whitehead, L. (1986) *Transitions from Authoritarian Rule: Prospects for democracy*, Baltimore: John Hopkins University Press.

O'Dwyer, C. (2004) 'Runaway state-building: how political parties shape states in postcommunist Eastern Europe', *World Politics*, July: 520–553.

— (2006) Runaway state-building: patronage politics and democratic development, Baltimore: John Hopkins University Press.

Offe, K. (1991) 'Capitalism by democratic design? Democratic theory facing the triple transition in East Central Europe', *Social Research*, 58(4): 864–881.

Orlović, S. (2002) 'Promene u spektru političkih stranaka', in V. Vasović and V. Pavlović (eds) *Postkomunizam i demokratske promene*, Beograd: Jugoslovensko udruženje za političke nauke, Fakultet političkih nauka.

— (2006) 'Demokratska konsolidacija Srbije' in S. Mihailović (ed.) *Pet godina tranzicije u Srbiji*, drugi svezak, Beograd: Friedrich Ebert Stiftung.

— (2008) Politički život Srbije: između partitokratije i demokratije, Beograd: Službeni glasnik.

Parrott, B. (1997) 'Introduction: Perspectives on postcommunist democratization', in K. Dawisha and B. Parrott (eds) *The Consolidation of Democracy in East-Central Europe*, Cambridge: Cambridge University Press.

Pavićević, Đ. (2010) 'Peti oktobar: nedovršena revolucija', in D. Pavlović (ed.) *Razvoj demokratskih ustanova u Srbiji – deset godina posle*, Beograd: Heinrich Boll Stiftung.

Pavlović, D. (2001) 'Populistički katanac', *Nova srpska politička misao*, 1: 229–242.

— (1996) 'The Flight from Modernization', in N. Popov (ed.) *The Road To War in Serbia*, Budapest: CEU Press.

— (2000) 'Modernizacija bez modernosti' in *Ljudi, događaji i knjige*, Biblioteka Svedočanstva, Vol. 1, Helsinki Committee for Human Rights, Beograd.

— (2006) 'Zarobljena država' in S. Mihailović (ed.) *Pet godina tranzicije u Srbiji*, drugi svezak, Beograd: Friedrich Ebert Stiftung.

Pavlović, D. and Antonić, S. (2007) *Konsolidacija demokratskih ustanova u Srbiji posle 2000. Godine*, Beograd: Službeni glasnik.

Pešić. V. (2007) 'Partijska država kao uzrok korupcije u Srbiji', *Republika*, May issue: 402–405.

Philip, G. (1999) 'Democracy and state bias in Latin America: some lessons from Mexico, Peru and Venezuela', *Democratization*, 6(4): 74–92.

Pierson, P. (2000) 'Increasing returns, path dependence and the study of politics' *The American Political Science Review*, 94(2): 251–267.

— (2004) *Politics in Time: History, institutions and social analysis*, Princeton and Oxford: Princeton University Press.

Popović, S. (2010) *One gorke suze posle,* zbornik tekstova sa portala Peščanik; Beograd: Peščanik.

Pop-Eleches, G. (2007) 'Historical legacies and post-communist regime change', *The Journal of Politics*, 69(4): 908–926.

Posavec, Z. (1993) 'The concept of democracy in the development of Yugoslavia 1918-1980', *Croatian Political Science Review*, 2: 64–70.

Pravda, A. (2001) 'Introduction', in J. Zielonika and A. Pravda (eds) *Democratic Consolidation in Eastern Europe: International and transnational factors*, Oxford: Oxford University Press.

Pridham, G. (2000) 'Democratization in the Balkan countries: from theory to practice', in G. Pridham and T. Gallagher (eds) *Experimenting With Democracy: Regime change in the Balkans*, London and New York: Routledge.

— (2001) 'Uneasy democratizations – pariah regimes, political conditionality and reborn transitions in Central and Eastern Europe', *Democratization*, 8(4): 65–94.

Primorac, V. (1994) 'Može li se upropastiti hrvatsko pravosuđe?', interview with Darko Hudelist for *Erasmus Journal for Culture of Democracy*, 7: 2–32.

Przeworski, A. (1991) *Democracy and the Market: Political and economic reforms in Eastern Europe and Latin America*, Cambridge: Cambridge University Press.

— (1995) *Sustainable Democracy*, Cambridge: Cambridge University Press.

Przeworski, A. and Limongi, F. (1997) 'Modernization: theories and facts', *World Politics*, 49(2): 155–183.

Puhovski, Ž. (1990) *Socijalistička konstrukcija zbilje*, Zagreb: Školska knjiga.

— (1993) 'Nationalism and democracy in the post-communist key', in Ž. Puhovski, I. Prpić and D. Vojnić (eds) *Politics and Economics of Transition*, Zagreb: Informator.

Pusić, V. (1994) 'Upotreba nacionalizma i politika prepoznavanja', *Erasmus Journal for Culture of Democracy*, 8: 2–21.

Putnam, R. (1993) *Making Democracy Work*, Princeton: Princeton University Press.

Rabushka, A. and Shepsle, K. A. (1972) *Politics in Plural Societies: A theory of democratic instability*, Ohio: Charles Merrill.

Radojević, M. (2002) 'Parlamentarizam u Srbiji' in V. Vasović and V. Pavlović (eds) *Postkomunizam i demokratske promene*, Beograd: Jugoslavensko udruženje za političke nauke, Fakultet političkih nauka.

Ragin, C. (1987) *The Comparative Method: Moving beyond qualitative and quantitative strategies*, University of California Press.

—   (2000) *Fuzzy Set Social Science*, Chicago: The University of Chicago Press.

—   (2004) 'Turning the Tables: How case-oriented research challenges variable-oriented research' in H. E. Brady and D. Collier (eds) *Rethinking Social Inquiry: Diverse tools, shared standards*, Lanham: Rowman & Littlefield Publishers.

—   (2011) QCA slides, from workshop held at the University of Luzern, May 2011.

Ragin, C. and Rihoux, B. (2009) (eds) *Configurational Comparative Methods: Qualitative Comparative Analysis (QCA) and related techniques*, London: Sage.

Ragin, C. and Rubinson, C. (2009) 'The distinctiveness of comparative research' in T. Landman and N. Robinson (eds) *Sage Handbook of Comparative Politics* in London: Sage.

Ramet, S. P. (1996) *Balkan Babel: The disintegration of Yugoslavia from the Death of Tito to Ethnic War*, Boulder: Westview Press.

—   (2010) 'Introduction' in S.P. Ramet (ed.) *Central and Southeast European Politics since 1989*, Cambridge: Cambridge University Press.

—   (2011) 'Serbia's Corrupt Path to the Rule of Law: An Introduction', in O. Listhaug, S. P. Ramet and D. Dulić (eds) *Civic and Uncivic Values: Serbia in the post-Milošević Era*, Budapest: CEU Press.

Ramet, S. P. and Wagner, F. P. (2010) 'Post-Socialist Models of Rule in Central and Southeast Europe', in S. P. Ramet (ed.) *Central and Southeast European Politics since 1989*, Cambridge: Cambridge University Press.

Rancière, J. (2011) 'Democracies against democracy', in *Democracy in What State?*, New York: Columbia University Press.

Rihoux, B. and Ragin, C. (2009) *Configurational comparative methods: Qualitative Comparative Analysis (QCA) and related techniques*, Los Angeles: Sage.

Roberts, A. (2005) 'Review: the quality of democracy', *Comparative Politics*, 37(3) 357–376.

Robertson, G. (2011) *The Politics of Protest in Hybrid Regimes*, Cambridge University Press.

Roeder, P. G. (1999) 'Peoples and states after 1989: the political costs of incomplete national revolutions' *Slavic Review*, 58(4): 854–882.

Rose, R. and Mishler, W. (1998) 'Negative and positive party identification in post-communist countries', *Electoral Studies*, 17(2): 217–234.

Rose, R. and Munro, N. (2009) *Parties and Elections in New European Democracies*, Colchester: ECPR Press.

Rose-Ackerman, S. (2004) 'The Challenge of Poor Governance and Corruption', Copenhagen Consensus, available at http://www.copenhagenconsensus. com/CCC%20Home%20Page.aspx. Last accessed April 23, 2013.

Rothschild, J. (1993) *Return to Diversity: A political history of East Central Europe since World War II*, Oxford: Oxford University Press.

Rueschemeyer, D, Stephens, E. H. and Stephens J. H. (1992) *Capitalist Development and Democracy*, Chicago: University of Chicago Press.

Rupnik, J. (2002) 'International Context' in L. Diamond and M. Plattner (eds) *Democracy After Communism*, Baltimore: John Hopkins University Press.

—— (2007) 'From democracy fatigue to populist backlash', *Journal of Democracy* 18(4): 17–25.

Rustow, D. A. (1970) 'Transitions to democracy: toward a dynamic model' *Comparative Politics*, 2(3):337-363.

Schedler, A., Diamond, L. and Plattner, M. F. (1999) *The Self-Restraining State: Power and accountability in new democracies*, London: Lynne Rienner Publishers.

Schedler, A. (2009) 'Electoral Authoritarianism' in T. Landman and N. Robinson (eds) *Sage Handbook of Comparative Politics*, London: Sage.

Schimmelfennig, F. (2001) 'The Community trap: liberal norms, rhetorical action, and the Eastern Enlargement of the European Union', *International Organization*, 55(1): 47–80.

—— (2005a) 'Strategic calculation and international socialization: membership incentives, party constellations, and sustained compliance in Central and Eastern Europe, *International Organization,* 59(4): 827–860.

—— (2005b) 'The Community Trap: Liberal norms, rhetorical action and the Eastern enlargement of the European Union' in F. Schimmelfennig and U. Sedelmeier (eds) *The Politics of European Union Enlargement,* London and New York: Routledge

—— (2007). 'European regional organizations, political conditionality, and democratic transfer in Eastern Europe' *East European Politics and Societies*, 21(1): 126–141.

—— (2008) 'EU political accession conditionality after the 2004 enlargement: consistency and effectiveness' *Journal of European Public Policy*, 15(6): 918–937.

Schimmelfennig, F, Engert, S. and Knobel, H. (2005). 'The Impact of EU Political Conditionality' in F. Schimmelfennig and U. Sedelmeier (eds) *The Europeanization of Central and Eastern Europe*, Cornell University Press.

Schimmelfennig, F. and Sedelmeier, U. (2005) 'Introduction: Conceptualizing the Europeanization of Central and Eastern Europe', in F. Schimmelfennig and U. Sedelmeier (eds) *The Europeanization of Central and Eastern Europe*, Ithaca: Cornell University Press.

Schimmelfennig, F., Engert, S. and Knobel, H. (2006). *International Socialisation in Europe*, London: Palgrave Macmillan.

Schmitter, P. C. and Karl, T. L., (1991). 'What democracy is… and is not', *Journal of Democracy*, 2(3): 75–88.

—— (2009) 'The nature and future of comparative politics', *European Political Science Review*, 1(1): 33–61.

Schöpflin, G. (1991). 'Post-communism: constructing new democracies in Central Europe', *International Affairs*, 67(2): 235–250.

Schumpeter, J. (1947) *Capitalism, Socialism and Democracy*, New York: Harper and Bros.

Sedelmeier, U. (2010) 'The EU and democratization in Central and Southeast Europe since 1989', in S. Ramet (ed.) *Central and Southeast European Politics Since 1989*, Cambridge: Cambridge University Press.

Sekelj, L. (2001) 'Prinudna demokratizacija kriminalizovane države' in I. Spasić and M. Subotić (eds) *R/evolucija i poredak: o dinamici promena u Srbiji*, Beograd: Institut za filozofiju i društvenu teoriju.

Sen, A. (1999) *Development as Freedom*, Oxford: Oxford University Press.

Sewell, W. (1996). 'Three Temporalities: Toward an Eventful Sociology', in T. J. McDonald (ed.) *The Historic Turn in the Human Sciences*, Ann Arbour: University of Michigan Press.

Šiber, I. (1993) 'Structuring the Croatian party scene', *Croatian Political Science Review*, 2: 111–129.

Sitter, N. (2002). 'Cleavages, party strategy and party system change in Europe, East and West', *Perspectives on European Politics and Society*, 3(3): 425–451.

Skocpol, T. (1979) *States and Social Revolutions*, Cambridge: Cambridge University Press.

Smith, K. E. (1997) 'The Use of Political Conditionality in the EU's Relations with Third Countries: How Effective?', Paper for the ECSA International Conference in Seattle, 29 May–1 June.

Somers, M. R. (1995) 'What's political or cultural about political culture and the public sphere? Toward an historical sociology of concept formation', *Sociological Theory*, 13(2): 113–144.

Špegelj (1993) 'War or Peace in Croatia', an editorial conversation between Tripalo, Špegelj, Gorinšek and Žunec, *Erasmus Journal for Culture of Democracy*, Issue 4.

Spendzharova, A. and Vachudova, M. A. (2011) 'Catching up or sliding back? Consolidating Liberal Democracy in Bulgaria and Romania after EU Accession', paper presented at the European Union Studies Association Conference, March 3–6, Boston.

Spohn, W. (2009) 'Comparative Political Sociology' in T. Landman and N. Robinson (eds) *Sage Handbook of Comparative Politics*, London: Sage.

Stevanović, V. (2004) *Milošević – the people's tyrant*, London: I.B. Tauris.

Stojanović, D. (1996) 'The Traumatic Circle of the Serbian Opposition' in N. Popov (ed.) *The Road to War in Serbia*, Budapest: CEU Press.

Stojarova, V. and Emerson, P. (2009) *Party Politics in the Western Balkans*, London: Routledge.

Stokes G., Lampe, J. and Rusinow, D. (1996) 'Instant history: understanding the wars of Yugoslav secession', *Slavic Review*, 55(1).

Štulhofer, A. (1998) 'Krivudava staza hrvatske privatizacije' in I. Rogić and Z. Zeman (eds) *Privatizacija i modernizacija*, Zagreb: Institut društvenih znanosti I. Pilar.

Subotić, J. (2010) 'Explaining difficult states: the problems of Europeanization in Serbia', *East European Politics and Societies*, 24: 595–616.

Szajkowski, B. (1992) 'The Albanian Election of 1991', *Electoral Studies*, 11(2): p. 157–161.

—   (2000) 'Macedonia: An unlikely road to democracy' in G. Pridham and T. Gallagher (eds) *Experimenting With Democracy: Regime change in the Balkans*, London and New York: Routledge.

Szajkowski, B. (2003) 'The parliamentary elections in Albania, June–August 2001', *Electoral Studies*, 22: 325–395.

—   (2007) 'The parliamentary election in Albania, July–August 2005', *Electoral Studies,* 26: 196–231.

Taagepera, R. and Shugart, M. S. (1989). *Seats and Votes: The effects and determinants of electoral systems*, New Haven: Yale University Press.

Tansey, O. (2007) 'Process Tracing and Elite Interviewing: A Case for Non-probability Sampling', Political Science & Politics, 4: 765–772.

Thelen, K. (1999). 'Historical institutionalism in comparative politics', *Annual Review of Political Science*, 2: 369–404.

Tismaneanu, V. (2007) 'Leninist legacies, pluralist dilemmas', *Journal of Democracy*, 18(4): 34–39.

Thomas, R. (1999) *Serbia under Milošević: Politics in the 1990s*, London: Hurst.

Tripalo, M (1993) 'War or Peace in Croatia', an editorial conversation between Tripalo, Špegelj, Gorinšek and Žunec, *Erasmus Journal for Culture of Democracy*, Issue 4: 11–27.

UN Human Development Indicators, available at http://hdr.undp.org/en/statistics/. Last accessed April 23, 2013.

UNESCO (2006) Education for All Global Monitoring Report, available at http://www.unesco.org/new/en/education/themes/leading-the-international-agenda/efareport/.

UNICEF (2001) Primary Education in the Federal Republic of Yugoslavia: Analysis and Recommendations, Belgrade: Belgrade UNICEF Office.

USAID NGO sustainability index, available at http://www.usaid.gov/locations/europe_eurasia/dem_gov/ngoindex/index.htm. Last accessed August 20, 2012.

US State Department Human Rights Reports.

—   (2000) Croatia Report.

—   (2003) Croatia Report.

—   (1995) Yugoslavia Report.

Uzelac, A. (1992) 'Zavisnost i nezavisnost: neka komparativna iskustva i prijedlozi uz položaj sudstva u Hrvatskoj', *Zbornik* PFZ, 42: 575–594.

—   (2000a) 'The Judiciary in War Times: the Case of Balkans', Gent Colloquium of the IAPL – International Association of Procedural Law, Gent (Belgium), 25–28 April.

—   (2000b) 'Role and Status of Judges in Croatia', in P. Oberhammer (ed.), *Richterbild und Rechtsreform in Mitteleuropa*, Wien: Manz, pp. 23–66.

—   (2001) 'Hrvatsko pravosuđe u devedesetima: od državne nezavisnosti do institucionalne krize', *Politička misao*, 38(2): 3–41.

—   (2004) 'The Rule of Law and the Judicial System: Court delays as a barrier to accession', in K. Ott (ed.) *Croatian Accession to the European Union*, Zagreb: Institute for Public Finance.

Vachudova, M. A. (2005) *Europe Undivided: Democracy, leverage, and integration after communism*, Oxford: Oxford University Press.

— (2009) 'Corruption and compliance in the EU's post-communist members and candidates', *Journal of Common Market Studies*, 47: 43–62.

Vachudova, M. A. and Snyder, T. (1996). 'Are transitions transitory? Two types of political change in Eastern Europe since 1989', *East European Politics and Societies*, 11(1): 1–35.

Vachudova, M. A. and Hooghe, L. (2009). 'Postcommunist politics in a magnetic field: how transition and EU accession structure party competition on European integration', *Comparative European Politics*, 7: 179–212.

Vasović, M. (2003) 'Post-tranzitivni šok: građani Srbije između društvenih vizija i ličnih aspiracija', in *Promene vrednosti i tranzicija u Srbiji: pogled u budućnost*, Beograd: Fridrich Ebert Stiftung and Institut društvenih nauka.

Vejvoda, I. (2000) 'Democratic despotism: Federal Republic of Yugoslavia and Croatia', in G. Pridham and T. Gallagher (eds) *Experimenting With Democracy: Regime change in the Balkans*, London and New York: Routledge.

Verdery, K. (1996) *What was Socialism, and What Comes Next?,* Princeton: Princeton University Press.

Vladisavljević, N. (2008) *Serbia's Antibureaucratic Revolution*, London: Palgrave.

— (2010) 'Mešoviti režimi, protesti i 5. oktobar' in D. Pavlović (ed.) *Razvoj demokratskih ustanova u Srbiji – deset godina posle*, Beograd: Heinrich Boll Stiftung.

Vujadinović, D. (2006) 'Tranzicijski procesi, politička kultura i civilno društvo', in S. Mihailović (ed.) *Pet godina tranzicije u Srbiji*, drugi svezak, Beograd: Friedrich Ebert Stiftung.

Welzel, C. (2003). 'Effective democracy, mass culture and the quality of elites', *International Journal of Comparative Sociology* 43(3–5): 269–298.

— (2006) 'Democratization as an emancipative process: the neglected role of mass motivations' *European Journal of Political Research,* 45: 871–896.

Welzel, C., Inglehart, R. and Klingemann, H. -D. (2003). 'The theory of human development', *European Journal of Political Research* 42(2): 341–380.

Wetzel, A. and Orbie, J. (2011) 'With map and compass on narrow paths and through shallow waters: discovering the substance of EU democracy promotion' *European Foreign Affairs Review*, 16: 705–725.

Whitehead, L. (2002) *Democratization: Theory and experience*, Oxford University Press, Oxford.

Wilkinson, R. and Pickett, K. (2010) *The Spirit Level: Why equality is better for everyone*, London: Penguin Books Limited.

Wood, E. M. (1995) *Democracy Against Capitalism: Renewing historical materialism*, Cambridge: Cambridge University Press.

World Bank (2000) *Anticorruption in Transition – A Contribution to the Policy Debate*, World Bank, Washington D.C.

World Bank (2006) *Anticorruption in Transition 3: Who is Succeeding... and Why*, World Bank: Washington D.C.

World Bank online dataset, available at http://data.worldbank.org/. Last accessed April 23, 2013.

World Economic Forum (2011) Global Competitiveness Report 2011–2012, World Economic Forum: Geneva.

World Values Survey (1995), dataset at http://www.worldvaluessurvey.org/. Last accessed April 23, 2013.

Yin, R. K. (2003) *Case Study Research: Design and methods*, London: Sage.

Zakaria, F. (1997) 'The rise of illiberal democracy', *Foreign Affairs*, 76: 22–43.

Zakošek, N. (1995) 'Organizirani interesi u Hrvatskoj', *Erasmus Journal for Culture of Democracy*, 11: 28–32.

— (1997) 'Pravna država i demokracija u post-socijalizmu', *Politička misao*, 4: 78–85.

— (2002) *Politički sustav Hrvatske*, Zagreb: Fakultet političkih znanosti.

— (2007) 'The heavy burden of history: political uses of the past in the Yugoslav successor states', *Croatian Political Science Review*, XLIV(5): 29–43.

— (2008). 'Democratization, state-building and war: the cases of Serbia and Croatia', *Democratization*, 15(3): 588–610.

Županov, I. (1994) 'Otkucava li moralna bomba?', *Erasmus Journal for Culture of Democracy*, 9: 28–32.

| index